U.S. SUBS DOWN UNDER

U.S. SUBS DOWN UNDER

BRISBANE, 1942–1945

DAVID JONES AND PETER NUNAN

Naval Institute Press
Annapolis, Maryland

Naval Institute Press
291 Wood Road
Annapolis, MD 21402

Library of Congress Cataloging-in-Publication Data
Jones, David, 1945 June 4–
U.S. subs down under : Brisbane, 1942–1945 /
David Jones and Peter Nunan.
p. cm.
Includes bibliographical references and index.
ISBN 1-59114-644-5 (alk. paper)
1. World War, 1939–1945—Naval operations—Submarine.
2. World War, 1939–1945—Naval operations, American.
3. World War, 1939–1945—Campaigns—Pacific Ocean.
4. Brisbane (Qld.)—History—20th century.
5. United States. Navy—History—World War, 1939–1945.
I. Title: United States submarines down under.
II. Nunan, Peter, 1938–
III. Title.
D783.J66 2004
940.54'26431—dc22
2004009007

12 11 10 09 08 07 06 05   9 8 7 6 5 4 3 2 ∞
First printing

To those who lived it

CONTENTS

FOREWORDS

U.S. Subs Down Under is more than the story of one small city in World War II. It is a tale that covers vast areas of the Pacific, the world's largest ocean, from Panama in the east to the Indian Ocean off the south and west coasts of Australia, and to the Philippines, the South China Sea, and Singapore to the north.

Peter Nunan and David Jones have brought together a body of submarine data that will enlighten a broad spectrum of the reading public. The story describes in detail wartime Brisbane and its submarine base, and the war patrols conducted by all U.S. Navy submarines that commenced or concluded their patrols in Brisbane. For those who were the submarine warriors of World War II, this book offers an opportunity to learn what other submarines accomplished in the Southwest Pacific, and to read fascinating accounts of what made the commanders plan and execute the war as they did. For all, there is considerable detail on what the Australian government, and the city of Brisbane in particular, did to support an effective shore establishment to host one or two submarine tenders and their submarines. Rest and recreation was provided for the returning submarine crews in Brisbane itself, in Toowoomba to the west, and at Surfers Paradise and even in Sydney to the south, while the tender and relief crews and the South Brisbane Dry Dock rejuvenated submarines after hard work at sea.

The authors have drawn upon definitive histories that present detailed accounts of all submarine war patrols in the Pacific from all operating bases as well as documents held in both U.S. and Australian archives.

They have buttressed this data with that from many books written by officers who fought the war both as commanding officers and as junior officers, and by several former enlisted men who served in the boats. In addition, they reached out to numerous officers and enlisted who gladly provided personal recollections of their service in the submarines and life among the Australian people who gave so much to help win the war. Finally, they have drawn upon oral histories by various officers involved with the submarines in Brisbane. Among these is the oral history of Adm. James Fife, the primary submarine commander in Brisbane, a unique document that provides insights into the relationships between many of the senior commanders who directed the war in the Southwest Pacific.

There are detailed descriptions of two submarines, *S39* and *Darter,* that were lost to grounding, and tales of heroic action by *Wahoo, Growler,* and others. The missions to many of the islands of the Solomons and in and around New Guinea in support of the coastwatchers, who were primarily Australian, are dramatic and hair-raising. The authors put the reader to sea in the small, cranky, World War I–design S-boats that, in spite of performance beyond the call of duty by their crews, were not up to the task of long-range patrols against a determined enemy. They do not hide the fact that the torpedoes that were provided to the larger fleet-submarines for the first two years of the war were atrociously inadequate.

As executive officer and navigator of *Drum* during her fifth patrol from Pearl Harbor to Brisbane, her sixth and seventh out of Brisbane, and her eighth from Brisbane to Pearl Harbor (after depth-charge damage), I can say proudly, "I was there and did that!" I can praise the outstanding support provided by *Fulton,* which I had the privilege of commanding in 1960. I can testify to the accuracy of the story of torpedo failures. I also decoded many of the "ultra" messages that provided accurate intelligence on Japanese ship movements. I spent untold hours verifying our position, sometimes under trying weather conditions, to a degree of accuracy that enabled us to respond to the frequent changes of station ordered in messages headed "From Fife to *Drum.*" Finally, I vouch for the excellent steak and beer (and golf) in the rural environment of the Toowoomba rest camp. I reveled on the gleaming white beaches of Surfers Paradise and endured the flight to Sydney in an Australian Air Force DC-3 riddled with bullet holes from encounters with the Japanese in New Guinea.

U.S. Subs Down Under also describes how the U.S. Navy closed down operations at New Farm Wharf early in 1945. Its talented team moved submarine tender operations first to Milne Bay, then to Manus Island and Mios Woendi in New Guinea, and finally to Subic Bay. The book concludes with a little-known story of derring-do by a detachment of six British XE midgets supported by HMS *Bonaventure,* ably described by Lt. Comdr. Max H. Shean, DSO and bar, American BS, RANR, commanding *XE4.*

Rear Adm. Maurice H. Rindskopf, USN (Ret.)

Having served in an RN submarine in the Pacific for four months in 1945, I found a wealth of information in *U.S. Subs Down Under* that was relevant to my operations but of which I had little knowledge. I am indebted to the authors for their enormous effort in researching and recording this information.

The authors' style of writing is most appropriate to this subject, neither casual nor heroic. Their recording of sources is a valuable indication to the earnest reader of where to find further detail, though the amount provided in this volume is comprehensive and should satisfy most of us. While knowing little of U.S. submarine design, I am confident, from what I did learn while serving under Rear Admiral Fife's command, that the authors have achieved a high standard of accuracy. Letters from crew members are among the many authentic sources quoted.

One of the aspects of U.S. submarine operations that impressed all of my shipmates in the closing months of World War II was the endurance of those fine new boats and that of their crews. Whereas RN submarines would return from a month-long patrol with thanksgiving, frequently a U.S. boat would signal a request to extend its patrol period. The improvement in design as the war progressed is clearly described, in line with my observation of the U.S. submarines' service and capability under Admiral Fife. It is revealed that the Brisbane-based boats had thin pickings within their patrol area and had to search diligently to achieve the results obtained, particularly as the Japanese antisubmarine efficiency was of a high order.

I commend this book to all who wish to be reliably informed on the course of the Allied submarine war and what it was like to be part of it.

Lt. Comdr. Max Shean, DSO and bar, RANR

PREFACE AND ACKNOWLEDGMENTS

For three years during World War II, submarines sailing from Brisbane were at the forefront of the war against Japan. Yet their story is not well known. At the time, men of the U.S. Navy's "Silent Service" were forbidden to speak of their operations, and when war ended, their Brisbane base had been closed for several months. Since then, Brisbane's role has been overshadowed by the larger Pearl Harbor and Fremantle task forces. This is unfortunate, as the story of Brisbane's submarine war is a proud one and deserves to be remembered.

The Brisbane submarine task force made a significant contribution to Allied victory in the Southwest Pacific and overcame disheartening hardships to achieve ultimate victory. But the most lasting achievement of Brisbane's submarine war is the warm bond of mutual respect and affection built between American submariners and the Australian people. This bond remains undimmed six decades later, reminding us of the friendship and shared values existing between our two nations, and encouraging us as new threats arise in our own time.

Even less well known is the story of the Royal Navy X craft that, after the U.S. submarines left, exercised in Queensland waters before sailing to a different kind of war off enemy harbors. Their exciting story is included.

At the outset we record our indebtedness and our deepest gratitude to many people who took part in Brisbane's submarine war and generously shared their experiences. They include American veterans who served in submarines, tenders, and on Brisbane's base, and ex-servicemen who served in Queensland waters with the Royal Navy's X craft. Also included are Australians who knew the sailors while they were here, worked with them, and befriended them on liberty.

We have been overwhelmed by the openness and enthusiasm of their support for our work, but it is they who created the story as they lived through the war years. We are deeply grateful to them for sharing it with us. All have now advanced in years, and sadly, some have passed away since we commenced our research. Without the support of these wonderful people, this book would never have been written. We hope that those who remain will gain great pleasure from the finished work that they commenced so long ago.

We particularly wish to thank Rear Adm. Mike Rindskopf and Lt. Comdr. Max Shean for honoring us with forewords and identifying so closely with our work. We particularly appreciate their expert advice, kindly and patiently given when our work was in a draft condition, and for their unstinting support throughout.

Special thanks are due to Jeanine McKenzie Allen, who, out of the tragedy of losing her father on war patrol out of Brisbane, so generously and cheerfully supported us with information from her own very extensive research in the U.S. National Archives and for so kindly and selflessly trawling through those archives on our behalf.

Les Cottman, Mary Lee Coe Fowler, Paul Snyder, and the late Tom Parks have given us long-term support, sharing their own experiences as well as introducing us to many others from the community of wartime submariners. For all their time and effort, as well as their friendship, we are most grateful.

We also wish to thank Dr. Michael White from the University of Queensland for his encouragement and advice from the earliest stages of our research.

Other veterans, American and Australian, who have contributed to our knowledge include former submarine and tender crewmen Charles Barlow, Glen Battershell, Dante "Don" Bisbano, Lt. Comdr. James Bishop, Sub-Lt. Ken Briggs, DSC, Comdr. R. L. Brown, Capt. H. H. Caldwell, Capt. B. D. Claggett, Claude Conner, Frank Davies, Willard Devling, Leonard Greenwood, Larry Hall, Clarence Hebb, George Hinda, Wayne Jemmett, Capt. Ira King, Stanley Larsen, J. H. Lewis-Hughes, OBE, Jack Lindsey, Jess Martin, R. D. Martin, Comdr. J. McGrievy, Frank Medina, Charles "Chuck" Meyer, Ed Packwood, Capt. D. C. Peto, Howell Rice, Comdr. George Schaedler, Charles Schechter, Warren Shaw, Howard Smay, Vic Spree, Comdr. Hugh Story, Paul Toper, William Turbeville, Arthur Ullrich, Bill Webb, Sid Wellikson, and Milton Weymouth.

Australians who knew the American submariners during the war and have also assisted with their recollections include R. Ball, Peter Brennan,

Yvonne Cottman, Luke Curtis, Marie Doyle, Elfrida George, Bryan Gormley, Lee Hebb, Thelma Heydon, Sophia Jordan, Peggy McLellan, Hope
Tweedale, Keith Williams, CMG, and Peter Winter. You will meet these
people and share their experiences as they speak through the pages of this
book.

Finally, we wish to thank the museums, libraries, and submarine veter-
ans organizations that have made information available to us and assisted
in our research. In particular our thanks go to the Queensland Maritime
Museum and the Queensland Branch of the Submarines Association–
Australia, as well as the U.S. National Archives, the National Archives of
Australia, the U.S. Naval Historical Center, the Royal Navy Submarine
Museum, the USS *Bowfin* Submarine Museum and Park, the Wisconsin
Maritime Museum, and the Oxley Memorial Library.

U.S. SUBS DOWN UNDER

INTRODUCTION

"Defend Australia against Japanese invasion"—this was the simple but daunting mission of the six U.S. submarines that arrived in Brisbane with their tender USS *Griffin* on 15 April 1942.

The news reported that day in the *Courier-Mail*, Brisbane's morning newspaper, underlined the mission's urgency.[1] "Japanese Gain Ground in Burma" and "Britain's Naval Losses Becoming Grave" headed an article on the features page. The editorial cartoon showed a mass of Japanese warships casting a black pall over Australia. A solitary gun was trained in defense. No caption was needed. In four months the Japanese had taken most of their planned objectives for the war's entire first year. This had cost them not the anticipated one-third of their fleet but a mere four destroyers and six submarines. It was a stunning achievement.

Although Australia had been at war for two and a half years, for most of that time Brisbane had taken the conflict on the other side of the world in its stride. But the radio news at 5:45 AM, 8 December 1941, of the events at Pearl Harbor snapped Australia awake. Other bulletins told of Japanese attacks on the Philippines, Hong Kong, and Malaya. The war was suddenly much closer to home. Broadcasting to the nation, Prime Minister John Curtin warned, "This is the gravest hour of our history." Most of the Australian services' effective units were engaged far from home. Their allies could give little help. Britain was fighting for its life in Europe. The U.S. Pacific Fleet was crippled. More than Australians in other states, Queenslanders followed the southward surge of Japanese conquest with mounting apprehension. On Christmas Day, Hong Kong surrendered. Kuala Lumpur and Manila fell in early January 1942. On the twenty-third of that month the Australian defenders of Rabaul were overwhelmed. The fall of Singapore on 15 February hit like a thunderclap, ending a campaign that had cost Australia more than eighteen hundred dead and sixteen thousand prisoners. Four days later, Japanese aircraft sank eight ships and killed 243 in two devastating raids on Darwin. The war had literally come home to Australia.

March brought more disasters. HMAS *Perth* and *Yarra* were lost, and air raids on Broome and Wyndham brought more carnage. On 9 March the Dutch East Indies surrendered. The day before, Japanese forces had taken Lae and Salamaua on New Guinea's north coast and Buka Island north of Bougainville. By month's end, Port Moresby was the only major coastal town in Papua New Guinea that remained in Australian hands.

Queenslanders were alarmed. The premier expressed his concern at the possibility of an early invasion. Some families fled the vulnerable north. Some men stayed but sent their wives and children south. Coastal regions were seen as susceptible to attack. The population of inland Toowoomba rose by five thousand, and Warwick's school enrollments rose by four hundred.

Stringent controls, including rationing, came into effect. A coastal "brownout" was imposed. Prime Minister Curtin warned, "Australians, you must be seized with the dire fact that we are in imminent and deadly peril. . . . What was but a threat yesterday may mean invasion and desolation in the very near future."[2]

This peril loomed large over Brisbane, a city well aware that it lay outside the military's core area to be defended. Up to December 1941, this city had slumbered on as the port capital of a primary producing state with a few processing industries. But Queensland's vast area had fostered the development of railway workshops and shipbuilding and repair yards.

In April 1942, Brisbane had a modest population of 350,000. But in just over two years of war the city's resident population had jumped by over 7 percent with the influx of transients and Australian and Allied servicemen. The City Council struggled to meet the demand for housing, transport, and water. Passengers on the public tramway system in 1941–42 were up by 15 percent over the previous year.

The problems of their new host city were unknown to the Americans as their squadron berthed at New Farm Wharf. Although they were only two and three-quarter miles from the city center, their arrival went unannounced and unreported. Only a small naval party greeted them. It was a marked contrast with the scenes a year before when the U.S. cruisers *Chicago* and *Portland* together with five destroyers began a tumultuous

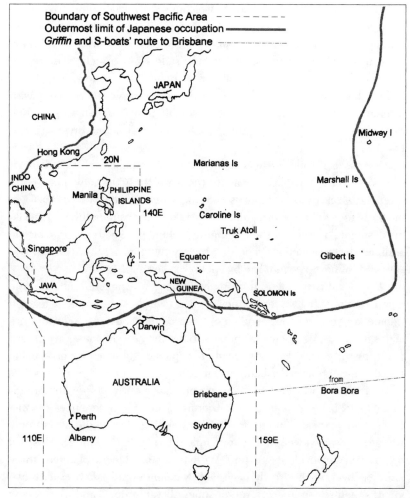

Boundary of Southwest Pacific Area ‑ ‑ ‑ ‑ ‑ ‑ ‑
Outermost limit of Japanese occupation ▬▬▬▬
Griffin and S-boats' route to Brisbane ‑‑‑‑‑‑

JAPAN

CHINA

Midway I

Hong Kong

20N

Marianas Is

Marshall Is

INDO
CHINA

Manila PHILIPPINE
ISLANDS

140E

Caroline Is

Truk Atoll

Singapore

Equator

Gilbert Is

JAVA

NEW
GUINEA

SOLOMON Is

Darwin

AUSTRALIA

from
Bora Bora

Brisbane

Perth

Sydney

110E

Albany

159E

The Pacific War Zone.

three-day visit on Tuesday, 25 March 1941. Ira King, then a young ensign on *Portland,* recalled, almost sixty years later, "Never have I seen such hospitality or had such a good time."[3]

Rear Adm. J. H. Newton's squadron had called first at Sydney, arriving on the day President Roosevelt signed the Lend-Lease Bill. This visit of warships of the then neutral United States was summed up by the *Christian Science Monitor* as a "pointed without being provocative" message to Japan and the Axis Powers. Admiral Newton's statement in Brisbane—"We are behind you in your struggle"—underlined the point.

Brisbane went overboard in its welcome. Immediately preceding the squadron's arrival, the *Courier-Mail* carried display advertisements welcoming the sailors. More than 250,000 spectators, some from as far away as Gympie and Toowoomba, cheered the sailors' city march. State receptions, balls, and informal hospitality overwhelmed the visitors.

But that was nine months before danger became reality. Now, with fears of invasion running high and censorship in place, there was not one word in the newspaper about the arrival of the small submarine force.

If the American sailors had read Brisbane's newspaper on 15 April 1942, what would they have learned about the world and their new home port? After the bleak news of Japanese advances and Allied naval losses, even the positive headline "Corregidor Guns Take Toll" would not have masked the desperate position of the Philippines defenders. The front-page article outlined the true picture, reporting twenty-two Japanese air raids in two days and "almost constant fire by enemy artillery."

Major local news focused on preparations for a Japanese attack. One report, announcing sweeping new police civil-defense powers, detailed Cabinet approval for the spending of £16,000 on civil-defense saltwater fire mains in Ann Street. Active responses to the threat went some way toward offsetting the gloom. A front-page photo depicted "sub-machine guns being tested at a camp near Brisbane yesterday."

Having been precipitated into war only four months before, the Americans would have seen in the *Courier-Mail* some consequences of Australia's two years of fighting. In the five weddings reported that day, only one groom was a civilian. The incomplete Greenslopes Military Hospital featured in an inside-page story. With two more blocks planned, three hundred beds were already occupied. Singapore had fallen exactly two months before, so reports on prisoner-of-war groups and Red Cross branches detailed membership increases. A more somber item was the Air Force casualty list of 147 names, most killed or missing overseas.

But life went on. Much of the newspaper was taken up with reports of produce sales, regional news, and sports, while the usual advertisements appeared, some adopting a patriotic slant. The oil companies announced that motor fuel would contain power alcohol. This, and a report on a charcoal burners' wage claim, pointed to efforts to conserve stringently rationed gasoline.

The news wasn't all serious. Only one war film was featured among the offerings at the many city and suburban cinemas. Other entertainment included a dance to support the town clerk's quest to win the "Ugly Man Contest."

The newspaper's reports would have reminded the newcomers that they were not the only American servicemen in Australia. The submarines were part of a rapid buildup of the American presence, which had started with the arrival of five thousand troops in the *Pensacola* convoy on 23 December 1941. In March the presence of twenty-five thousand men was officially acknowledged, so "Home News from the USA" and "U.S. Sports News" now featured in the *Courier-Mail*.

Two reports, more pertinent to the new arrivals, ran in the paper that day. American Maj. Lynn Cowan argued for Sunday entertainment for the U.S. Army, with Australia's chief of chaplains, Maj. John E. Kinney, supporting him. Chaplain Kinney also announced an instruction to all U.S. commanders to "do everything in their power" to discourage marriages between servicemen and Australian women. Kinney made five points, including the authorities' duty to protect immature young people and the fact that any Australian wife would need to apply for admission to the United States. The chaplain eventually won on the matter of Sunday entertainment. He was resoundingly defeated on the marriage front.

So as well as news of the war, the newspaper gave good insights into the country and the apprehensive, determined city that was the submariners' new base.

1
FIRST ARRIVALS

At the time of Pearl Harbor, most American submarines, including all the modern ones, were already deployed in the Pacific to counter expected Japanese aggression. The most powerful contingent, twenty-nine submarines, was based in the Philippines. This consisted of twenty-three modern submarines and six smaller and older S-class boats. They were very soon fighting for their lives.

The remaining twenty-one Pacific submarines were stationed at Pearl Harbor. They survived the attack unscathed and were quickly patrolling Japanese-occupied islands in the western Pacific and Japanese home waters. In the Atlantic were around thirty operational submarines and a handful of training units. All were older vessels, mostly S-class of World War I design, with a range of only five thousand nautical miles, outdated equipment, and poor habitability.

New fleet-submarines were joining the fleet slowly, with only eight added in the Pacific in the next six months. The only submarines available to reinforce those already fighting the Japanese were those in the Atlantic.[1] However, the Atlantic submarines were already on a war footing. Since the middle of 1941, U-boats had operated freely off the U.S. east coast, sinking American ships. U.S. submarines were deployed on anti-U-boat patrols from bases spread from Newfoundland to Cuba and Panama.

Capt. Ralph Waldo Christie's Squadron 5 was the most proficient Atlantic squadron. Tall and handsome, Christie had a distinguished presence. His impressive record of accomplishment in more than twenty-seven years of naval service included a Master of Science degree in mechanical engineering. Much of his career had been devoted to the

Capt. R. W. Christie (*left*) congratulates Lt. Comdr. J. R. Moore,
captain of *S44*, aboard USS *Griffin* in Brisbane.

Official U.S. Navy photo, U.S. National Archives, Record Group 80-G, 12171

technical aspects of torpedo development and production. He also had
extensive experience in submarines, commanding his first at the end of
World War I. Submarine Squadron 5 (SubRon 5) was his country's main
operational submarine unit in the Atlantic Ocean.

The flagship of Captain Christie's squadron was the tender USS *Griffin*
(Comdr. S. D. Jupp). *Griffin*, very recently converted from commercial
service, arrived in Newfoundland late in November 1941. Her squadron's
eighteen submarines were scattered among Newfoundland, Bermuda, and
U.S. east coast ports. *Griffin* had been on station for only ten days when
Pearl Harbor was attacked and the Pacific Fleet devastated. At a stroke, all
plans for SubRon 5 dissolved while the United States turned to battle a
new enemy in the Pacific. *Griffin* moved immediately to Newport, Rhode
Island, to refit and provision while her submarines concentrated in the
Panama Canal Zone. *Griffin* joined them there on 20 February 1942.

With SubRon 5 forming up in the Panama Canal Zone, Adm. Ernest King, commander in chief of the U.S. Navy, issued directions for the squadron's next move. Reflecting the fluid nature of the war at that time, his dispatch of 28 February 1942 read, "Direct SubRon 5 to proceed . . . toward Brisbane. Ultimate destination later." The desperate shortage of Allied warships dictated that no escort would be furnished.[2]

Putting Admiral King's directions into effect was difficult, as the S-boats' limited range barely allowed them to reach halfway across the Pacific. As well, a similar deployment in 1921 of eleven of the then new S-class from the eastern states to the Philippines took seven months, with every one of the vessels breaking down. Added to this were the real dangers of encountering Japanese warships and their refueling stop, "Bobcat," falling into enemy hands.

Captain Christie issued his orders for the trans-Pacific voyage on 28 February 1942. Accompanying *Griffin* would be a second tender, *Antaeus*, and ten submarines from Submarine Divisions 52 and 53. Sailing for the submarines was scheduled for 5 March. "Bobcat" was identified in orders opened at sea as Bora Bora, 4,652 nautical miles from Balboa at the Pacific entrance to the Panama Canal. As this distance was close to the limits of endurance of both the S-boats and *Antaeus*, careful instructions were given for the submarines and tenders to travel at their most economical cruising speed. Their departure dates were therefore staggered.[3] To extend the S-boats' range, some ballast tanks were converted to fuel tanks. This modification prevented the submarines from diving safely, and to prevent accidents, their Kingston (diving) valves were padlocked shut.

However, these plans were not final. At the last minute Admiral King ordered Christie to detach *Antaeus* and the four submarines of Division 52 to help defend Alaska. This left only six submarines of Division 53, *S42* through *S47*, to accompany Christie to Brisbane.[4] *Griffin* and the six remaining boats passed through the Panama Canal, and the submarines set off for their long Pacific crossing on 5 March 1942. Two days after her six boats, *Griffin* sailed from Balboa to join them, laden with torpedoes for all American submarines in Australia, radar parts for surface vessels, and all types of spares required to service submarines. At her destination, *Griffin* would be self-sufficient in providing all the refit, repair, and supply needs of her squadron.

On the other side of the Pacific the twenty-nine Asiatic Fleet submarines had been under pressure. Their base at Cavite in Manila Bay was heavily bombed within three days of Pearl Harbor, with one submarine sunk. The

Japanese invaded, and two days before Christmas, General MacArthur ordered the withdrawal to Bataan.

Retreating first to Java, then to Darwin, the hard-worked submarine force was swept back until the survivors found safe haven at Fremantle and Albany in Western Australia. Five of the six Asiatic Fleet S-boats now remained. They had been pushed hard and their crews exhausted by the constant activity, ever-present enemy, and lack of time or facilities for repairs. These submarines, *S37* to *S41*, constituting Submarine Division 201, arrived in Fremantle between 9 and 19 March 1942.[5]

Fremantle provided welcome safety. However, these old submarines had only a short range, and Japanese shipping in the East Indies was too far away. With Christie's division of S-boats already crossing the Pacific for the east coast of Australia, it was natural to send their sisters in Western Australia east to form a homogeneous task group. On 15 March, Capt. J. Wilkes, commanding the submarines gathering in Fremantle, issued the necessary orders. After they recovered from their retreat, the five old submarines sailed for Brisbane.[6]

Six months earlier no one would have dreamed that Brisbane would so soon become a major submarine base. The war was far away in Europe and the Mediterranean, and the bulk of Australia's armed forces were overseas. Furthermore, although Brisbane was an important port, Australia's naval base was in Sydney, with only a small reserve unit in Brisbane. Finally, after three short-lived efforts, the Royal Australian Navy no longer operated submarines. Nevertheless, Brisbane was well suited for its role as a submarine base, with well-established port facilities, including South Brisbane Dry Dock, capable of handling most U.S. submarines. It was also beyond the range of Japanese aircraft in New Guinea.

The early stages of *Griffin*'s trans-Pacific voyage were promising, with the squadron sailing over calm seas in fine weather. Four days out, *Griffin* crossed the Equator. In time-honored tradition, King Neptune came aboard to carry out his inspection. No one was immune from Neptune's authority, and even Captain Christie was ignominiously inducted into the mysteries of the deep.

On 18 March, in midocean, the squadron overtook an ancient vessel, crawling along under full sail. Howard Smay, making the passage aboard *Griffin*, recalled the occasion: "We sent a signal over, told them to stop, and they didn't respond. Finally we sent a boarding party over.... They'd been under way for three months. They didn't even know there was a war on."[7] The stranger was the American six-masted schooner *Star of Scotland*, carrying cotton to the Far East. Advised of the war situation, she was allowed to proceed.

On 26 March, *Griffin* and her S-boats reached Bora Bora, the journey's halfway point. They remained three days for refueling and rest in the pristine lagoon overshadowed by spectacular peaks before commencing the remaining stage to Brisbane.

Conditions remained calm and fine throughout the voyage until the evening of Friday, 14 April, the day before the squadron's arrival in Brisbane. A violent storm arose, lashing the convoy with hail and sixty-knot winds. No damage was done, and at 8:36 on the following morning *Griffin* passed Cape Moreton lighthouse and embarked a pilot, securing to New Farm Wharf that afternoon. *Griffin* and her submarines had arrived at their new home.

Howard Smay aboard *Griffin* had vivid recollections of the occasion as the lines were first secured in Brisbane: "We had been issued information booklets which described in great detail the wonders of Australia and the gracious hospitality of Australians. . . . To this we had added our own fantasies, night and day for forty-two days, of what a glory it would be to finally set foot in this land of enchantment. . . . I waited impatiently at the after gangway, resplendent in my finest uniform and flush with cash, tensely waiting for the magic word, 'Commence liberty.' Instead the crushing announcement was, 'There will be no liberty tonight.'"[8] For Howard Smay, Brisbane would have to wait. Immediately after *Griffin*'s arrival, he transferred to *S47*, and there was urgent work to be done making ready for war patrol.

Awaiting Captain Christie in Brisbane was the Asiatic Fleet's *S38*. She had arrived from Fremantle at 8 AM that same day escorted by USS *Tulsa*, a veteran China gunboat. At Bretts Wharf a store-ship, USS *Gold Star*, waited to load torpedoes from *Griffin* for the submarines in Western Australia. The remaining four Asiatic Fleet S-boats joined during the following week. *S37* and *S40* arrived on 20 April escorted by HMAS *Goulburn*, and *S39* and *S41*, in company with HMAS *Warrego* and *Rockhampton*, reached Brisbane three days later.[9]

The delivery of the aging SubDiv 53 to Brisbane complete and intact, in only six weeks, was a major achievement. They had crossed 7,778 nautical miles of ocean without mishap, and the S-boat crews had endured tropical heat and arduous conditions in their small vessels during almost six weeks at sea.

But Captain Christie and his men were allowed no time for celebrations. Japanese forces were on the move, and the threat of enemy invasion was rapidly taking shape on Australia's northern borders.

USS *S44* was the most successful Brisbane S-boat,
sinking three enemy ships including the heavy cruiser *Kako*.
Official U.S. Navy photo, U.S. National Archives, Record Group 80-G, 36130

Already established on the northern coast of New Guinea, the Japanese
intensified their bombing of Port Moresby. At the same time, intelligence
was predicting an assault on Port Moresby early in May 1942. Aerial
reconnaissance reported a buildup of Japanese forces in Rabaul, and radio
intelligence provided accurate, though incomplete, decrypted enemy radio
messages. By 17 April the Allies recognized that an amphibious invasion
with aircraft carrier support was timed for the first week of May. Its objective was clearly Port Moresby together with other points in the Solomons.

General MacArthur in Australia and Pacific Fleet commander Admiral
Nimitz at Pearl Harbor were determined to commit all the forces at their
disposal to stop the Japanese advance. By the end of April a force of American and Australian warships centered around two aircraft carrier task
groups was gathered in the Coral Sea.

The Japanese offensive was exactly the threat the submarines in Brisbane had been sent to counter, and Captain Christie hurried to get as
many as possible to sea. No effort was spared, and by the end of the month

four submarines had left Brisbane seeking battle. By the time the Japanese invasion convoy sailed, all four had taken up positions off southern Papua, New Britain, and New Ireland.

First to sail was Howard Smay's S47 (Lt. Comdr. J. W. Davis), departing on 22 April 1942, only seven days after her long Pacific crossing. With a major battle looming, Captain Christie charged S47 with a dangerous mission in the heart of enemy activity. Davis's orders were to "penetrate St George's Channel to attack enemy vessels vicinity of main base at Blanche Bay [Rabaul]. . . . Your primary mission is to DESTROY ENEMY VESSELS. Your secondary mission is information. Make contact reports if and when their importance outweighs the loss of security involved in the use of radio."[10]

Howard Smay remembered the crew's feelings about their old submarine as they set out on this, the very first war patrol from Brisbane: "We kept her shining. . . . We thought she was a *fine* ship, state of the art, absolutely invincible. We'd go out there, we'd chase a battleship if necessary, or half a dozen tin cans [destroyers], take 'em on, lay waste to the Japanese navy."[11]

S47 arrived off New Britain on 30 April and on the following evening made her first enemy contact. A Japanese submarine was sighted on the surface, but with Davis unable to close the distance, the Japanese drew away. On the following night S47 entered St. George's Channel, only seven miles wide, between New Britain and New Ireland, and morning saw S47 lying close in to the entrance to Blanche Bay, the anchorage for Rabaul. There Davis saw firsthand the buildup of enemy shipping for the coming assault. Blanche Bay was dangerous for a submarine. Not only was the area heavily patrolled, but the bay was relatively shallow, and pockets of fresh water made depth-keeping difficult.

During the day S47 saw first an escorted tanker, then a pair of destroyers, and finally a cruiser entering the bay. Davis attempted to bring S47 into a position to attack, but the vessel passed by out of range each time. S47's people were discovering one of the realities of war in their old submarine: "We were making two knots submerged and chasing after something doing twenty and he never got us within range. They would outrun us all the time."[12]

While S47 maneuvered to attack the cruiser, an electrical fault prematurely fired a torpedo, revealing the boat's presence. On the following morning four warships came out of Rabaul on a three-hour antisubmarine search, frequently dropping depth charges. It was a further lesson in the reality of battle for S47's crew, as Howard Smay recalled: "We never were trained in depth-charging [before] the war was on. . . . We were being depth-charged, and we'd never heard one. . . . We were getting really banged up pretty good, and we didn't even know what they were."[13]

Tom Parks, a veteran of S39 in the Asiatic Fleet and later of *Sailfish* in Brisbane, described a depth-charge attack: "There is no other experience with which I can compare a depth-charging. I experienced quite a few air raids in Manila and Surabaya, Java, and they don't come close. The noise when a depth charge explodes is almost deafening. Water doesn't compress, and the force of the charge hits the boat like a huge hammer. If the charge [was] close, the click of the detonator pistol could be heard before the charge exploded. That was the time to be really nervous. The screws of the destroyer passing overhead could be heard if we weren't too deep."[14]

Caught in shallow water by four enemy warships, S47 was in a precarious position. After running aground several times, Davis worked his submarine clear and escaped. S47 moved on to a quieter patrol position off New Hanover while the crowd of vessels she had seen in Rabaul made ready for sea.

The Port Moresby invasion convoy sailed from Rabaul late on 4 May. Already at sea was a strong Japanese force of surface warships and an aircraft carrier squadron in the Solomon Islands. To the south, in the Coral Sea, was an Allied force of two aircraft carriers, eight cruisers, and thirteen destroyers.

The submarine captains were advised of their aircraft carriers' presence, and they were also kept informed of significant movements of enemy shipping. However, the S-boat crews, confined within their steel hulls, could not see the big picture of the battle unfolding to the south of them. For them each day carried the same hazards and the same routine. Their purpose was simply to sink any Japanese ships they could find.

The Battle of the Coral Sea reached its climax on 7 and 8 May 1942 while the Port Moresby invasion convoy was still north of the Louisiade Islands. It became famous as the first occasion when a Japanese seaborne invasion was repelled. The battle was also historic as the first ever fought between aircraft carriers when ships of the opposing fleets never came within sight of each other. Although it was not apparent for some time, the battle marked the only occasion when Japanese surface warships penetrated south of the Solomons and into the Coral Sea. It was the Japanese surface fleet's closest approach to eastern Australia.

Although an Allied strategic victory, the battle had a bitter taste due to the loss of the aircraft carrier USS *Lexington*. To this day she is the largest U.S. warship ever sunk by enemy action. Also lost were the destroyer USS

Sims and the fleet oiler USS *Neosho*. More than one hundred survivors from these two vessels were brought to Brisbane, where they were accommodated aboard *Griffin*.

Cruising in the vicinity of New Britain, New Ireland, and Buka, the S-boats were largely in the background of the battle. However, as the invasion convoy returned to Rabaul on 8 May, both S44 and S47 made torpedo attacks without scoring a hit.

It was not until 11 May that Brisbane's S-boats had their first success. S42 (Lt. Comdr. Oliver Kirk) was patrolling off Cape St. George at the southern end of New Ireland. As he peered through his periscope in driving rain in the predawn gloom, Kirk made out the shape of a ship. Kirk called his observations to S42's attack team, rapid calculations were made, and four torpedoes were fired. At 4:52 AM, only thirteen minutes after the first sighting, S42's crew heard three explosions.

Their victim was the large minelayer *Okinoshima* (4,400 tons), flagship of Rear Admiral Shima, leading a small convoy bound for Nauru and Ocean Island. *Okinoshima* was hit in the boiler room and quickly lost power. Fires broke out, and she began to list. The Japanese took *Okinoshima* in tow, but next morning the fires broke out again with renewed ferocity, and she capsized and sank. The Brisbane submarines had achieved their first success.

Meanwhile, two escorting destroyers began searching, and within twenty-five minutes their sonar had located S42. She was subjected to depth-charge attacks for more than six hours, and sonar probing continued for a further three.

S42 received a pounding. Close depth charges loosened hatches and plates, causing leaks into her control room that increased as the day progressed. Through this ordeal S42 lay silent with watertight doors closed, fans and blowers shut down, servo motors turned off, and helm and diving planes under manual control. The sound operator listened intently to the movement of the escorts above while Kirk plotted and directed each evasive move.

The air inside the submarine became heavier as the oxygen diminished, the temperature soared, and bodies sweated. Condensation dripped from overhead surfaces, mixing with streaming sweat to make the decks wet and slippery. So high did the temperature climb that one sailor suffered a fit and others later collapsed from heat exhaustion. Four hours after the last sound of her attackers, at the end of a long day of depth-charging, evasion, and oppressive conditions, Kirk brought his weary submarine to the surface.

The hammering had taken its toll. On the next dive the crew could not keep a steady depth, and the leaks continued, forcing a return to Brisbane. S42 spent eighteen days in South Brisbane Dry Dock repairing her battle damage.[15]

Lieutenant Commander Kirk and S42 had achieved the Brisbane submarines' first success, and a significant one it was. The destruction of Okinoshima, the major unit of the Nauru and Ocean Island invasion force, delayed that operation for more than three months. But in the process S42 had endured possibly the most severe depth-charging received by any of Brisbane's S-class submarines.

S42's success led to another victory on the following day. The repair ship Shoei Maru was sent from Rabaul to attempt to salvage Okinoshima. After the big minelayer foundered, Shoei Maru was returning to Rabaul when S44 (Lt. Comdr. J. R. Moore) sighted and sank her. Shoei Maru's trawler escort dropped sixteen depth charges in retaliation, but Moore brought his submarine away undamaged.

By 13 May 1942, ten of Brisbane's eleven submarines were at sea to counter the mortal threat represented by the thrust against Port Moresby. But by this time the Battle of the Coral Sea was over. On 20 May, S39 inspected Deboyne Island off Papua, which the Japanese had used as an advanced seaplane base. However, they had evacuated the island a week earlier, and S39 found nothing.

The focus of sea warfare shifted from the Southwest Pacific in the latter half of May toward Midway Island in the central Pacific. There, a month after the Coral Sea battle, another and more decisive battle was fought. The Battle of Midway saw the decimation of the aircraft carrier force that spearheaded the Japanese advance over the first six months of the war. Thereafter the complexion of the Pacific war changed. From the middle of 1942 the war at sea became a bitter struggle fought at close quarters. Its outcome would not be determined for many months, and during this phase the focus swung once more to the Southwest Pacific.

Although S-boat sailors found the battle against the Japanese difficult, they soon discovered that they faced other enemies in Brisbane's submarine war. These lurked in the age and wear of their own submarines and their primitive equipment, and in the hardships of wartime submarine life. Accumulated damage and breakdowns had already taken their toll on S37. After four war patrols in the Far East without proper repair and maintenance, she spent her first two months in Brisbane undergoing an extensive overhaul.

At sea, *S44* was first to suffer tribulations. Sailing on 24 April 1942, *S44* was only three days out from Brisbane when her port engine failed. For thirty-six hours the crew labored to dismantle and repair this engine. Then the submarine continued her patrol and took her place in the Coral Sea battle. *S38*'s radio failed after leaving Brisbane, and she could not communicate with base until her final day in the patrol area. A different kind of enemy struck *S46* after leaving Brisbane when her cook fell ill with the mumps. The close confinement turned one man's illness into an epidemic, and *S46* was immobilized at Townsville for six days until the submarine was disinfected and her sick crew recovered.

However, *S43* had the worst experience of all. Her air compressors broke down while she was in the heart of enemy territory in May. With the submarine drifting helplessly, her crew struggled for two nights to repair the compressors, while during the day she lay submerged and inactive. Eventually one compressor was repaired sufficiently to allow *S43* to start her diesel engines and crawl away from enemy waters. With persistent leaks and water-contaminated fuel oil adding to her woes, *S43* limped back to Brisbane on one engine at one-third speed.[16]

In their first month the venerable submarines of Brisbane's Task Force 42 had fought in a major sea battle and sunk two enemy ships. On the other hand, two of their number were forced to return home heavily damaged, and all had experienced hardship and frustration in submarine performance and combating the enemy.

2
THE NAVY COMES ASHORE

Preparation for Brisbane's first U.S. Navy establishment had begun three weeks before the submarines arrived. The first indication Brisbane authorities had that their port would be used as a submarine base came in a letter dated 29 March 1942 from the secretary of the Australian Navy Board to the district naval officer in Brisbane. The letter foreshadowed the arrival of *Griffin* and eleven submarines around 15 April and requested that specified facilities be requisitioned and placed under guard.[1]

After isolated Pinkenba Railway Wharf was rejected, the navy took possession of Brisbane Stevedoring Company's New Farm Wharf and its associated wool sheds on 14 April 1942.[2] Royal Australian Navy officers' tentative selection of Townsville as operations base was also rejected, and Captain Christie ordered both maintenance and operations to be based in Brisbane. Eleven miles from the river mouth, navigation to New Farm Wharf required care. Here the Brisbane River is 550 yards wide with a 120-degree bend a mile and a half downstream. Tides range up to eight feet with strong tidal currents. Flows become much stronger in the wet season with storm runoff and flooding from cyclonic rains. Stanley Larsen, who served aboard *Greenling* and the shore base, still remembers a flood rising nearly to the level of New Farm Wharf's decking. The river allowed little margin for error in a submarine captain's ship-handling. Mishaps occurred, but fortunately none was serious.

From its small beginnings at New Farm Wharf the U.S. Navy's presence in Brisbane grew until the base became the biggest in Australia, and one of the biggest in the Southwest Pacific area. Supply and repair offices and workshops shared the wharf's storage sheds with offloaded stores. Two weeks after arrival, a Newmarket service station became the task force's garage, and the supply depot spread to a store in South Brisbane in June. By November, warehouses were under construction at the inner northern localities of Hedley Park, Swan Hill, and Perry Park. Perry Park, close to both New Farm Wharf and the city center, became the main supply depot, eventually including a large administration building, three warehouses, and barracks. Closer to the base in New Farm Park, work began on base headquarters, and construction of a receiving station began in September.[3] In the city, rooms in the Bank of Sydney building became force headquarters in July, and the enlisted men's clothing store moved into Ascot Chambers during November.

At other wharves, loading and unloading merchant ships remained an important function, increasingly so as war materiel poured in. Brisbane Stevedoring Company's August request for the return of its mobile crane, taken over with New Farm Wharf, therefore received prompt attention. On 22 August the Navy Board in Melbourne approved purchase of a replacement crane for the submarine base.

S40, between 29 April and 1 May, was the first submarine to use South Brisbane Dry Dock. Two other former Asiatic Fleet boats followed in the next two weeks. All eleven S-boats had passed through the dock by 26 July. The dock register records the same entry for each of them: "Repairs to props, cleaning and painting."[4] Yet time on the blocks varied from two days to S42's eighteen, spent repairing severe depth-charge damage after sinking *Okinoshima*. A clue to some of the other work carried out lies in the request of the RAN officer in charge, Brisbane, to Melbourne for approval of the manufacture of tail shafts for "S type U.S. submarines" between June and October.[5]

Work on warships at the state government–owned dry dock began when HMAS *Swan* and *Katoomba*, damaged in Darwin air raids, arrived for repair in February 1942. The local engineering firm Evans Deakin, which had commenced shipbuilding in Brisbane in 1940, was appointed coordinating contractor for ship repair, setting up their ship repair depot upstream of the dock. By war's end the dock's work, not only on submarines but also on Australian and Allied warships, merchant vessels, and dredges, had made a great contribution to victory.

Griffin arrived in Brisbane at a time of change. The Southwest Pacific area was being formed under Gen. Douglas MacArthur as supreme commander. This area covered all of Australia as well as the Solomon Islands, New Guinea, the Dutch East Indies, and the Philippines. Since early February 1942 Vice Adm. Herbert Fairfax Leary, USN, had commanded Allied

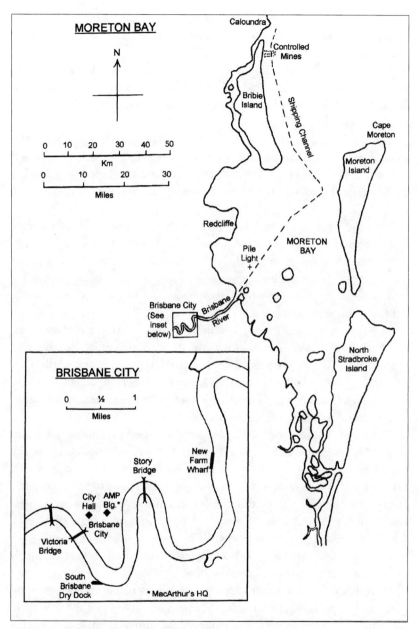

Brisbane City and Its Approaches through Moreton Bay.

naval forces in the area from Melbourne. In April the admiral had a combined Australian, Dutch, and American force of seven cruisers, fifteen destroyers, and thirty-one submarines.

In Brisbane, Christie's immediate superior was Rear Adm. F. W. Rockwell, who commanded all American naval forces in eastern Australia, designated Task Force 42. Like his submarine commander, the admiral set up headquarters on *Griffin*.

The bulk of the American submarines that had escaped from the Philippines were in Western Australia, and Rear Adm. Charles Lockwood took command of these in May. His responsibilities included command of all Allied naval forces in the west and Commander Submarines Southwest Pacific.

With the addition of the Asiatic Fleet's S-boats, Captain Christie's command expanded to eleven submarines. These formed Task Group 42.1, which was the major component of Rear Admiral Rockwell's Task Force 42. As Rockwell had no experience in submarines and Lockwood was far removed in the west, Christie had considerable freedom in operational control of his vessels.

In July 1942 Admiral Leary came to Brisbane with General MacArthur, and both established their offices in the AMP Building on the corner of Queen and Edward Streets. Two months later Rear Adm. Arthur S. ("Chips") Carpender, USN, replaced Leary and moved from Perth to take over "MacArthur's Navy." He worked closely with the general, who appreciated the value of submarines to his campaign.

The rapid buildup taxed both the navy and the city. Consider Comdr. Arthur McCollum's experience as he journeyed to join Admiral Carpender's staff. Ordered to Southwest Pacific Force headquarters as operations officer, McCollum was surprised to meet the officer he was to relieve at Pearl Harbor. He then discovered that the headquarters were no longer in Melbourne but "in a place called Brisbane."[6] After an arduous flight delayed by false starts and engine breakdowns, he reported to Admiral Carpender, to be forcefully told that his assignment was not operations officer, in which he had experience, but intelligence officer.

From his billet in Lennons Hotel, McCollum noted another looming problem for the headquarters and Brisbane: accommodation for Admiral Carpender's growing staff. Newspaper columnist John Lardner also observed the comings and goings at Lennons early in 1942: "For every colonel or pilot or major with a mission who checked out, [the proprietress] saw two colonels, three pilots, or four men with missions waiting in line at the desk."[7] The mass of real and aspiring top-level guests, from the

MacArthur family down, always exceeded the number of rooms. It was a citywide problem. The flood of servicemen was overwhelming.

Griffin's crew had brought their accommodation with them. Captain Christie also remained on board—at a convenient remove from the growing base, command, and theater headquarters, but just a pleasant drive from MacArthur's and Carpender's offices, which he visited daily to meet with the staff and collect intelligence.

A scattered collection of houses, flats, and hotels accommodated the submarine crews. Bill Ruhe was unimpressed with his room at the Gresham Hotel, "a mid-Victorian fright [with] heavy furniture . . . no john . . . and a straw or worse mattress." The five-course breakfast was some compensation.[8]

As the submarine base grew in size and complexity, so did "the Compound" at New Farm Wharf. It functioned as a base within the larger base of Brisbane. So when *Sailfish* arrived from Fremantle on 2 September with a sailor injured in rough seas, his broken jaw and teeth were treated not in a hospital ashore but on *Griffin*.

A major step forward was initiated by ComInCh order 00928 of 6 September directing the setting up ashore at New Farm Wharf of a Submarine Repair Unit. In close cooperation with the Australian authorities, work began on adapting the buildings and collecting machine tools.

The submarine sailors explored Brisbane. New Yorker David Peto remembered "a town which seemed to me to be like a set in a U.S. Western movie of an earlier generation or two."[9] Hugh Story compared Brisbane with his homeland: "Brisbane was tropical, and I recall some of the larger homes along the river were up on stilts as they tended to be in the American South."[10] The lack of sewerage and the backyard "little houses" also attracted attention.

Possibly the bleakest impressions of Brisbane are those of Stan Larsen, who recalled a city under the pressures of war: "In Brisbane there was a large water pipe going down one side of the street. It had been put in to help fight fires in case of bombing raids early in the war. There was very little to buy, and the store windows had very little to display. I think there was plenty of food, so hunger was not a problem, but getting a beer was a waiting game as the pubs were only open a few hours a day as the supply was limited and it was quite a rush to get in when the bar opened."[11]

At the personal level, Americans found that some adjustments were needed. Columnist John Lardner described contemporary Brisbane as seen through American eyes. Combining incisive observation with a light touch, he gave the American people an early insight into the city that was becoming a temporary home to more and more of their sons, brothers, and husbands. Some highlights:

"The girls of Australia are fine, handsome, fresh in the best sense of the word, and intelligent."

"Order coffee in any form and you do so at your own risk."

"A casket agency is a place where you buy lottery tickets."

"Brisbane is a fine place to spend leave . . . [and] mud crabs . . . make fine eating."

"The comic strip field is thin [with] . . . the best [being] . . . Ben Bowyang . . . and . . . Bluey and Curley."

"Newsprint is strictly rationed . . . and . . . news of baseball results in America must be telescoped."

"Sunday [is] a 'blue day' here without movies."[12]

While the welcome extended by Brisbane's citizens was warm, there was culture shock. Howard Smay, who had sailed into Brisbane on *Griffin*, recalled his experiences between the patrols he made in *S47*:

As the ship's cook . . . I had the advantage over other of my shipmates. I dealt directly with the merchants of Brisbane in procurement of food for our patrols. Each shipment that I received aboard invariably contained a number of surreptitious messages such as . . . "Dear Yank, My name is Gloria. Please call me at any time at 17694. PS I love you." . . . Food was scarce there as everywhere else during wartime. Although we marveled at how delicious our meals always were in restaurants . . . it was quite another matter in attempting to load a submarine with the submariners' favorite delicacies. Not a bite of mutton, goat, or rabbit had ever before been served in the *S47*. However, my order for beefsteak, boneless chicken breasts, pork, shrimp, lobster, etc. was filled instead with mostly freshly butchered old sheep and rabbits (complete with bones, feet, etc.). . . .

Another disappointment was the beverage that was substituted for the fruit juices that I had ordered. It was called bitter orange, bitter lemon, etc. The crew reckoned that the bitterness derived from the trees that were squeezed in the processing. This beverage came in glass bottles which promptly broke during the first storm or depth-charge attack, producing hazardous glass shards and sticky decks. . . .

[A] mouth-watering memory is of fresh corn-on-the-cob that I brought back from a weekend visit to a farm of my dear friend, Mr. Sheehy. . . . His beautiful field of corn was at its peak, and all of it had been destined for animal feed until he allowed me enough for one meal for my mess.[13]

Brisbane's charms and hospitality became lasting memories for many. Corwin Mendenhall, who arrived in *Sculpin* on 27 August, recalled, "While in Brisbane those few days we met a number of Aussies who outdid themselves with hospitality. Tennis and picnics were much in vogue."[14] Mendenhall had just been promoted to lieutenant, and, unable to obtain the silver collar badges for his new rank, he cut the bars from an Australian florin. The embossed portions of the coin were admired by many, but much later he was ordered to wear regulation insignia, and his "two-bob" badges were discarded.

Bobette Gugliotta, wife of Guy, then a junior officer on S39, records that crew's time in Brisbane in her book *Pigboat 39*. All hands appreciated Brisbane's goodwill and climate—more tropical than Perth, but less oppressive than the Philippines and Java. With its many outdoor toilets and horse-drawn vehicles—more now that gasoline rationing had begun to bite—a number of the Americans compared Brisbane with the cities of their childhood. They were charmed by the flowering trees, the iron lace railings, the exotic wildlife nearby, and the girls. S39's officers happily made use of their guest memberships in all the city's clubs. There they met hospitable new friends like Stewart Tait, who took them to the races at Albion Park followed by dinner at home. "Pud" Thurlow, manager of the Bulimba Brewery, treated them to a brewery tour and later to a dinner, where more invitations flowed.

For S39's sailors, Brisbane was a mixed bag. There were girls and beer, but in Perth the submariners had little competition for either. Here, there were thousands of GIs as well as other sailors. The Australian servicemen also included veterans returned from North Africa. Sure, the submariners—paid 50 percent more than other U.S. sailors—had bulging wallets, but this fueled resentment as more and more servicemen competed for a finite number of girls and a rationed quantity of beer.

S39's Filipino mess stewards faced another problem. Given Australian attitudes of the 1940s, they and the other Filipino, Guamanian, and black servicemen found the city a lonely place. With their country under enemy rule, even mail call brought no comfort to the Filipinos.[15]

Ships' parties soon became a source of friction with the city police. Throughout the war and well into peacetime, alcohol was banned at

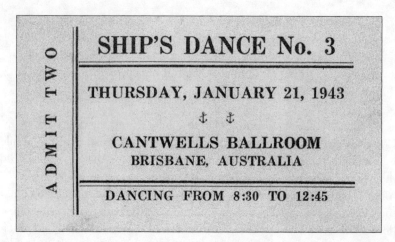

Courtesy of L. L. Cottman

dances. The Asiatic Fleet sailors had enjoyed lavish parties in Manila and on the China coast. Now, last flings before hazardous patrols sometimes stretched the local limits of decorum. Bill Ruhe later wrote of an August New Farm party, "[It was] terrifically wild [with] movie kisses [and] a fight in the head [that looked] like in the movies."[16]

Civil police disquiet was voiced after a constable was refused admission to *Tulsa*'s dance on 24 June in violation of the agreement allowing such visits. More serious was the fallout from *Griffin*'s dance at the Ritz Ballroom, home of Addie Cantwell's Dance Studio, on 8 October. Constable Heffernan reported "most disgusting" conduct on the part of forty sailors and twenty women in the street at the foot of the studio's stairs.[17] After *S40*'s dance at the same venue on the thirteenth, Police Commissioner C. J. Carroll had complained to the U.S. Justice Department in Washington. An arrangement was worked out between the navy and the commissioner, a twice-wounded veteran of World War I: liquor would be permitted at parties if attendance was restricted to sailors and their guests.

It wasn't just the parties. Beer at baseball games in New Farm Park also attracted police attention. So did alcohol at public dances. Constable F. J. White arrested Hugh James of *Sperry* at the popular Trocadero Dance Hall on 11 January 1943. The incident followed a familiar pattern. Acting on a complaint, White confronted James, who not only was uncooperative but "became very abusive." When Chief Ellison of the shore patrol arrived, James continued to abuse the policeman but answered his countryman's questions and left with him. The bottle, later found to contain pure alcohol, stayed behind. The Queensland police forwarded the report to the American authorities but took no further action.[18]

As Brisbane's population of lonely young men soared, requests for permission to marry started to arrive from sailors who had fallen in love with local girls. But there were hurdles to be negotiated before the marriage could take place. Commander Southwest Pacific had stipulated three conditions to be fulfilled before any of his sailors could marry an Australian:

1. The force commander must give his permission.

2. Six months must elapse between receipt at headquarters of a letter of intention to marry and the ceremony.

3. The force commander must establish the lady's good reputation. (In his time at Fremantle, Admiral Lockwood checked with the ladies' pastors. He also tried, unsuccessfully, to reduce the "cooling-off" period to three months.

Most Australian–American relationships did not reach the point of matrimony. Peggy McLellan worked in the Elizabeth Street offices of Metro Goldwyn Mayer. On the night the first submarines arrived, she and her sister attended the dance at City Hall. There they met two *Griffin* sailors, Johnny Waddill of Alabama and Alvin Whitehouse of California. From that night until *Griffin* sailed, the two were part of the McLellan large extended family. The girls worked as ushers at the Alderley movie theater on Saturday nights. The sailors happily spent those evenings talking with Mrs. McLellan, who had quickly developed a special affection for those young men so far from home. Often the sailors slept on spare beds on the verandah. These times away from *Griffin*'s crowded mess decks were capped with leisurely Sunday mornings spent sitting in the sun eating homemade biscuits.

Johnny and Al returned the hospitality. Within a month of their meeting, the sailors hired a car to drive the girls around Brisbane and Redcliffe—a rare treat in a city where few families owned private cars and stringent gasoline rationing restricted their use. Candy and flowers and rides in taxis were frequently part of movie and dance dates. Peggy's MGM job facilitated the movie dates. Live shows at the Cremorne, just over the Victoria Bridge, roller-skating at the nearby Blue Moon Rink, and dances at such venues as Cloudland in Bowen Hills, City Hall, and the Navy Ammunition Depot at Mount Coot-tha (with truck transport there and back) made for a lively time. At times an Orange Alert enforced by military police and the shore patrol would intrude and force an end to the evening. Then the sailors would send the girls home in a taxi before returning to New Farm Wharf.

3
S-BOATS

In their first month, Brisbane's S-boats had turned in a mixed performance. S42 and S44 had shown that they could make a useful contribution, but experience had also shown that the old submarines were struggling, with many hardships to be overcome.

The S-boats had been designed for service in the Atlantic Ocean, cooperating with surface units in fleet battles. However, exercises had shown that they were unsuitable for fleet operations, and they were assigned largely to coast defense. Japan's expansionist policies between the wars resulted in America's focus turning to the Pacific, and subsequent submarines were larger with a longer range.

Brisbane's S-boats came in two slightly different designs. S37 to S41 had a standard displacement of 850 tons and an overall length of 219 feet, while S42 to S47 were a little larger, displacing 900 tons and 225 feet long. All had a narrow beam of only 20.5 feet, making them cramped inside and prone to roll in a seaway. Brisbane's eleven S-boats were laid down between 1918 and 1921, but construction was slow, and all took four years to complete.

Their appearance was angular, and their dull black paintwork gave them a sinister look. However, the deck casing and conning tower visible above the surface were only a minor part of the vessel. Their essential body, lying largely unseen below water, was the cylindrical pressure hull enclosing the crew and the submarine's operating equipment. Inside the pressure hull were six watertight compartments. The "sharp end" of the submarine was the torpedo room in the bow containing the primary weapons, four 21-inch torpedo tubes and twelve torpedoes. Each torpedo carried a 500-pound warhead and had a range of two miles. Their design was old, but they were of proven performance.

The nerve center of the S-boat was its control room, in the center of the submarine directly below the bridge. Controls for operating and fighting the submarine were fitted here, including diving and trim controls, navigation, sonar and plotting equipment, and periscopes. The radio enclosure and the accommodation for the four or five officers adjoined the control room.

At each end of the control room were the forward and aft battery rooms that provided, on a deck above the battery cells, the living space for more than forty crewmen. Accommodation was cramped, and in an S-boat the mess tables folded up overhead and were let down only at meal times. If a crew member wanted to sit and read, it usually had to be in the forward torpedo room. Although the S-boats' complement was originally thirty-eight men, wartime conditions expanded this to forty-seven or more in the latter half of 1942.

The rearmost compartments, representing more than a third of the vessel's length, were occupied by the propulsion systems. These were the engine room, containing two big Nelseco diesel engines for running on the surface, and the motor room with two GE electric motors for submerged propulsion. Below floorboards were two massive banks of 120 wet-cell batteries powering the electric motors. Also below deck were some fuel and ballast tanks, and compressed air to blow out ballast tanks for surfacing.

The diesel engines also powered generators that recharged the batteries depleted after submerged operation. S-boats originally had an underwater speed of eleven knots, but maximum submerged power could be supplied only for short periods before the batteries were drained. In practice, submerged speed was around three knots. By the time they arrived in Brisbane, age had reduced their surface speed to 11 knots from their original maximum of 14.5 knots. Within the U.S. Navy the S-boats inherited the unglamorous nicknames of "pig-boats" and "sewer pipes."

S-boats were not well suited to their war duties from Brisbane. They were not designed for long Pacific distances and tropical heat, and their age showed in outdated equipment and advanced wear. Their range of five thousand nautical miles was inadequate for the Southwest Pacific. To operate off Rabaul, the S-boat had to cover sixteen hundred nautical miles, taking at least a week on passage. With an endurance of four weeks, this left only two weeks for operations.

Designed for shorter-range operations, the S-boats' food storage and refrigeration were minimal. Fresh meats crammed into the inadequate freezer froze into a single chunk and were gone after two weeks at sea. Then the crew survived on canned and powdered food. On occasions this almost ran out before the submarine returned to port.

The Brisbane S-boats' equipment was far from being state of the art for fighting their savage total war. With no radar or echo sounder, navigation was difficult. Within the first six weeks of the war, S36 had been lost after stranding on a reef in the Dutch East Indies, and some of her crew were now aboard Brisbane S-boats.

Lacking radar, the S-boats relied on a human observer (the "Mark 1 eyeball") for sighting the enemy through the periscope by day or from the bridge at night. Periscopes fogged up in high humidity or leaked. They also vibrated, making sighting difficult. The torpedo fire control system was basic. The "is-was" ("This is where the target was"), a plastic slide-rule device, calculated the course to the attack position by depicting the relationship between the submarine and the target. The Mark VIII angle solver (nicknamed the "banjo" because of its shape) helped the firing control party determine the lead angle to fire the torpedo to intercept the target. William Ruhe, who worked with these instruments on two patrols in S37, described the torpedo firing calculations as "bow-and-arrow guesstimates."[1]

S-boats were also poorly equipped for evading counterattacks. Their noisy diving planes meant that under silent-running conditions, they had to be operated manually. This was hard work for the operators in stifling conditions. Their evasive speed during silent running was limited to two knots, and their sonar gear was inadequate.

Listening sonar apparatus was in a hydrophone on the foredeck with its shaft extending into the forward torpedo room. The apparatus was hand rotated to find the direction of the sound. The limitations of the S-boats' manual sonar equipment became obvious when four Japanese warships attacked S47 at Rabaul early in May 1942. With the sonar able to bear on only one vessel at a time, the operator had to judge which one was making the attack and estimate when it was starting its run so that the captain could take evasive action. The sonar operator could track other vessels only by rapidly turning the cumbersome apparatus by hand to each vessel in turn.

The S-boats' outdated design made little provision for crew hygiene. Washing facilities were virtually nonexistent. There were no showers and only two toilets, one for the four or five officers and one for more than forty other crew members. A bath was a few cups of water in a bucket and a sponge. Although the submarine had evaporators for distilling fresh water, this was used for the batteries, which consumed enormous quantities of double-distilled water.

Tom Parks described the toilet: "There was only one head (toilet) for the crew, and it was smaller than a telephone booth. The waste was ejected by compressed air, and it almost took an engineer to operate it without getting what we called a 'flareback.'" The consequences of a "flareback" can be imagined, but the difficulty of accessing and using this facility resulted in constipation being an occupational hazard of the S-boat.[2]

Disposal of garbage also caused a problem, as floating waste could be recovered and alert the enemy. Consequently, any garbage likely to float was put into weighted bags. Some S-boats found themselves with insufficient weighted bags and were forced to hold garbage on board, adding to the existing smells.

S-boat berthing was very cramped at the best of times. During the war, extra crew meant that there were not enough bunks for all. So two sailors had to alternate in one bunk—"hot-bunking." It was just another hardship for the crews when a sailor, weary after his turn on watch, had to rest on a piece of canvas left hot, smelly, and sweat-soaked by its previous occupant.

Any sickness or injury on patrol could be treated only by other crewmen with first-aid training. Medical aids were minimal, and serious cases were held until the submarine returned to base. In rare cases the submarine came off patrol to address the emergency. When a crewman aboard S38 developed acute appendicitis on 30 September 1942, the submarine was redirected to meet a Catalina flying boat to evacuate him to a hospital.[3]

Another hardship of S-boat living was the hordes of cockroaches that infested the inner compartments and prowled around (and over) the crew. William Ruhe reported on the sickening sight of his sandals covered with small brown creatures ravenously feeding on the salt deposited by his sweaty feet. Sufficient cockroaches always survived vermin eradication to regenerate the population.[4]

The worst shortcoming of the S-boats was their unsuitability for tropical conditions. Poor ventilation and a lack of air conditioning made every patrol a test of physical stamina. Only one S-boat, S44, possessed an air-conditioning unit, which her crew had bought and installed themselves.[5]

Smells were pervasive. Tom Parks of S39 remembered, "There was no air conditioning, and the boat really heated up in tropical waters. The ventilation system was very inefficient, and there was no way to really scrub the foul air. After ten hours submerged, the air was *really* foul."[6] The smells, particularly that of diesel oil, would cling to the submariners' bodies and clothing, accompanying them even when they went ashore. Paul Snyder remembered, "We were so used to the smell that we didn't realize the diesel body fragrance that we had. Often ashore and in our dress blues a girlfriend . . . would remark about how they knew we were submarine sailors just by our diesel scent. We certainly did not need the dolphin emblem on our sleeve for them to know—the diesel bouquet was really the qualifier."[7]

But although the smells could be tolerated, the heat and humidity of tropical waters damaged both men and machines. All Brisbane's S-boat operational areas were within 10 degrees of the Equator. They had to remain submerged throughout the day in these tropical seas. Inside, the temperature would rise above 100°F, humidity would climb to 100 percent, the inside pressure would steadily increase as air-powered equipment was used, and the air would become heavier as its oxygen content was depleted.

The humidity resulted in moisture condensing on the hull's inner surfaces, dripping onto men and equipment and making decks slippery. Whiskers of mildew grew on food and clothes, and rust attacked metal items. Men would be covered in a lather of sweat that soaked seats and bedding and dripped onto whatever they were working on. "Guam blisters" (heat rash) would break out and fester on their sweating bodies. Despite salt pills to restore losses through sweat, the hot, humid conditions sapped energy, making every effort an ordeal.

In his report on S37's first patrol from Brisbane, Lieutenant Commander Reynolds described the effect of humidity on S37's equipment:

> The insulation on most electrical equipment and wiring throughout the ship is in poor condition. . . . Source of the trouble is rotten insulation on cable ends and where passing through lumber [sic] holes in ship's frames. Moisture collecting here soaks the rotten insulation and grounds the cable. . . . In the midst of the noise from tank vents and the activity of getting the ship secured from dive, the weak points in the circuits now break down, . . . fires occur everywhere, sometimes alarms short out, fans take off, lights burn out, meters blow up, and bedlam results. It is often several days before all burnt places are found.[8]

The years had taken their toll on the S-boats, which as well as being obsolete were now showing advanced wear. Decayed electrical systems were prone to breakdown and dangerous fires. In addition, the riveted plates of their pressure hulls had been thinned and pitted by corrosion, and their weakened structure leaked. The weakened plates made the submarines more vulnerable to depth-charging and also limited their diving depth, making them more prone to detection.

When she sailed from Brisbane for the Battle of the Coral Sea, S38 was still carrying damage from a battery explosion in the Philippines more than four months earlier. The condition of S37 was too bad to allow her to undertake a patrol, and accumulated defects kept her under repair for more than two months. After heroic activity in Asiatic waters, S39 experienced a succession of breakdowns on her first patrol out of Brisbane, with main engine failures being the most serious. Repairs were protracted, and attempts to sail on patrol on two successive occasions were frustrated by breakdowns in each of her main engines. Even after a six-week refit in Brisbane, S41 was forced to return for repairs before reaching her patrol area.

Despite their successful trans-Pacific voyage, the submarines of Division 53 from the United States were in little better shape. As an example, in the six months before her arrival in Brisbane, S44 spent 127 days or 70 percent of her time at sea. This was on war patrols to counter German U-boats, and constant wear and delayed maintenance were beginning to make an impact.[9]

Battle damage to S38 on 1 July 1942 was caused as much by her own age and infirmities as by the enemy. Just arrived in her patrol area, S38 was lining up to make her first attack when she was attacked with depth charges. She was able to evade, but the depth charges loosened corroded plates, causing leaks, making depth control difficult, and sending a stream of bubbles to the surface. These bubbles were soon seen by a patrolling aircraft, which also attacked, creating further mechanical troubles. Lieutenant Commander Munson had no alternative but to end his patrol and take S38 straight back to Brisbane. Once there, she underwent urgent repairs in South Brisbane Dry Dock, with her crew working day and night without liberty before she sailed for her next patrol.

The constant stream of breakdowns coupled with the poor living conditions and limitations of the S-boats took a heavy toll. The toll was particularly punishing on the officers and the captains who had ultimate responsibility for the effective operation of their vessels, the safety of the men, and achieving patrol objectives. Several captains returned from patrols mentally exhausted.

The oppressive heat and long hours of extra work repairing breakdowns also bore heavily on the crews. William Ruhe observed sailors at close quarters through two patrols on S37: "Even though the S-boats are quite broken down, their men aren't in equally poor shape. In fact, they continue to function well. They are stable psychologically, have above average IQs and are competent at fixing things while at sea and are cool in combat. The crew is far more important to a submarine's success than its

S44's crew relax on her foredeck in Brisbane on 1 September 1942.
Note the dome of the sound-listening device on the left submarine
and the bow plane recessed into the hull on the right submarine.

Official U.S. Navy photo, U.S. National Archives, Record Group 80-G, 16109

equipment."[10] Looking back after many years, Tom Parks said this of his
life aboard *S39*: "We got along in this intolerable way because we knew we
had to. There were occasional flare-ups of temper, but they died down
quickly. . . . Despite the lack of creature comforts, we loved the ships, and
we felt that we were a breed apart."[11]

These fine men at a very young age took their ancient S-boats to the
enemy's doorstep at a time of great need and made their presence felt.
They were all that was available to keep up the fight.

Before proceeding on patrol, each S-boat undertook a test dive in Moreton
Bay to check tightness and readiness for action. Such a test was essential
because it quite frequently revealed leaks or other defects requiring further repairs. The dive was also an important exercise to polish veterans'
skills and to indoctrinate new hands.

Diving is one of the most dangerous evolutions undertaken by a submarine. The crew must act as a team dependent on every man doing his job on a split-second basis. When the klaxon sounded to dive, the diesel engines were shut down, hull apertures were sealed off, and vents at the top of the ballast tanks were opened. Water flooded the tanks from openings at the bottom, forcing the air out, reducing the submarine's buoyancy, and allowing her to submerge. The diesel engine air intake had to be closed before the water reached it. The air intake could not be closed until the main engines had been completely shut down, as they would suck all the air in the submarine into the engine, creating a vacuum.

A panel of lights in the control room called a "Christmas tree" showed red when critical valves and hull openings were open and green when they were shut. A "green board" meant that all openings were secure and it was safe to dive. When a green board appeared, the chief petty officer on watch bled a small amount of high-pressure air into the boat to ensure that no hull openings remained. Meanwhile, electricians shifted the main motors to battery power, and the diving planes were manned and angled down until the submarine reached the required depth.

Having satisfactorily completed her test dive, the S-boat disembarked her pilot and headed out to sea. An alert lookout was needed for enemy submarines, which had opened their campaign off the eastern Australian coast with a midget-submarine attack on Sydney Harbour on the last night of May 1942. Four days later I-29 was sighted off Moreton Island, and from then on reports of submarines real and imagined were received on a regular basis.[12]

An S-boat's course took her east of Frederick Reef into the Coral Sea. On passage the crew exercised torpedo handling, gunnery, practice dives, surfacing, and damage control. Passing 15°S, about the level of Cooktown, the submarine was considered to be entering enemy waters. Until passing this point on the return journey the S-boat remained submerged during the day, surfacing an hour after dark to refresh the air and charge the batteries. The submarine submerged again an hour before sunrise and ran through the day solely on battery power.

In enemy waters some submarines completely changed their routine, to one known as "reversa." Under "reversa," daylight hours when submerged would be regarded as night, with lights dimmed and all but the duty watch stood down and resting. On station the submarine operated at minimal speed, periodically coming to periscope depth to search visually while maintaining a constant sonar listening watch for ships. A constant watch was also needed to ensure that the submarine remained at her required depth and trim. Adjustments of trim and depth were made by pumping ballast and also by up or down movement of the diving planes. The S-boats normally maintained a depth of eighty feet in enemy waters, rising to periscope depth of forty-five feet only for periodic periscope scans.

Over the course of the day the S-boat heated up, pressure and humidity rose, smells accumulated, and air deteriorated as oxygen was used up. After dark the captain checked that all was clear, then surfaced to replenish the air and recharge the batteries. When the conning tower hatch was first opened, steamy, foul air rushed out of the submarine as the pressure was released. The diesel engines were then connected so that the batteries could be recharged and cool, fresh air could be sucked through the submarine.

At night on the bridge the captain, a watch officer, and two lookouts peered through binoculars into the darkness for any sign of the enemy. The noise of the boat's own diesel engines made the listening watch more difficult. However, it was at night on the surface that the submarine was able to receive radio messages. Every night Captain Christie radioed his captains at sea advice on current enemy movements, weather reports, and any fresh orders. This regular broadcast was known as the "Fox" schedule. Messages on this circuit were sent up to six times in case some submarines on patrol had been forced to submerge, preventing reception, at a particular time. Submarines maintained radio silence on patrol unless reporting enemy contacts or when ordered to acknowledge.

On the date directed in patrol orders, the submarine would leave her patrol area to return to Brisbane, reporting her estimated time of arrival off Cape Moreton on passage. Sleeping compartments that had been kept dim while on station were fully lit, and the order "up bunks" began a general cleanup. This was known as "field day," and all of the crew would turn to for housekeeping and cleaning ship. Despite the difficulties of leaks and mildew, every effort was made to make the S-boat spotless and tidy for the return to base. The navy ideal of cleanliness being next to Godliness, drummed into sailors at their boot camps, prevailed, even after an arduous patrol in enemy waters.

After the rigors of three weeks on patrol, the trip south across the Coral Sea could prove a mixed blessing. Although surface running during the day and fresh air were welcomed, the open sea sometimes brought exposure to heavier swells than crews had experienced previously in protected waters among the islands. The narrow-beamed S-boats rolled badly, and rough seas would make watch on the exposed bridge miserable and require hatches to be closed against minor flooding.

The wink of Cape Moreton lighthouse was recognized with relief as the sign that they had made it home. Passing up the Brisbane River, the submarine was greeted by friendly waves from shore and a welcoming party and band waiting on New Farm Wharf. The band might be playing the old Gene Autry cowboy tune "Back in the Saddle Again" for their return, matched by "Empty Saddles in the Old Corral" for their departure.[13] Once mooring lines were attached, the crew were greeted with fresh fruit, ice cream, mail, and, best of all, liberty.

To Captain Christie, his submarine force's role was straightforward. The Japanese were strongly established in New Guinea and the nearby islands, and they were well placed for further advances on Australia. Although one advance had been beaten back, it was only a matter of time before more would follow. It was a matter of urgency for his submarines to hit as hard as they could in the Japanese-occupied islands.

Christie's operation plans and orders required his task group to "establish and maintain submarine patrols in the waters off New Guinea, Bismarck Archipelago, Solomon Islands area, and wage unrestricted submarine warfare . . . [;] 'unrestricted submarine warfare' means that you may attack with torpedoes or guns, without warning, any enemy vessel except such ships as are given safe passage by proper authority and hospital ships."[14]

The concept of unrestricted submarine warfare was a sensitive one to Americans. During World War I there had been public outrage over the losses of then neutral American lives and property from German U-boats waging unrestricted submarine warfare. Ultimately it was a major factor in bringing the United States into the war against Germany. More recently, in 1941, similar outrage had been caused by losses on the east coast of the United States through German U-boats again conducting unrestricted warfare.

After World War I, efforts were made to prohibit unrestricted warfare, culminating in the London Treaty being signed in 1930 by the major powers, including the United States and Japan. This treaty required all warships, including submarines, to warn and stop enemy merchant vessels encountered in time of war so that the safety of their crews and passengers could be assured before the merchant vessel was sunk.

Throughout the interwar period, American submarines were seen as an adjunct of the fleet to be used against enemy warships. Accordingly, the U.S. submarine service had not studied how a policy of unrestricted warfare could be applied, nor had there been any training in its operational aspects. Nevertheless, such was the sense of outrage, first at the German U-boat war, and then at the surprise Japanese attack on Pearl Harbor, that the U.S. Navy carried out unrestricted submarine warfare from its entry into the war.

Captain Christie, following general practice in the U.S. Navy, assigned priorities for targeting enemy shipping, with warships first, followed by tankers, supply ships, and troopships. His orders also relieved pressure on submarine captains to risk their boats to save survivors, and no Japanese prisoners were to be taken. Submarines should go to the rescue of survivors of friendly vessels only when it was safe to do so.[15] The sinking of enemy shipping was the overriding purpose of every American submarine and remained so throughout the war. Their crews summed the mission up as "Find 'em, chase 'em, sink 'em." Any other tasks such as special missions were seen as distracting submarines from their real job of sinking ships.

Typically, S-boat patrols were in the vicinity of the Japanese strongholds on New Britain and New Ireland. Focal points off Cape St. George, St. George's Channel, and off Kavieng and Buka were covered on a regular basis, and submarine captains were also advised of the routing of Japanese shipping from Truk Atoll to Kavieng and Rabaul, and from Rabaul to Lae.

After the Guadalcanal campaign began in mid-August 1942, S-boats were also deployed farther down the Solomon Islands to positions off the Shortland Islands, New Georgia, and Savo Island. A few S-boat patrols had a defensive objective to intercept possible Japanese moves against Milne Bay, Guadalcanal, or Noumea.

These were dangerous waters to patrol. Seas between the islands were narrow, strewn with reefs, and prone to strong tidal currents. Charts held by S-boat captains dated from the turn of the century and lacked detail. Some S-boats sailed without any charts at all for part of their patrol area.

The waters north of the Louisiade Archipelago were strongly patrolled by Japanese aircraft based at Rabaul, forward airfields, and seaplane bases spread throughout the islands. The Japanese had perfected their aerial reconnaissance technique before the war, and little that moved on the sea surface would escape their notice.

At this time New Guinea and the Solomons represented the front line between Japanese and Allied forces. The presence of escorts and the speed of warships made it very difficult for an S-boat to achieve success. Invariably, any torpedo attack resulted in the submarine suffering a depth-charge counterattack.

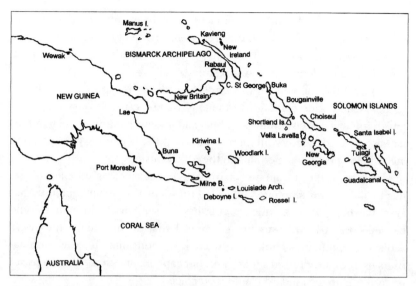

Operational Area in Waters of New Guinea, Bismarcks, and Solomons.

After returning from their first patrols from Brisbane, most S-boats needed extensive repairs while the Japanese strengthened their position in the islands. Repairs kept them in port for periods ranging from four to ten weeks. However, *S44* and *S47* completed their refits quickly and departed on their second patrols little more than two weeks after returning from their first.

Captain Christie kept two submarines in enemy waters throughout most of the next two months until events in the Solomons in August changed the character of the war in the Southwest Pacific. During this period the Brisbane S-boats continued to suffer defects and breakdowns, but they also continued to build upon their earlier successes.

S44 (Lt. Comdr. J. R. "Dinty" Moore) emerged as the star performer of the Brisbane S-boats when she sank her second ship, the naval auxiliary *Keijo Maru*, off Guadalcanal on 21 June 1942. Tom Parks, who served with "Dinty" Moore later in the year aboard *Sailfish*, considered him an outstanding leader whom the men totally respected and loved. His priorities were the U.S. Navy, his ship, and his crew, a balance that assured success.[16]

The sinking of *Keijo Maru* was a frightening experience, as the ship exploded while *S44* was passing below. Diving beneath the hail of debris, the boat was rocked by a near miss from a bomb, which started a number of leaks. Worse still, nothing could be seen from number 1 periscope. When the boat surfaced later, the crew were relieved to find that the damage was not as bad as feared. When a Japanese sailor's coat was removed from around the lens, vision was restored.[17]

In July, Brisbane submarines undertook their first special missions to support clandestine operations in enemy waters, especially assisting Australian intelligence coastwatchers. Special missions continued as an important aspect of Brisbane's submarine war until the beginning of 1945, proving to be of great strategic value to the Allied cause.

However, as far as Captain Christie was concerned, his submarines' job was to sink enemy shipping. Achieving this objective was paramount, and every patrol report was critically examined to see how performance could be improved. Christie was not convinced that all his submarines were achieving as much as could be expected. Responsibility for each submarine's performance rested squarely on her captain, and those who were not performing up to standard would be replaced.

The first captain to attract Christie's disapproving attention was Lieutenant Commander Davis. His S47 was first to return to Brisbane on 20 May 1942 after a grueling and disheartening patrol. Despite repeated efforts, S47 failed to make a successful torpedo attack, and she had been damaged outside Rabaul Harbor. Howard Smay described the effect of Christie's displeasure on his captain: "A few nights after we limped back home we were having a ship's party in Brisbane. As the party was winding down in the wee hours of the following morning, I approached . . . Davis who was sitting all alone and in deep thought. I excused myself and asked him what Commodore Christie thought of our abortive patrol. . . . Davis replied, 'He hasn't even received me yet.' I noticed that Captain Davis was softly sobbing as I left him."[18]

Happily, Davis retained command of S47 and went on to considerable success later in command of *Raton*. Three other S-boat captains were not so fortunate, being relieved of their commands in July and August for not showing sufficient aggression or not achieving results, while a fourth stood down voluntarily because of stress. Although success was sorely needed at this stage of the war, one can sympathize with these officers who had to overcome the breakdowns and inadequacies of their own boats before they could even engage the enemy.

Submarine captains were not the only ones expected to meet high standards. In the confined space aboard a submarine it was important that every crew member fit in with submarine life and be able to live in harmony with his shipmates. If a crew member could not cope with the pressure or caused friction with his fellows, that man was removed from the submarine as soon as she returned from the patrol. Many such men went on to successful careers in surface vessels.

4

S-BOATS IN THE SOLOMONS

After the Battle of the Coral Sea, the next South Pacific arena was the Solomon Islands. Brisbane's S-boats played their part. The immediate threat to Australia had lessened, so the force's mission became to help disrupt enemy surface operations and supply lines into the Solomons.

In an appreciation of Japanese forces dated 26 June 1942, Christie noted, "A landing field is being prepared on the north coast of Guadalcanal Island."[1] This merited more than a line in Task Force 42's orders. The airfield was a threat to the Australian–American supply line. Washington therefore acted.

With the tide of the Japanese advance still flowing, a bold decision was made to capture the airfield on Guadalcanal before it could be completed. Tulagi nearby would also be recaptured. Speed was of the essence, and the date set for the assault was only a month away.

To many, including General MacArthur, this timetable seemed too ambitious. Although the Allied attack would be bitterly contested and its outcome would not be resolved for six months, Guadalcanal marked the turn of the tide against Japan. Early on 7 August 1942 the 1st Marine Division stormed ashore on Tulagi and Guadalcanal. Surprise was complete, and both objectives were soon taken. However a strong, immediate reaction was expected from Japanese forces.

After the wear and damage of three months' intensive operations, the Brisbane S-boats could provide only limited support for this major Allied assault. On the day of the landings only two American submarines were on station in the Bismarck Archipelago, with another, S46, just leaving at the end of her patrol. S41 and S47 should have been there, but both had returned to Brisbane for emergency repairs. Despite these disappointments, S38 and S44 would make a positive contribution to the Allied offensive.

At the time of the landings, S38 (Lt. Comdr. Henry Munson) was between New Britain and Bougainville, well placed to intercept any movements to the Allied beachhead. Immediately upon hearing of the Guadalcanal landings, Vice Admiral Mikawa, the Japanese commander at Rabaul, gathered all his available forces for a counterattack. Air attacks commenced later in the day, and a cruiser force assembled to attack the Allied invasion fleet. More than four hundred troops embarked aboard the transport *Meiyo Maru,* which set off that night under escort to reinforce the Japanese defenders on Guadalcanal.

Around midnight on 8 August, Munson detected *Meiyo Maru's* convoy. He dived to evade the escorts and fired two torpedoes that hit, sending *Meiyo Maru* to the bottom with 342 sailors and troops. Sinking the transport with troop reinforcements for Guadalcanal was a significant success. The remainder of the convoy turned back, giving the American marines a vital breathing space.[2]

S38's success was also lucky. Munson had taken his submarine deep and fired torpedoes on the bearing of *Meiyo Maru's* sound emissions. Although this technique was widely encouraged and practiced in peacetime exercises, it was rarely successful under wartime conditions.[3]

The night after the successful landing, the first Japanese hammer blow fell. In the Battle of Savo Island off Guadalcanal the U.S. Navy suffered its greatest ever defeat at sea.

On 7 August, S38 radioed a sighting report of Admiral Mikawa's hastily assembled reaction force of seven cruisers and a destroyer racing south from Rabaul. The submarine could not attack, because the force actually steamed over her. Munson's report and another from an RAAF Hudson were not given the weight they deserved.

On the night of 8/9 August, in a short, murderous assault off Savo Island, the eight Japanese ships cut through the Allied covering force. When they withdrew after forty-five minutes the enemy had achieved a stunning victory. Three U.S. cruisers as well as the Australian *Canberra* had been sunk, leaving 1,024 Allied sailors dead and 763 wounded. All of this cost thirty-five Japanese deaths and fifty-one wounded. It was a small price to pay for such a crushing victory—but more was to come.

The next morning off Kavieng, S44 (Lt. Comdr. J. R. Moore) sighted four of the victorious cruisers approaching in two columns. With their slow underwater speed, submarines—like Munson's S38 just days before—often could not achieve a firing position against fast targets. But this was different. S44's position was good, and Moore maneuvered to make it better. He chose the second ship in the second column. Waiting until he could clearly distinguish the white-uniform-clad officers on the bridge, he fired all four bow tubes' reliable old Mark 10 torpedoes from seven hundred yards. All four hit. Within five minutes, the heavy cruiser *Kako* slid beneath the waves. S44's crew later reported that the concussion of the torpedo hits and the cacophony of the ship's boilers exploding and bulkheads collapsing alarmed them more than the depth-charging as they crept away.

Kako was quite a prize. The cruiser had participated in the Japanese victories at Guam, Wake Island, and Rabaul and in the Coral Sea battle. The night before, she had torpedoed *Chicago*. S44 had taken some revenge for Savo Island and the other reverses, but her success was more notable than that. This was the first time a U.S. submarine had ever sunk a major enemy warship.

On Moore's return to Brisbane the executive officer, Lt. C. W. Flenniken, received the Silver Star. Moore's Navy Cross was not his only reward. He was transferred to command the fleet-boat *Sailfish*, whose previous commander, Richard Voge, had been detached to become the first staff officer at Pearl Harbor with combat experience.

One of the first S-boats sent to the new Solomons theater was S39. She never reached her patrol area and became the first Brisbane submarine to be lost.[4] Commissioned in 1923, S39 was assigned to the Philippines the next year. She arrived in Brisbane from Fremantle on 23 April 1942 with three war patrols on her record.

A fruitless fourth patrol ended alongside *Griffin* on 6 June. In his patrol report Lt. Comdr. Francis Brown recommended that, for further operations in these poorly surveyed waters, a fathometer be installed. His request was not granted.

After five weeks of extensive overhaul, S39 began trials in Moreton Bay on 14 July. Brown, an engineering specialist, judged the work satisfactory and set course for the boat's fifth patrol in the New Ireland–New Britain area. Only one hour later, the rudder indicator jumped gears and the port engine stopped. S39 returned to *Griffin*. Next day they sailed again, but the starboard engine broke down. After twenty-four hours of work, the vessel again limped back to *Griffin*.

On 3 August the submarine again headed out. Relief at being under way was tempered by the number of heavy colds among the crew. The executive officer, Lt. Larry Bernard, was so ill that he was confined to his bunk, leaving S39 one watch-keeping officer short. As heavy rain increased and sea conditions deteriorated, so did Bernard's condition. Worried, Brown radioed Brisbane. He was ordered to head for Townsville. Three days of plowing through heavy seas ended in meeting HMAS *Bendigo,* and Bernard, now suffering from pneumonia, was transferred for treatment in Townsville.

Finally, with Lt. Guy Gugliotta as executive officer and Lt. Monk Hendrix as acting navigator, S39 turned for her new patrol area west of Bougainville. The machinery was running better than most could remember, and the weather improving.

But the good weather did not last. Strong southeasterly winds and heavy seas returned. Low cloud and poor visibility restricted the new navigator's position sights. At midnight on the night of 13/14 August, with the ship's dead-reckoning position estimated to be well east of the Louisiade Archipelago, course was changed. On the pitching conning tower, the watch strained their eyes into the inky black night.

Shortly before 2:20 AM, a lookout reported possible breakers ahead. The officer of the watch at first identified them as low cloud, then, realizing his mistake, ordered "back emergency." It was too late. At speed, and with strong following winds and seas, S39 rode up on a reef south of Rossel Island. It was almost the peak of high tide.

In seconds, as his ship listed to port, Brown was on the bridge where he fought to keep the stern to the pounding sea. At 3:15 he radioed Brisbane. In spite of all efforts the boat slewed partly broadside to the seas. The crew donned life jackets and readied the three boats. Then, a breaking wave swept one boat away, slamming Seaman R. Ray against a protruding pipe, opening his left leg from buttock to knee.

With the clear dawn the navigator fixed their position as 3.2 nautical miles west of Adele Island. The list eased to 5 degrees. Still, the position looked so bad that the captain ordered all secret publications burned. At 6:40 AM Brisbane requested details and instructed that torpedoes were to be the last items jettisoned. Brown used the time to high tide to jettison other munitions, most of the food, fuel, and ballast.

Forty minutes of backing and twisting began at 10:30 AM. The vessel moved about fifty feet, but the list increased to 40 degrees. With the batteries almost drained, Brown ordered ballast and trim tanks flooded to hold their position.

The radiomen had been trying unsuccessfully to contact Brisbane, finally transmitting "any stations" calls. It was a relief to hear a reply. RAN Radioman Dan Dryer on Thursday Island relayed their message. The reply stated that HMAS *Katoomba* would arrive the next day. If refloating efforts failed, she would embark the crew and *S39* would be destroyed.

Katoomba (Comdr. A. P. Cousin, RANR[S]) was escorting a troop convoy to Milne Bay with HMAS *Arunta* when she was detached at 12:50 PM to go to the aid of *S39*. Three hundred nautical miles to the west and butting through rough seas and a strong headwind at her best speed, the corvette would take a full twenty-four hours to reach the scene.[5]

The crew settled down to wait. Twenty-foot breakers pounded the hull. Leaks developed in the oil tanks. The battery charge did not go well. *S39's* position deteriorated.

The next morning, Brown made a last effort to break free unassisted. All torpedoes were deactivated and fired onto the reef. With all ballast blown, both motors backed full. The only result was a swing broadside to the swell, and a greater tilt to 60 degrees. Now the ship seemed not only doomed but in danger of capsizing.

Brown gave permission for any who wished to make the hazardous swim through the surf to the comparative safety of the reef. Nobody went. He then decided to land the injured Ray and all the nonswimmers there.

It was not an easy transfer. Lieutenant Hendrix battled the swirling seas to take a light line to the reef. Then Chief Commissary Steward Walter Schoenrock joined him to land and make fast a heavy mooring line. By noon, as the rising seas widened the hull leaks, all the crew except for the captain, two officers, and twelve senior sailors were safely on the reef.

Katoomba arrived at 1:10 PM, finding *S39* "on weather reef with heavy seas breaking over her. . . . On approaching the reef the height of the breaking seas was estimated at from 15 to 20 feet. . . . Large submerged rocks were close under her starboard quarter and also on the port quarter, and seas were continually pounding right over her. Thirty-two men were standing on the reef proper which was not dry but apparently had about 18 inches of water over it."[6]

Nevertheless, *Katoomba* prepared to pass a tow wire to *S39*. Then, at 2 PM, an explosion rocked the submarine, and water poured in. A jettisoned 4-inch shell had detonated under the engine room. At 2:18 Brown signaled the corvette, "Ready to evacuate."

But dragging her anchor, *Katoomba* was also in danger. Deciding that his boats would not survive in the heavy seas, Cousin signaled Brown that he would sail to the island's lee side. He asked Brown to have those on the reef wade three-quarters of a mile across the lagoon for him to pick them up. Cousin would put to sea for the night, prudently not anchoring after dark in enemy waters. Those remaining would have to spend a wet night on the reef.

As the reef party set off, the crew on board smashed what machinery and fittings they could and poured oil and alcohol over the rest. Essential records, some sentimental items, and supplies for the night on the reef, including half a dozen bottles of brandy and whiskey, went into waterproof cans. When the rest had reached the reef, Brown fired a flare down the hatch to ignite the oil- and alcohol-soaked interior of his submarine. Then he joined them.

By 7 PM, twenty survivors were aboard *Katoomba*. Carrying the injured Ray, they had waded across the lagoon to meet the corvette's whalers at a narrow pass in the reef.

As darkness fell, the twenty-seven remaining on the coral passed the bottles and began a sing-along. By midnight the song list was exhausted, the wind had increased, and the tide was above the men's knees and still rising. As the water reached their waists, cold added to their discomfort. In spite of that, some men fell asleep standing up. Their shipmates grabbed them as they slumped into the water.

Around 2:30 AM the tide began to ebb. The water was just lapping their ankles when *Katoomba*'s whaleboat came into sight at dawn. Passing the last bottle around, the weary group waded across the lagoon to meet it. *Katoomba* sailed from Rossel Island at 11:30 AM, 16 August, with all of S39's crew aboard. The submarine's destruction was judged so complete that the corvette did not shell the smoldering hulk. However, Brisbane later ordered bombers to pound the wreck.

Exhausted, the submariners spent most of the three days to Townsville sleeping. *Katoomba* berthed at 9:38 AM, and S39's crew returned to Brisbane by train. Commander Cousin recorded his "admiration for the exemplary conduct and behaviour of S39's personnel and particularly for the captain, Lt. F. E. Brown, USN, and the 26 other officers and men who remained standing over knee-deep on the reef throughout a dirty squally night."[7]

Katoomba's boiler-room crew had happy memories of the rescue. The Americans' soaked clothes had been hung there to dry, and most of the loose change in the pockets had fallen into the bilges. At the next bilge cleaning the chief stoker was inundated with volunteers for this normally unpopular job.[8]

In Brisbane, crew members were reassigned to other boats. The subsequent inquiry exonerated Brown, and he was soon at sea again in command of S43. However, the captain of the only S-boat lost from Brisbane was not so fortunate the next time. On 7 October 1943, Brown went down with S44 in action off the Kuriles.

The crew of USS S39 gathered on the stern of HMAS *Katoomba*.
Courtesy of Dr. R. McLeod collection

The month before S39 was lost off New Guinea, S37 came within five seconds of destruction on Brisbane's doorstep.

The Asiatic Fleet veteran became, in February 1942, the first U.S. submarine ever to sink an enemy destroyer. Two months later she limped into Brisbane. Four hard war patrols had produced defects that included sixteen burned-out main engine bearings.

After extensive work, S37 (Lt. Comdr. J. Reynolds) moved to Moreton Bay on 22 June for tests. *Griffin's* repair officer suggested that Reynolds dive his boat to 135 feet—only half her design depth, but a prudent figure for the condition of the hull. Water poured in through hull leaks, through the forward toilet, and around the periscopes. Back at periscope depth, Reynolds donned a raincoat and sou'wester hat before stepping under the shower to make his observations. He then surfaced and returned to New Farm Wharf. More work was obviously needed.

The next day S37 sailed on her fifth war patrol and her first from Brisbane. Returning four weeks later, she began her entry into the Port of Brisbane in predawn darkness. What happened next is described by two participants.

The captain's report for 21 July 1942 states, "0225—After challenge by Port War Signal Station, encountered great difficulty in establishing identity. Created a grave situation in approaching protective devices before being identified. Signal Station ordered ship to stop. Stopped one half mile south of N.W.1 buoy. Required one hour lying to and boarding ship by port examination officer to clear identity. Pilot vessel almost rammed the S37, requiring this ship to back emergency and rig the ship for collision."[9]

Bill Ruhe, S37's engineering officer, recalled the incident in more colorful detail:

> I was sleeping peacefully when the collision alarm snapped me awake. All the bulkhead doors were slammed shut and tightly dogged before I could get to the control room. . . . The 37 was moving frantically—backing, stopping, going ahead, then backing full. Finally, at secure from collision, the doors were opened, and [another officer] came aft to explain what happened.
>
> As he related it, we had started up the swept channel in Moreton Bay without having exchanged any recognition signals with the shore station guarding the entrance to the bay. When the 37 passed over a detection coil in the channel, a controlled mine in the channel was automatically activated to blow up the intruder. The shore station, alerted by a signal from the detection coil, illuminated the 37. Recognition signals were exchanged, and the activated mine was turned off. The shore station blinked over to the 37, "You were lucky this time. There were still five seconds to go before you triggered our mine."[10]

Upon arrival at New Farm, Lieutenant Commander Reynolds requested relief from command of S37 because of stress. On her two later patrols from Brisbane S37 was commanded by Lt. T. Baskett, an urbane lover of poetry whose party piece was a recitation of Milton's elegy *Lycidas*.[11]

As the Guadalcanal campaign gathered momentum, the S-boats struggled in the now fast-moving war. Japanese destroyers on overnight supply runs to Guadalcanal and offensive action swept by the S-boats too fast or out of range. S-boats were located in defensive positions off Savo Island to ambush Japanese raids. This was a focal point for both sides and placed S-boats in danger from friend and foe alike. S37, S41, and S42 all found themselves sharing this billet with an enemy submarine. This represented a danger to their survival and also identified their location, which was then avoided by Japanese warships. Brisbane's S-class submarines failed to sink any more ships in the Southwest Pacific.

By the end of September all remaining S-boats were due for a thorough refurbishment. Fleet-submarines were becoming available, and Brisbane's S-boats could be released or relegated to defensive patrols off Milne Bay, Noumea, or Fiji. During September and October, *S37, S38, S40,* and *S41* patrolled back to Pearl Harbor via the Gilbert and Ellice Islands. With years of service in the Asiatic Fleet, their crews looked forward to seeing home again. After refueling in Noumea, *S37* reconnoitered enemy activity in the Gilbert Islands en route to Hawaii. The long haul exceeded the submarine's official cruising range by ten nautical miles. Sure enough, the tanks ran dry at almost that distance from Pearl Harbor, and the batteries brought the boat in.

S42, S45, and *S47* sailed on their last Solomons patrols in mid-October. Then, at 11:30 AM, 11 November, Brisbane River pilot Neill took *Griffin* to sea accompanied by *S43, S44,* and *S46.* A week later SubDiv 53 rendezvoused at Suva. After voyage repairs, *Griffin* led her six boats in retracing their path of eight months earlier back to Panama via Bora Bora, arriving on 7 January 1943. There they parted. The submarines transited the canal to the Atlantic. *Griffin* headed for Oakland, California, for modernization.

USS *Griffin* (Capt. S. D. Jupp) had a proud Brisbane record, performing fifty submarine refits and repairs over seven months. Throughout this period *Griffin* was hard pressed servicing her S-boats because of the extent and frequency of their breakdowns, wear, and damage. Her June workload was eight or nine S-boats refitting for most of the month and six or seven at any one time in July and August. When Fremantle submarines started to arrive in September, refit and voyage repairs were provided to them as well.

The work was heavy and unrelenting, and *Griffin's* men worked long hours to keep their aged submarines at sea. However, not all were satisfied with the tender's work. *S39's* crew blamed poor workmanship by *Griffin* for some of the July breakdowns that delayed their fifth war patrol.

As the only American repair ship available, the workload of the "Grimy G," as *Griffin* was known to her crew, expanded beyond submarines. In September the versatile tender overhauled Mark 13 aerial torpedoes before dispatching them to Townsville and Darwin. Another task was the overhauling of guns on forty-five Allied merchant ships. The most unusual undertaking was the salvaging of all the armament from *Rufus King,* wrecked off Moreton Bay's South Passage in July 1942. *Griffin's* people successfully transferred her weapons to the shore.

Attached to Task Force 42 was the old gunboat USS *Tulsa* (Lt. W.

Porter). Small and slow, she provided useful escort and training support. In this latter capacity *Tulsa* acted as a target for submarines practicing sonar approaches and attacks.

Over seven months, eleven overage S-boats made thirty-seven patrols from Brisbane ranging from thirteen to forty-two days. Their six confirmed sinkings amounting to 29,874 tons were not impressive, but against superior forces in waters suited to the enemy, they had held the line. Their attacks included some critical successes, and their presence forced the Japanese to take precautions.

Their crews had done well to achieve such results with such old vessels. Official naval historian Samuel Eliot Morison summed up the difficulties they had to overcome as slow speed, primitive torpedo control, poor diving performance, telltale oil leaks, and poor habitability. He continued: "Navigating an S-boat was accomplished more by smell and feel than through science. There was no radar, no fathometer, and only inferior sound gear. Submergence all day in unpredictable currents threw off dead reckoning, and without bubble sextants star fixes could not be obtained at night; even their horizon sextants were almost worn out so that twilight fixes were uncertain."[12]

The S-boats were primitive, unsanitary, and prone to equipment failure and malfunction. Nevertheless, their crews battled adversities to keep their vessels at sea and make their contribution to the Allied cause. Despite such conditions, the crews' morale was high. When fifteen men on *S37* were offered transfer to a new submarine under construction, only two accepted.[13]

Others too appreciated the S-boats' efforts. As *S37* exited the Brisbane River to begin her sixth patrol, she met entering port the New Zealand–manned cruiser HMNZS *Achilles,* one of the vanquishers of the German battleship *Admiral Graf Spee.* Honors were exchanged as their bows crossed, and *S37*'s crew were stunned as cheers thundered out from the cruiser's decks above. The heroes of the war's first great sea battle in the South Atlantic were saluting their brave little ally of the South Pacific.[14]

And so the S-boats departed. Although some later returned as training boats, they were replaced in Brisbane by newer submarines. *S39* had been the only loss, and not one sailor had been killed. Milton's *Lycidas,* Captain Baskett's party piece, had been written to honor a drowned friend. No Brisbane submariner had ended like Lycidas, "dead, ere his prime . . . in that perilous flood." Not yet.

5

NEW TASKS

"DESTROY ENEMY VESSELS"—the block letters in S39's patrol orders bluntly stated the primary mission for all submarines.[1] When Lieutenant Commander Brown took S39 out on 10 May 1942, his predominant mission was to sink ships. But throughout the Brisbane base's life its submarines carried out other vital roles grouped under the intentionally vague term "special missions." Such diversions from a submarine's primary mission were frequently justified: "It was neither profitable nor proper to avoid all missions of mercy, or in support of clandestine war, or many other special tasks for which submarines were best suited. The trick was to maintain a balance which did not divert too much submarine effort from their major job."[2]

When S39 sailed just two days after the climax of the Coral Sea battle, her orders stated, "A large number of enemy transports strongly supported by men of war of all types including aircraft carriers has been sighted . . . particularly in the vicinity of DEBOYNE ISLAND."[3] Deboyne was in the middle of S39's Patrol Area Victor. Sensibly, she was ordered to reconnoiter. In powerful currents and heavy seas, solid overcast and haze, S39 spent days examining Deboyne and its neighbor, Misima. As the seas abated she circumnavigated the island, then radioed Brisbane that no ships had been sighted. Some Japanese were on Misima, but Deboyne's beaches appeared unsuited for landings. Then S39 resumed her primary mission.

There was another source of intelligence in the islands. In 1919, Capt. C. J. Clare, district naval officer, Western Australia, suggested organizing civilian volunteers along Australia's remote coasts to form a coastwatching service. In wartime they would report shipping movements, suspicious activity, and any other information of value.[4] The proposal was adopted and extended to include Papua New Guinea and the Solomon Islands. By 1939 the coastwatching service of civilian volunteers reporting by radio was in place. Lt. Comdr. Eric Feldt, an inaugural graduate of the Royal Australian Naval College, now warden of the Wau goldfields, was mobilized to command them. As the volunteers watched for German and Italian raiders, in anticipation of Japan's entry into the war he worked with the director of naval intelligence, Comdr. R. B. Long, on improving the screen.

From these beginnings the small coastwatching service made a contribution to victory in the South Pacific out of all proportion to its size. Brisbane's submarines provided vital support to the coastwatchers.

When the Japanese occupied the islands, Feldt acted quickly to protect his operatives, now behind the lines of a brutal enemy. He arranged service commissions to regularize their status and worked to retrieve those in immediate danger. At the top of this list were A. K. Kyle and G. M. Benham on New Ireland and J. L. Woodroffe on Feni Island forty miles to the east.

On 27 June 1942, Feldt, with Lt. Comdr. I. Pryce-Jones, RANR, called on the commander of Task Force 42, Rear Admiral Rockwell, to ask for assistance from a submarine. Pryce-Jones reported, "The admiral was understandably reluctant to withdraw a submarine from offensive operations. When, however, he ultimately agreed to authorize the mission, his co-operation and that of his officers was whole-hearted."[5] Lt. Comdr. E. R. Hannon's S43 was assigned to the mission, sailing from Brisbane with Pilot Officer C. J. Mason aboard to contact the coastwatchers.

On the night of 19/20 July, Mason landed on the east coast of New Ireland and gathered information from the local people before reembarking. He discovered that Kyle and Benham were prisoners of the Japanese. S43 then landed Mason on Feni Island, where, according to his New Ireland contacts, Woodroffe was hiding in the bush. Mason spent all the next day on an unsuccessful search. He passed a note to an islander to deliver to Woodroffe telling him to be on the beach the following night.

Returning to the submarine, Mason accidentally holed his boat on launching it and barely made it back to the beach before it sank. A rubber boat was dispatched from the submarine to recover a soaked, exhausted Mason. As the coastwatcher stumbled aboard, Hannon pointed to a flashing light on the beach. Was it Woodroffe a day early? The rescuers weighed the options. Mason, who had not slept for thirty-six hours, was at the end of his endurance. They decided to stick with the plan and wait.

The next night Mason paddled ashore to keep the rendezvous. When

S43 returned after midnight, a Japanese patrol boat was in the area. At
1:30 AM, S43 was in her pickup position off the beach. No one came. The
boat returned at the appointed time on the next three nights. Lights seen
on the last night did not conform with the plan. Nevertheless, Hannon
signaled. Receiving no reply, S43 resumed her war patrol. It was later
learned, as Pryce-Jones reported, that both Woodroffe and Mason had
been captured.[6]

This tragic mission brought home to the submariners the hazards their
passengers faced ashore. The sailors had risked their own lives attempting
to retrieve the coastwatchers. That S43 was not attacked showed that
Mason had returned their loyalty.

Special missions, as dedicated missions or added to a war patrol, were
not popular. They took submarines away from their primary task of sinking
enemy ships. They involved discomfort as more men and equipment were
crammed into already cramped boats. Closing poorly charted enemy shores
at night, they exacerbated the dangers of an already hazardous service.

The submariners carried out all the special missions assigned willingly
and professionally, and there was an unplanned, enduring by-product:
packed together, American sailors and the mainly Australian coastwatchers developed a mutual understanding and admiration.

The night Mason began his fateful mission on New Ireland, Sub-Lt. Malcolm Wright completed another special mission on New Britain. Wright,
a patrol officer in New Guinea since 1936, was assigned to a pioneering
mission from 12 to 19 July 1942. His commander, Eric Feldt, described this
mission frankly: "His first assignment, to land at Adler Bay, was authorised
by the High Command with the object of obtaining intelligence of the
Japanese buildup at Rabaul. I knew he would not get any worthwhile
information on that subject but I did want to try out the possibilities and
find out the difficulties of landing parties from submarines. The most
important information was the likely attitude of the natives which was
then unknown. Malcolm's landing provided this and other information on
the practical side which made other landings possible."[7]

In his meetings with local people during a week ashore, Wright
achieved all his chief's aims. He even dispelled Feldt's doubts about the
mission's chances of obtaining intelligence on Rabaul. A young Chinese
man who had worked in a labor gang gave Wright a detailed layout of
Japanese installations in the town.

The night before his return to the submarine, Wright received tangible
proof of the "attitude of the natives." Before an appreciative audience of

village men, Nugilei, the chief, addressed the former patrol officer: "Master Wright, until you came we believed that all the white men were dead. The Japanese had told us so. But we have seen you . . . and we know that they lied. Now we know that someday the Australians will return and bring good times back with them." Giving Wright a small package, Nugilei went on: "We would like you to send this to the King. Tell him that we are still his people and we look forward to the day when the Australians return to New Guinea." When he reached Brisbane, Wright forwarded the fine piece of tapa cloth to the governor general. The king later received it. When the Australians did return in 1945, Nugilei was presented to the Duke of Gloucester. The old man was overwhelmed when he shook hands with the "brother belong king."

The night after Nugilei's speech, at the end of a tense week spent deep within enemy territory, Wright rowed to the waiting S42. Approaching, he hailed the boat, and "the sound of the American voices answering me was like beautiful music." Wright became good friends with S42's commander, Oliver Kirk, and his executive officer, Francis Gambacorta. On their return to Brisbane, the three spent much of their leave together.[8]

S43's rescue attempt, S39's reconnaissance, and S42's coastwatcher landing and retrieval were typical of later special missions. But some were different.

In mid-October 1942, *Amberjack* (Lieutenant Commander Bole) was near the end of her first war patrol when a radio message diverted it to Espiritu Santo, where Bole was briefed for a unique mission. On beleaguered Guadalcanal, aviation fuel was in desperately short supply, and Japanese forces thwarted any chance of surface resupply. If the planes could not fly, the balance would tip in favor of the Japanese. *Amberjack's* crew loaded nine thousand gallons of aviation gasoline into two fuel tanks, then sailed on 22 October with two hundred bombs and fifteen army pilots and ground crew.

Cautiously closing Guadalcanal three days later, Bole was ordered to divert to Tulagi. The reason became obvious when three Japanese destroyers sped past to pour fire on the American marines and drop supplies to their troops before racing off. At dusk, *Amberjack* surfaced to discharge her vital cargo of men, munitions, and fuel. Then, just after midnight, the relieved crew began their voyage to a well-deserved leave in Brisbane. This was the only time in the war a U.S. submarine was used as a fuel tanker.

Coastwatchers played a vital role during the early months of desperate struggle following the American landing at Guadalcanal.

Lt. W. J. ("Jack") Read, in north Bougainville, 480 miles from Guadal-canal, was on the flight path from the Japanese air base at Kavieng. Lt. Paul E. Mason, a former planter, was above Buin in the island's south athwart the route of attackers from the other main base at Rabaul. He also overlooked the anchorage where the enemy assembled ships for the dash to Guadalcanal. Their warnings enabled American defenders to inflict heavy losses on raiders.

The Japanese had little room to maneuver. To make the long round-trip in daylight, their raids occurred around midday. With the distance close to the range of their aircraft, they could not vary their route. The enemy took the obvious solution of developing airfields at Buka and Kahili in Bougainville's south, closer to Guadalcanal. In addition, land patrols from Kahili forced Mason to move so that ships and planes could slip by.

In late August, Australian and American intelligence decided to improve the network by placing coastwatchers on the closer islands of Vella Lavella and Choiseul. Henry Josselyn, Guadalcanal's former assistant district offi-cer, volunteered for Vella Lavella. Nick Waddell, former Choiseul district officer, was the other obvious choice. Aircraft insertion was deemed unsafe, so the submarine *Grampus* (Lt. Comdr. J. R. Craig) was chosen to deliver the parties. Two men were required on each island, so the Australian for-mer patrol officer, Sub-Lt. John Keenan, joined Josselyn, and Waddell chose Sgt. Carden Seton, "a physical giant of a man" who had managed plantations on Choiseul.[9]

The parties had to be self-sufficient for at least three months. Major limiting factors were the thirty-inch diameter of the submarine hatch and the fact that each party's two men had to land and carry the stores at night on an unknown shore. Tele-radios and all other articles susceptible to water damage were sewn into canvas and waterproofed. All packages except batteries and their charging engine were restricted to fifty pounds. Multiple items were spread among packages to avoid "putting all their eggs in one basket." Each party took ten two-man Mark III food packs. To protect tins from puncture, packs were enclosed in buoyant wooden crates. The men found that using local food supplements doubled a pack's life to two weeks.

On 6 October a truck took the groups' stores and personal gear to New Farm Wharf. Loaded onto *Grampus* with the ship's stores, they were kept separate in the after torpedo room. That night two seven-man rubber boats and a small collapsible canoe for each party went aboard. The canoes were made in Brisbane, copied from a museum outrigger exhibit, and "aged" to look exactly like a well-used local craft.

Josselyn described their embarkation: "We ourselves boarded the submarine depot ship USS *Griffin* at 2000 hours on the 6 October in uniform. In order that four British officers might not be seen by any curiously minded persons boarding a United States submarine and not disembarking again, we rigged ourselves as U.S. seamen before going aboard."[10] Walter Lord gave more detail: "It was at this point that Waddell had a brilliant inspiration. Since they had to dress like gobs, why not *act* like gobs? So they spent a final glorious evening on the town, ultimately stumbling aboard in most authentic fashion." The performance was a little marred by the pronounced English and Australian accents of the "gobs." Waiting below to give them a final briefing was the Allied Intelligence Bureau's head, a disapproving Col. C. G. Roberts. All merriment ceased forthwith.[11]

At this stage of the war any special mission in the New Guinea–Solomons area was added to the prime focus of the submarine's patrol, the war against shipping. So the four coastwatchers who sailed from Brisbane on *Grampus* experienced, in Josselyn's words, both "an unsuccessful attack on an enemy vessel, and . . . an unsuccessful attack on us" before they disembarked.[12]

On 13 October, *Grampus* cautiously approached Vella Lavella's poorly charted coast, spending the afternoon looking for a break in the reef for the landing that night. A Japanese destroyer appeared at about 3 PM and lay off the coast for four hours before sailing. Did the enemy know of their plans? Had the ship put a party ashore? Should the landing be postponed?

As the submarine charged batteries that evening, the men decided to go ahead. At 1 AM *Grampus* hove to three miles off Sauka Point in perfect weather: no moon, good visibility, and only an oily swell disturbing a flat calm. The combination of the swell and the dark, slippery deck complicated the loading of the two rubber boats and the canoe. In the hurry to load the second boat, a case punctured the rubber. Insulation tape only partially sealed the leak, so some supplies had to be left aboard.

Josselyn paddled off in the canoe using a line around his waist to tow the boats, with Keenan plugging the leak. With two thousand pounds to tow, they made slow progress, and it was two and a half hours before they reached the reef. Unable to find a passage before the rapidly approaching dawn, they decided to shoot the surf, coming through unscathed, although the damaged boat capsized with the loss of some supplies. The pair unloaded and hid the boats just before a Japanese flying boat flew low along the beach.[13] (Later in the war a wire radar target and walkie-talkies allowed a submarine to track and direct boats to the shore. Then they were dragged back by a light line.)[14] Five nights later Waddell and Seton landed on Choiseul, and *Grampus* resumed her war patrol.

Over the succeeding months new coastwatchers joined their comrades on other islands to report aircraft and ships transiting the Slot. They performed other functions, too. On 6 August 1943, Sub-Lt. R. Evans, RAN, on Kolombangara rescued the captain and ten crew members of a PT boat sunk four days before in Blackett Strait. Evans met the skipper again in 1961, when he flew to the United States to meet President John F. Kennedy in the White House.

The coastwatchers' rescue total in these fiercely contested waters was high. Josselyn and his partner hosted 31 aircrew and 165 survivors of the cruiser *Helena*. Waddell and Seton had, by 2 March 1944, a score of twenty-three airmen rescued.[15] Coastwatchers sometimes took enemy lives in gun battles, but this was against Feldt's policy of covert observation. He had deliberately named his organization Ferdinand after Walt Disney's bull who preferred sniffing flowers to fighting. Coastwatchers could make a much greater contribution to victory by staying out of fights.

The coastwatchers' contribution was great and freely acknowledged:

"Large share of our success against enemy due splendid men in coastwatcher service."   (Adm. R. K. Turner, USN)

"The intelligence signaled from Bougainville by Read and Mason saved Guadalcanal, and Guadalcanal saved the South Pacific."
                                                      (Adm. W. F. Halsey, USN)[16]

Less known was the vital support submarines gave the coastwatchers. But the coastwatchers knew it and acknowledged it in their reports. Josselyn wrote, "Our relations with Lieutenant Commander Craig, his officers and men, were of the highest order. We owe them much."[17] Keenan reported, "They did everything possible to make our effort a success."[18]

Sadly, five months after the landings, *Grampus* was lost with all hands. Other boats continued the special missions.

Since the beginning of the war Lieutenant Read had been transmitting intelligence from the north of Bougainville, and with the American invasion of Guadalcanal, his messages had given up to two hours' warning of air attacks. Yet as 1942 drew to a close, Read had the pressing problem of Allied civilians who had been unwilling or unable to escape before the enemy occupation. They were now hiding in bush camps, and Read wanted them safely away, not only for their own sakes but also because their capture and ill treatment by the Japanese "would have caused most undesirable effect on native opinion."[19]

Four of the fugitives were American nuns, Sisters of St. Joseph of Orange, California. The two nurses and two teachers had started the order's first foreign mission on Buka Island in 1940. After Pearl Harbor, they ignored evacuation orders, believing that their religious status protected them.[20] Following the March 1942 killing of a plantation owner and the arrest of a priest, the nuns hid in the mountains until Read arranged their escape to a camp one hundred miles south. Reports of the capture, mistreatment, and murder of other nuns and priests forced a further flight inland to the mountains on 3 December.

For almost four more weeks the nuns, together with some Marist sisters and two old priests, stayed in their jungle retreat while Read and an American priest, Father Lebel, worked on their evacuation. In a radio message to Admiral Halsey, Lebel pointed out that the nuns were American citizens. To relieve Read of his burden, at 4 AM on 29 December, Halsey's headquarters radioed USS *Nautilus* (Lieutenant Commander Brockman), patrolling nearby, to evacuate them. The next day the party began its trek to Teop Harbor. The jungle journey over steep slippery paths was taxing, but at dusk on 31 December, Father Lebel led fourteen nuns and two other priests to link up with six other men, three women, and three girl evacuees.

Nautilus surfaced three miles off the harbor entrance and with guns manned awaited the signal. When the fire flared at exactly 10 PM, Lieutenant Lynch and two others set off in the submarine's power launch. They towed astern a rubber boat filled with supplies for Read. Then a broken rudder delayed them for an hour. Read, waiting anxiously ashore and hearing a faint noise in the harbor, paddled out to find the launch stuck on a reef. It was soon free, but Read remembered the moment: "The memory of my brief acquaintance with these men will cling. They reminded me that we were just entering the New Year of 1943 and I was invited to join with them and honour the occasion in good old traditional manner. We did right there in the middle of Teop Harbour; and then got down to the business in hand."[21]

After Read's stores were landed, he and Lieutenant Lynch conferred. Commander Brockman's orders had specified only seventeen women evacuees. Could he safely take the rest? They decided that the launch would take the women out while canoes took the men into the harbor to await its return. At 5:35 AM a relieved Commander Brockman headed *Nautilus* out to sea with all aboard.

For three days before their transfer off Guadalcanal, the ladies occupied the officers' quarters while the men took crew bunks. The pharmacist's mate treated various ailments, including malaria. From Guadalcanal the Australians and the American nuns eventually reached home. Three years later the sisters returned to Buka.

Nautilus resumed her interrupted war patrol. Two days later an aircraft alert forced the boat to dive, leaving Assistant Officer of the Deck Philip Eckhert and lookout J. F. Rossi on deck. As the diving officer, Eckert knew he would soon be missed, and both men were back on board within half an hour. No mention of the incident appeared in the log or patrol report.[22] The report did record a successful attack on a destroyer and the unsuccessful stalking of a cruiser, ruined by malfunctioning torpedoes.

Nautilus ended the patrol in Brisbane on 4 February 1943. There the ship's officers received a letter of thanks signed by all the evacuees, expressing the hope that they could all meet after the war. For some the wish was granted sooner. Before the war ended some of the signatories hosted a party for *Nautilus* at Brisbane's Victoria Park.

There was a surprise for Jack Read when he unpacked the stores *Nautilus* had landed. The crew had added their own gifts of tobacco, clothes, and toiletries. In his report he wrote, "It was a most thoughtful act for which I now record my thanks."

6

NEW SUBMARINES ARRIVE

From the landings on Guadalcanal and the disastrous losses of the Battle of Savo Island, it was clear the battle for the Solomons would be bitterly contested. Both sides poured in troops, aircraft, and shipping to gain the ascendancy. It was another six months before the final outcome of the battle for Guadalcanal would be decided.

Despite two successes at the outset, Brisbane's S-boats were out of their class in the intense fighting later. More submarines of the best type were needed in the Solomons. The nearest submarines available to reinforce Brisbane were the twenty fleet-submarines based in Western Australia. They were patrolling the Dutch East Indies, Indochina, and the Philippines, but found success elusive. One of the two Western Australian squadrons, Squadron 2, would be redeployed to Brisbane, its individual boats transferring progressively as they returned from patrol.

Squadron 2 joined the Asiatic Fleet in the Philippines just before the outbreak of war, and it had been in the forefront of the fighting as the Japanese advance swept them back to Australia. The tender *Holland* was constantly on the move providing a base for her submarines, anchoring successively at Balikpapan, Makassar, Surabaya, Darwin, and Tjilatjap, keeping one step ahead of the Japanese advance. She finally arrived at Fremantle on 3 March 1942, traveling on to Albany two weeks later.

After two months of retreat, the American sailors felt that arriving in Fremantle was like entering heaven. The friendly people were wonderful hosts, the Australian beer was outstanding, and the late summer weather was perfect. They were also free of the threat of Japanese air attack, and they could regroup and return to the fray.

To date, Squadron 2's war against shipping had not gone well. Although none of the squadron had been lost, successes were few and hard won. Too often submarine captains had seen their valuable torpedoes miss, and many believed they were running too deep, passing harmlessly under their targets. In June and July, tests were conducted by *Skipjack* and *Saury* at Albany that proved their fears to be justified. The torpedoes were running ten feet deeper than their setting.

On 12 August 1942, five days after the landing at Guadalcanal, USS *Sculpin* (Lt. Comdr. L. H. Chappell) berthed in Fremantle to be greeted with orders to draw stores sufficient for a six-month detachment to another base. Frantic activity over the next few days allowed her to sail on 17 August, and once at sea, Chappell announced that she was bound for Brisbane. The voyage would take her nonstop south of Tasmania until she reached Brisbane, some twenty-nine hundred nautical miles later.

Sturgeon followed two days behind *Sculpin,* and before the month was out *Sailfish* departed from Albany for Brisbane. It was winter in the Southern Ocean, and at this time of year the weather south of Australia was usually bad. *Sculpin*'s crew were pleasantly surprised by calmer conditions than expected, although cold temperatures were a bracing change from the tropical heat they had endured for the past year.[1]

By the time *Sailfish* made her passage, the weather had turned, and her crew had a very rough trip. Big waves crashed over her bridge, slamming a lookout against the steel superstructure, breaking his jaw. In agony, he was taken below, where the pharmacist's mate could do nothing but administer painkillers until they arrived in Brisbane a week later.

The pressures on the submarines sent east are further illustrated by five recruits who joined *Sailfish* in Albany. They were assigned without undertaking the usual induction course at the navy's Submarine School. Prior to the war, all American submariners were volunteers, and they had to pass essential training at the Submarine School at New London, Connecticut. Under wartime pressure, some, like these, were "shanghaied" direct to the boats. Despite bypassing their basic training, four of these trainees qualified aboard *Sailfish*.[2]

When *Sculpin* moored at New Farm Wharf on 27 August 1942, she was the first fleet-submarine seen in Brisbane, contrasting starkly with the ancient S-boats. Sleek and graceful, she was big, and she was new. Completed four years earlier, *Sculpin* was half again as large as the S-boats, with a displacement of 1,450 tons, a length of 310 feet, and a 27-foot beam. She packed twice the punch, with eight torpedo tubes, four in the bow and four aft. Her twenty-four Mark 14 torpedoes were more advanced than the S-boats' old Mark 10s, containing a complex and highly secret magnetic exploder in addition to their contact detonator.

Sculpin was designed for Pacific service, and her range of twelve thousand nautical miles could take her from Pearl Harbor to Japan and back without refueling. Her patrol endurance of sixty days more than doubled that of the S-boats, and living conditions were much improved. *Sculpin* was roomier than the S-boats and fully air-conditioned. Effective air conditioning improved the atmosphere surrounding the submarine's delicate equipment and also made tropical patrols easier for crewmen. Her six officers and sixty-five enlisted men had mattresses on their bunks, fixed mess tables, showers, and toilets. But living conditions remained austere. With water scarce, shaves and showers were limited to once every four days. Showering entailed a little water on to get wet and soap down, then water on again to rinse off, with less than a gallon used in all. Only forty-six bunks for sixty-five enlisted men meant that "hot-bunking" continued, with some sailors on different watches sharing the same bunk. The distinctive submarine smell of battery acid, diesel fumes, cooking odors, and unwashed bodies remained.

Sculpin's power plant was also a major advance on that of the S-boats. On the surface, four GM Winton diesel engines of around 1,200 hp each, coupled to 1,000-kW generators, could be linked in various combinations to two GE electric motors for propulsive power or to recharge the submarine's batteries. These drove *Sculpin* at a top surface speed of twenty knots, half as fast again as the S-boats. However, their submerged speed of nine knots was no improvement, although 252 wet-cell batteries doubled capacity over the S-boats, giving *Sculpin* a greater endurance on battery power.

New items of equipment, lacking in the S-boats, enhanced *Sculpin's* fighting qualities. A torpedo data computer (TDC) processed information on the bearing, range, and angle on the bow of the target vessel to set and fire torpedoes accurately. Data was input from periscope or sonar, and the TDC automatically portrayed the submarine and target, and computed the proper gyro angle to send to the torpedo room to continuously set it into the torpedo until the moment of firing. The TDC vastly improved the probability of success.

Another improvement was a basic form of air warning radar. *Sculpin's* radar was an early version of SD radar that, in good conditions, could detect aircraft at up to ten miles' distance, far beyond the lookouts' visual range. However, SD radar provided no information on the direction of the contact. Lookouts would search around the compass to find it. SD could also register birds and was prone to breakdowns. Some submarine officers doubted SD radar's usefulness, but it was a start.

Fleet-submarines like *Sculpin* were the backbone of the American submarine force throughout the war. They followed a continuous line of development from 1933 to the end of the war, with successive versions showing incremental improvement on a standard design. Altogether 266 fleet-submarines were completed during this period. Compared with other nations' submarines they were large, befitting the vast Pacific, and the living conditions they offered were unrivaled. They proved reliable and hardy and were well suited to the war conditions they would face.

The term "fleet-submarine" reflected the U.S. Navy's original intention, practiced in prewar exercises, to use submarines to scout ahead of the fleet in surface battles. This concept was discarded during the war, and it was in independent action against Japanese seaborne communications that fleet-submarines made their greatest contribution to victory.

However, in August 1942 the battle over Guadalcanal was shaping up as a struggle between the major warships of the U.S. and Japanese navies. High hopes were held for the contribution America's fleet-submarines would make to the success of this struggle. But this would be difficult. After escaping the Japanese advance and being at sea for nine months of war, Squadron 2's submarines badly needed proper repairs and maintenance. Furthermore, in the Solomons they faced the Japanese navy's best warships in narrow waters. Many of the difficulties already encountered by the S-boats confronted them, too.

Sculpin put to sea on her first Brisbane patrol on 2 September 1942, and *Sturgeon* followed two days later. However, three days out, one of *Sculpin*'s main motors broke down, and she returned to Brisbane. Two days later she departed again. *Sailfish* fared no better. On 10 September she was being swung from her New Farm berth when the tug's towrope broke and the river current carried her into the wharf, where she bent a starboard propeller blade. The propeller was straightened and reinstalled two days later, enabling *Sailfish* to sail. But the damaged propeller vibrated, handicapping *Sailfish* throughout the patrol.[3] Despite these early setbacks, the three fleet-submarines were on station by the second half of September 1942. Each had an eventful patrol.

First on the scene was *Sturgeon* (Lt. Comdr. H. A. Pieczentkowski), patrolling to the west of Bougainville. Within a week she had made two attacks, missing a large cargo ship and possibly damaging a tanker. At dawn on 1 October she achieved a major success, scoring three torpedo hits on the seaplane ferry *Katsuragi Maru*, which sank. This was an important kill, as it struck at the seaplane patrols that the Japanese were using to advantage in the New Guinea and Solomons areas. But *Sturgeon* underwent a vicious depth-charge attack and thereafter leaked oil, revealing her presence to enemy destroyers.[4]

Arriving in her area on 14 September, *Sculpin* spent the next five weeks between New Britain and New Ireland. After her first attack, four very close depth charges caused a leak and extensive internal damage in all compartments. Altogether *Sculpin* made five separate attacks, expending all of her torpedoes. Although four sinkings were claimed, only two ships were confirmed in postwar records. Nevertheless, this represented the best result to date for Task Force 42.

Sailfish had bad luck throughout her patrol largely due to the noisy propeller announcing her presence to listening equipment on Japanese escorts. Three days after arriving south of Bougainville, *Sailfish* fired three torpedoes at a minelayer, but they missed and she was badly shaken up by the depth-charge counterattack that followed. After that, she saw many Japanese targets and destroyers but was unable to get close enough to attack. *Sailfish* suffered several more depth-charge attacks as well as a near miss by aircraft bombs. Her patrol was extended by a week, and it was a tired and battle-weary crew that finally returned to Brisbane.

Tom Parks, a crewman on *Sailfish* during this time, described what it was like on board a submarine during a torpedo attack: "After a long and boring period, the sighting of a target provided some excitement, and when word was passed to man battle stations there was a big adrenaline rush. Most of the crew did not know what was going on during an attack. The crew in the control room watched and listened as the attack progressed, and the torpedomen had some clues from the number of tubes to make ready and the depth setting of the fish."[5] Throughout the attack, both the approach and withdrawal, the submarine would be "rigged for depth charge," with watertight doors and ventilation flaps shut and with machinery, pumps, and fans stopped to reduce noise. "The atmosphere inside . . . was stifling," Parks recalled. In tropical waters with air conditioning shut off, the temperature would rise to as much as 110°F.[6]

Developing the attack was a team effort, with the captain playing the central role. The sound operator provided information on the target and escorts from the listening devices, and the captain took quick looks through the periscope. Data were continuously input to the TDC, which displayed the relevant firing solution, and the TDC operator made recommendations to the captain on positioning the submarine and torpedo settings. In some boats independent calculations were made by another officer on the familiar and simpler devices, the "banjo" and the "is-was." The captain made decisions based on recommendations of his attack team.

However, it was he alone who made the essential decisions on every attack, and it was finally the captain's skill and resolve that determined its success.

Once torpedoes were fired, the sound operator listened to check whether they were running "hot, straight, and normal." All aboard waited anxiously as the time for the torpedo run ticked by. An explosion at the right time indicated a hit, which was heard and cheered by all. This was frequently followed by further sounds of tearing metal and explosions as the target sank.

A successful attack brought great satisfaction to both captain and crew, and every aspect was discussed for days afterward in the messes. If the attack failed, there was general deflation throughout the submarine. For the captain these feelings were even stronger. One described how the high of a successful attack had only a limited life: "Then, when you miss the next one, you hit rock bottom again."[7]

It was essential that the sonar operator follow the escorts' movements, as the torpedo wakes pointed to the submarine's location, immediately attracting escorts to counterattack. Rapid evasive action was essential after every torpedo attack on an escorted target. The captain sat at the plotting board, calculating from sound data the three-dimensional movements for his boat. It was in escaping from depth-charge attack that the captain's skill, composure, judgment, and leadership were put to their greatest test.

Tom Parks recalled Lieutenant Commander Moore's leadership in evading a frightening ten-hour depth-charge attack by three warships on *Sailfish*: "I think that the greatest fear that we had was showing fear. The captain gave us our cue. He appeared calm and coolly gave orders. I especially remember 'Dinty' Moore. . . . Captain Moore acted as if this were an exercise in escape tactics instead of the real thing. I was really scared and trying not to show it. I was staring at the captain wondering what we were going to do, and he looked up, caught my eye, winked, and grinned. I knew then that we were going to make it."[8]

Elsewhere sailors were confined at their battle stations, sweltering in watertight compartments. They heard the depth charges but had no idea how long the ordeal would last. A key to coping with being depth-charged was having something to do to occupy one's attention. Occasionally a sailor became comatose from shock while under attack, slowly recovering after the battle was over. In this case he was transferred off submarines immediately upon return.

August and September 1942 saw the spotlight of the Pacific war focus on the Southwest Pacific. On land the Japanese followed up their advance over the Kokoda Track with an assault on Milne Bay at the eastern tip of Papua. This was bitterly opposed, and in a fortnight of fierce fighting in torrential rain, the Japanese were forced to withdraw. It was the first time during the war that a Japanese invasion was defeated. During September, Australian soldiers finally held the Japanese advance over the Kokoda Track, and the slow process of driving them back began.

The struggle for Guadalcanal remained on a knife-edge. Despite wave after wave of Japanese attacks, American marines held strategically vital Henderson Field, from which American aircraft dominated the skies during daylight. At night the sea belonged to the Japanese, who repeatedly rushed warships through the Solomons at high speed to land fresh troops and bombard Henderson Field.

At sea the Americans were bleeding. In the seven weeks to the end of September 1942, the American fleet lost the aircraft carrier *Wasp*, while two more carriers, *Saratoga* and *Enterprise*, and the modern battleship *North Carolina* sustained heavy damage. Only one aircraft carrier, *Hornet*, and one battleship, *Washington*, remained on line to meet the Japanese fleet. Submarines were desperately needed to tip the balance in the Allies' favor.

With the arrival of the first three fleet-submarines, Christie was able to send ten submarines on patrol from Brisbane in September 1942. This equaled the number of patrols sailing that month from the main Pacific base at Pearl Harbor. Unfortunately, results were poor, with only three vessels sunk, all by Brisbane's newly arrived fleet-boats.

As the Solomons battle accelerated, reinforcements arrived at a painfully slow rate. The next three submarines, *Grampus*, *Grayback*, and *Gudgeon*, left Albany together and arrived in Brisbane on 3 October. All were en route to their patrol areas in the Solomons within the next five days. Squadron 2's remaining submarines, *Swordfish*, *Saury*, *Snapper*, *Seadragon*, and *Sargo*, reached Brisbane at the end of October. *Spearfish* arrived on 11 November. With her squadron transferred to Brisbane, the tender *Holland* left Fremantle for Brisbane at the end of October. She did not complete the journey, damaging her rudder on passage and diverting to Melbourne for repairs.

Moving Squadron 2 to Brisbane depleted the Western Australian task force from twenty submarines to eight. This task force's commander, and also nominal commander of all Southwest Pacific submarines, Rear Adm. C. A. Lockwood, was dismayed at losing so many vessels. His force's area north of Fremantle was immense and potentially productive. With only eight submarines left, he believed he could not maintain an effective campaign in Southeast Asia. A dynamic and proactive leader, Lockwood immediately took up the case to keep the submarines in the west with Vice Admiral Carpender, who commanded all Southwest Pacific naval forces. His arguments fell on deaf ears. He then argued that, being admiral commanding submarines in the Southwest Pacific area, he should exchange with Christie, his subordinate, to command the largest concentration of submarines, now in Brisbane. These arguments also failed. A strong personality clash originating when Carpender and Lockwood were together in the west appears to have been the main reason for the failure of Lockwood's arguments.[9]

Events moved on, and in six months Lockwood was appointed to command the Pacific Fleet's submarines at Pearl Harbor. He held this command for the remainder of the war. Much loved by his men, he was the driving force behind the phenomenal success of American submarines later in the war and their enormous contribution to the ultimate victory.

In September, Lockwood flew to Brisbane to discuss strategy and common issues with Carpender and Christie. Although the uneven distribution of submarine commands was mentioned, an even more pressing reason for his visit was an acute shortage of submarine torpedoes in Australia. Stocks of the fleet-submarines' sophisticated Mark 14 torpedoes were reduced when 230 were lost at the Cavite Navy Yard in the Philippines. Since then Lockwood's submarines had fired torpedoes at a much greater rate than supplies could be delivered. Production of torpedoes was slow, and delivery from the United States, half a world away, was spasmodic and miserly.[10]

With no immediate solution to the supply problem, several measures were taken to keep Australian submarines effective at this critical stage of the war. Most important of these in Brisbane was issuing the S-boats' older Mark 10 torpedoes to fleet-submarines and rationing supplies, resulting in submarines sailing without a full torpedo load.

Mark 10 torpedoes were not a great success on fleet-submarines, equipped as they were with different connections from the TDC to the torpedo gyros. Time and again attacks were abandoned because torpedo gyros could not be set in time to allow an accurate firing. This was critical where targets were either fast-moving warships or heavily escorted merchant ships.

Rationing could be severe. S38 was reduced to only four torpedoes when she sailed on 21 September 1942. In her single patrol from Brisbane, *Seadragon* (Lt. Comdr. W. E. Ferrall) carried twenty torpedoes instead of twenty-four, and all were older Mark 10s. During this patrol Ferrall was forced to abort four separate torpedo attacks because the gyros could not be set quickly enough to make the shot. Aboard *Seadragon* this was put down to the age of the torpedoes and a mechanism worn by repeated practice over the years. *Sculpin* experienced similar frustration in attempting to fire Mark 10 torpedoes. Her officers believed the problem was that the motors used for setting the gyros of Mark 14 torpedoes were not strong enough for the mechanism on the Mark 10s.[11]

With war in the Southwest Pacific at such a critical stage, Christie deployed his submarines to achieve best results. Competing priorities pressed upon him. First was the savage struggle to control the Solomons. Against this, General MacArthur was demanding submarines to assist the Allied campaign in New Guinea. Following prewar American doctrine of using submarines with the surface fleet, Christie positioned them off Japanese bases and along the enemy's route to Guadalcanal. In this way submarines should pick off enemy warships, reducing their numbers before they met American surface forces. Unfortunately, Christie's submarines did not live up to expectations. Although there was no shortage of enemy vessels sighted, heavy escorts, fast targets, poor torpedoes, limited space for maneuvering, and the need to remain submerged in the face of strong enemy patrols all contributed to the submarines being unable either to attack or to succeed.

However, a major cause of the failure of Christie's fleet-submarines at this stage was limited strategic vision. Distinguished submarine historian Clay Blair described this failure:

> By September, when the first three [fleet-submarines] left Brisbane, it was clear from codebreaking information and other intelligence that the Japanese were using Palau and Truk as bases for operations in the Solomons. There was heavy traffic—both men-of-war and merchant shipping—between those islands and Rabaul and Kavieng. Rather than attack this traffic on the high seas, with open water and plenty of leg room, Christie chose to position the boats off the terminal points, where air and sea antisubmarine measures were heaviest. As a result, the skippers were forced to remain submerged a great deal of the time in shallow and dangerous waters, wasting two prime assets of the fleet boat: speed and mobility.[12]

7
BOATS FROM PEARL HARBOR

Through October and November, while Australian troops inched their way over the Kokoda Track, American marines grimly held Henderson Field against persistent, determined Japanese attacks.

The battle at sea became more intense as Japanese and American warships met repeatedly in bloody and savage night battles. The aircraft carrier fleets clashed again in late October, with heavy losses on both sides. The climax came in the middle of November, when the Japanese attempted to bombard Henderson Field and run a convoy of reinforcements to Guadalcanal. In three days twenty-six ships, from battleships to destroyers, including all convoy transports, were sunk.

The Guadalcanal crisis brought changes to Brisbane's submarine war. Control of the task force changed, and the number of American submarines increased. Guadalcanal lay in the South Pacific, part of the Pacific area under the supreme control of Admiral Nimitz, while New Guinea and the Bismarck Archipelago were in the Southwest Pacific area controlled by General MacArthur. Task Force 42 was part of Southwest Pacific forces, but to ensure the best coordination of all naval forces available it was essential that Christie's submarines supporting the Guadalcanal battle come under the direction of the South Pacific Command.

On 18 October 1942, Vice Adm. W. F. "Bull" Halsey, an energetic and aggressive leader with an impressive record, took command of Allied forces in the South Pacific area. Soon afterward Admiral Nimitz placed Christie under Halsey to integrate Task Force 42 into the overall Pacific strategy, particularly in the Guadalcanal campaign.

Captain Christie's situation became anomalous and unique. He was the only Pacific task force leader responsible to two different commanders. Assigned to the Southwest Pacific, he was under General MacArthur. His additional responsibility was to Vice Admiral Halsey in the broader Pacific naval battle, which had reached a crisis. The situation was fraught with potential conflict and confusion.

MacArthur, seeing himself losing the submarines, one of his most significant naval assets, was not happy. Further, he was planning a seaborne advance up the northern coast of Papua and wanted submarine support. To keep the submarines he saw as his, MacArthur wrote directly to Admiral King, commander in chief of the U.S. Navy, over the heads of the naval commanders in his own area and in the Pacific.[1]

Admiral King ordered that six submarines always be available to meet General MacArthur's needs. The conflict was resolved by Vice Admiral Halsey's cooperative attitude and Christie's diplomatic skills. Christie remained in full control of his submarines, ensuring that needs were met in both areas of his responsibility.

Vice Admiral Halsey was, in Capt. James Fife's opinion, one of the great Allied leaders in the war against Japan.[2] He also had the common touch, identifying with and inspiring his sailors. Paul Snyder remembered Halsey visiting *Guardfish* after one of her Brisbane patrols:

> Halsey sent down word that he was coming aboard, but no one was to be in other than a working uniform. He sat in the after battery [crew's mess] and visited with several sailors. . . . We had . . . soldered a silver dollar to . . . the deck so that as a person stepped through the hatch . . . the silver dollar was the first thing he saw, and with great amusement always the crew would watch the effort of someone trying to pick up the dollar. We forgot about it when Halsey stepped through the hatch and held our breath as he made several tries to pick it up and finally even kicked at it. When he found out the joke, he laughed as heartily as the rest.[3]

Events in Guadalcanal were developing fast, and more submarines were badly needed. Fleet-submarines were slowly becoming available from Western Australia, but they were handicapped by torpedo shortages and the need for overhaul.

The demand was met by sending submarines from Pearl Harbor to patrol off Truk Atoll, the main Japanese base supporting their Guadalcanal operations. Off Truk, submarines were expected to target Japanese warships. However, the increased emphasis given to Truk meant that the Pearl Harbor command had to reduce the number of patrols sent to Japanese home waters.

Most Pearl Harbor–Truk patrols continued through the Solomons or New Guinea waters to Brisbane. In the last three months of 1942 almost half of Pearl Harbor's submarine war patrols ended in Brisbane. This was part of a deliberate increase in strength of Brisbane's submarine force to participate in the crucial Solomons battle. The move also replaced time-expired or obsolete submarines with fresh, modern vessels. Two new submarine tenders were sent directly to Brisbane, and their squadrons of fleet-submarines would join them from patrols off Truk and the Solomons. They replaced *Griffin* and her inadequate S-boats, and Squadron 2's vessels would rotate home for much-needed dockyard refits and leave for crews.

The tenders transferred to Brisbane were *Fulton* and *Sperry* with their respective SubRons 8 and 10. *Fulton* (Capt. E. C. Bain) and *Sperry* (Capt. R. H. "Red Hot" Smith) were large, purpose-built submarine tenders of 9,734 tons' displacement fitted with heavy lift cranes and workshops capable of carrying out a wide range of repairs to submarines. They carried all facilities necessary to render their squadrons self-sufficient at any port. *Sperry* was only five months old and *Fulton* seven months older.

Fulton's shakedown cruise had come to an abrupt end on 7 December 1941 as she began to zigzag to Panama. Clarence Hebb, a "plank owner" (aboard the ship from her first commissioning), recalled the time:

> What followed was a hurried loading of material in Panama to build a refueling station in the jungle in Nicaragua to keep the PBY Catalina flying boats in the air patrolling the waters off the Panama Canal. . . .
>
> With the completion of this first assignment *Fulton* was ordered back to Panama to once again load up all necessary equipment and supplies to build a duplicate PBY refueling station on one of the islands in the Galapagos Islands group.[4]

Then the tender sailed for Pearl Harbor, arriving there on 15 March. Her skilled tradesmen were soon assisting the restoration of USS *Nevada* and *California*. More promising developments occurred the next day when *Fulton* began the work she had been built for. *Drum* was her first customer.

Fulton's most exciting assignment came during the Battle of Midway, when she was rushed to sea to meet the aircraft carrier *Yorktown*, crippled by Japanese aircraft, burning, and listing without power. *Fulton* raced to the scene to embark the then-abandoned *Yorktown*'s survivors off rescuing warships and carry them to safety. The operation, begun on 6 June, was extremely dangerous because of the presence of enemy submarines. To counter the threat, *Fulton* remained under way while embarking survivors by breeches buoy, continuing by boat at night in total darkness. By the morning of 7 June, *Fulton* was steaming back to Pearl Harbor with 1,891 survivors of *Yorktown* and the destroyer *Hammann* aboard, receiving a resounding welcome upon her arrival.

Fulton then returned to her primary task of servicing submarines, establishing an advanced base at Midway Island on 12 July. On 17 October, she left Midway and hurried to Pearl Harbor for a quick docking. All hands worked through the night to scrape and paint the big tender's bottom before sailing the next day. Loaded with a full stock of supplies, torpedoes, and spare parts, as well as additional personnel for relief crews, she and *Sperry* left Pearl Harbor on 26 October 1942 for a secret destination. It was an anxious trip, and some thought that two tenders were being sent to ensure that if one was torpedoed the other would get through. In Pearl Harbor they had been reminded of enemy submarine activity with the new battleship *North Carolina* and the aircraft carrier *Saratoga* in dry dock repairing recent torpedo damage.

The submarine threat was real enough. At 8:47 AM on 3 November, after the escort had departed, *Fulton*'s war diary records, "Maneuvered to avoid torpedo from starboard." "General quarters" was sounded, and a few minutes later *Fulton* was forced to maneuver again "to avoid submarine on our port bow."[5] Robert Heath was standing watch on *Fulton*'s port bow, and he recalled what happened:

We were steaming with *Sperry* on our port side on a zigzag course. The *Fulton* had just started on the starboard leg of our zigzag with the *Sperry* slightly ahead. The *Sperry* suddenly sounded a long blast on her whistle and started backing full-speed. Being on lookout watch, I had a pair of powerful binoculars. The *Fulton* of course started backing full. I looked through my binoculars and observed two torpedo wakes pass close in front of the *Sperry* headed in our direction. One passed about two or three hundred feet in front of our bow, and the one that barely missed *Sperry*'s bow came on and caught us on the port side of the bow. It made a definite bang, metal to metal—kind of like hitting the side of the ship with a sledgehammer.[6]

The torpedo attack was not repeated, and they continued, lucky to have escaped. (When *Fulton* was next dry-docked some eighteen months later, crew members saw a dent in her bow where the torpedo had hit but failed to explode.)[7] But the alarms were not over. At around 2 AM the following night, "general quarters" sounded again as an unidentified vessel appeared. Fortunately, this turned out to be USS *Stack,* one of their escorts, meeting them earlier than expected. The next day *Sperry* diverted to Noumea while *Fulton* continued.

On 7 November, *Patterson* and *Bagley* relieved *Stack,* and the destroyers made several sonar contacts before reaching Brisbane. Dawn on Monday, 9 November, revealed the welcome sight of Moreton Island, and the pilot boarded at 8:37 AM. Asked "Do you have blackouts here?" the pilot replied, "Oh, we have a bit of a brownout." So for the first time in eleven months *Fulton*'s crew would sleep with fresh air coming through open portholes. After the lonely wilderness of Nicaragua, the Galapagos, and Midway, and the clangor of a rebuilding Pearl Harbor, a berth at New Farm Wharf, a short tram ride to downtown Brisbane, was most welcome.

Fulton's arrival in Brisbane was memorable. With her crew ceremonially lining the deck, large crowds of people gathered on shore to warmly welcome the fine, big ship with waving and cheering. Radioman Les Cottman recalls, "The welcome we got was terrific, ship's whistles, horns, sirens, and hordes of people waving and shouting, a grand reception and a sample of the generous nature of the Australian people."[8]

Early on 11 November, Captain Christie broke out his flag as commander of Task Force 42 on *Fulton.* Later that morning his previous flagship *Griffin* got under way to return to the United States. On 13 November, *Sperry* berthed astern of *Fulton* at New Farm Wharf. She remained for the next two months, and during this period Brisbane's submarine base reached its peak.

The arrival of the first three Pearl Harbor submarines in Brisbane was unplanned and underlined the difficulties faced by the Allies in the South Pacific. All three arrived in the month before *Fulton.*

The first was *Trout* (Lt. Comdr. L. P. Ramage), forced to seek urgent repairs after an eventful month off Truk. On 3 October 1942 she had come to periscope depth for a navigational sight when she was hit by a completely unexpected explosion. Another followed as *Trout* dived away to safety. A Japanese aircraft had surprised her and put both periscopes out of action. Ramage had to leave the area and have the vital periscopes repaired at the nearest repair base, Brisbane, arriving on 13 October. Initially Christie sent *Trout* to Fremantle for repairs, but the battle for Guadalcanal was reaching its climax, and the submarine was recalled

The Brisbane submarine base at New Farm Wharf
with *Fulton* and eight fleet-submarines.
Official U.S. Navy photograph, in collection of *Bowfin*
Submarine Museum and Park, Honolulu

from Bass Strait. Two S-boat periscopes were installed at New Farm
Wharf, but they were short, barely protruding above the periscope shears,
and one had distracting dirt in its lens. With these stopgap repairs *Trout*
was sent into the heat of the battle around Guadalcanal.[9]

Another emergency visitor to Brisbane was *Plunger*. While on patrol in
the Solomons she unexpectedly hit the seabed on 2 November, destroying
her sonar equipment and damaging her hull. Sent to Brisbane for repairs,
she entered South Brisbane Dry Dock on 15 November. Far different was
the case of *Amberjack,* which was diverted to Brisbane after delivering aircraft fuel and reinforcements to Guadalcanal. Her precious cargo safely
delivered, *Amberjack* arrived in Brisbane on 30 October.

Purposeful patrols from Pearl Harbor to the Southwest Pacific termi-
nating in Brisbane began in October 1942 when *Silversides, Growler,* and
Flying Fish departed for the south. Most patrolled via Truk, but some were
assigned directly to positions in the Solomons or Bismarck Archipelago,
involving an outward passage of nearly three thousand nautical miles.

Patrolling from Pearl Harbor took these submarines into the South
Pacific command area of Admiral Halsey. The change in control took place
at the latitude of Truk, where Pearl Harbor submarines transferred to the
direction of Task Force 42 in Brisbane. Communication through the
evening "Fox" schedule was not affected as messages were broadcast to all
submarines at sea.

These submarines were modern vessels with experienced crews. They carried the latest equipment, and most were fitted with new SJ surface search radar, which enabled submarines to detect and track vessels at night and in poor visibility. The first patrol to terminate in Brisbane was *Silversides* (Lt. Comdr. C. Burlingame), mooring at New Farm Wharf on 25 November 1942. In the Caroline Islands she had seen plenty of action but had sunk nothing. Another seven submarines followed her in to Brisbane during December, two more in January, and finally *Guardfish* on 15 February 1943.

As with Squadron 2's submarines now operating from Brisbane, high hopes were held for the Pearl Harbor boats' success. However, like their predecessors, the new arrivals found success hard to come by. Kept down by constant aircraft patrols, *Growler* was unable to close the few ships she saw, and *Tuna* saw only one ship throughout her patrol. *Gato* unsuccessfully attacked a convoy and was savagely depth-charged and bombed as a result. The newcomers told of heavy enemy patrol activity keeping them submerged all day, strong escorts, and poor charts of the narrow island waters.

However, one Pearl Harbor submarine achieved a notable sinking on her voyage to Brisbane. *Albacore* (Lt. Comdr. R. C. Lake) was assigned to patrol off the northern coast of New Guinea in support of General MacArthur's Buna campaign. Initial results were disappointing, as she made several attacks that failed and was depth-charged and damaged after one of these. On 18 December, *Albacore* was cruising off Madang. It was a dark night, and peering through the gloom, Lake saw shadows of two ships. He fired torpedoes at both, hitting the larger vessel, which blew up and sank. Although *Albacore* was unable to identify the vessel, debris found the next morning was from the light cruiser *Tenryu*. This was a valuable success, as *Tenryu* had been in the forefront of the Japanese occupations of Wake Island, Kavieng, Buka, Tulagi, and Buna, participating also in the Coral Sea, Savo Island, Milne Bay, and Guadalcanal battles.

October, November, and December 1942 saw Brisbane's submarine task group reach its peak. Thirty-seven different submarines came under Task Force 42's control in that period, and twenty submarines patrolled during each of these months.

The remaining S-boats made their final patrols from Brisbane and by mid-November were on their way back to the United States. Squadron 2's submarines, having completed a twelve-month tour of duty, returned home for a major refit. They left Brisbane from late October, reversing the track of the Pearl Harbor submarines, many of which would replace them as permanent members of Task Force 42. Last of Squadron 2 to leave Brisbane were *Swordfish*, sailing on 9 January 1943, and *Snapper*, finally getting away on 27 January after being delayed by a main motor breakdown. Squadron 2's tender *Holland* also left from Melbourne for the United States on 9 January.[10]

Despite much activity in 1942's final quarter and the urgency of the Guadalcanal battle, results were poor. *Sculpin* and *Sturgeon* made a promising start early in October, but it was not maintained. As more fleet-submarines entered the Solomons, only one more Japanese ship was sunk in the next eight weeks, *Choko Maru*, sunk by *Gudgeon* (Lt. Comdr. W. S. Stovall) on 21 October off Kavieng. Throughout November 1942, with the Guadalcanal battle reaching its bloody climax, not one Japanese ship was sunk by any submarine patrolling to or from Brisbane.

One Task Force 42 submarine did meet the Japanese fleet during the mid-November battles. This was *Trout* (Lt. Comdr. L. P. Ramage), which had called at Brisbane for emergency repairs to her periscopes six weeks before. She was cruising north of Santa Isabel Island on 13 November when Christie, acting on radio intelligence, ordered her to an intercept position. The next morning *Trout* met the battleship *Kirishima* encircled by a strong escort, but the attack was frustrated when the battleship zigzagged away. Ramage made another attack during the afternoon, firing five torpedoes that missed, and *Trout* was forced deep to escape the counterattack. Although *Kirishima* survived this attack, *Trout*'s plain-language contact report brought up an American battleship task group that sank the Japanese battleship that night.

Results improved in December. Squadron 2's *Seadragon* (Lt. Comdr. W. E. Ferrall) sank the Japanese submarine *I-4* with old Mark 10 torpedoes. *Grayback* (Lt. Comdr. E. C. Stephan) failed to score with torpedoes, but early on Christmas Day she found four Japanese landing barges off Vella Lavella and sank them by gunfire. However, submarines arriving from Pearl Harbor achieved better results, sinking six Japanese ships including *Tenryu*, sunk by *Albacore*, and three torpedoed by *Greenling*.

Greenling (Lt. Comdr. H. C. Bruton) had an excellent record when she left Pearl Harbor on 9 December 1942 for the Southwest Pacific. Soon after reaching Bougainville, she attacked a tanker, sinking one of the escorts. *Greenling* then moved to New Ireland, attacking a convoy and sinking two freighters. However, Bruton did not have it all his own way. On 10 January 1943 *Greenling* damaged another escorted tanker but was driven off by gunfire without sinking the ship. Within the week *Greenling* had made up for this by sinking another freighter, then surfacing and sinking the freighter's escort with her deck gun. Finally she scouted two islands in the Admiralty group for possible enemy activity.

Greenling and Bruton were among the most successful U.S. submarines and captains up to that time. Their eleven ships totaled 54,564 tons, all confirmed by postwar research. *Greenling* had also earned a Presidential Unit Citation, the highest award possible for a U.S. warship, for her previous patrols.

It was a busy patrol, and after all the fighting there was a sweet taste to *Greenling*'s arrival in Brisbane on 31 January 1943. David Peto, her communications officer, recalled the scene: "I shall always remember steaming up the river to our berth alongside the submarine tender USS *Fulton*. There was a light rain falling, and the green country was such a welcome sight. There were cows grazing near the riverbank. In short order after reading our mail from home and receiving our pay from several weeks at sea, several of us boarded the tram for downtown Brisbane."[11]

Last of the Pearl Harbor transfers was another submarine with a record matching *Greenling*'s. This was *Guardfish* (Lt. Comdr. T. B. Klakring), also with a Presidential Unit Citation. By her arrival in Brisbane on 15 February 1943, *Guardfish* was credited with eleven ships sunk.

Early in January, *Guardfish* reached her patrol area off Kavieng, where she sank two destroyers and a small freighter. However, the patrol's highlight was her attempt to penetrate Rabaul Harbor on 28 January 1943. Throughout 1942, Rabaul was a safe haven for Japanese shipping, guarded by air and sea patrols, shore guns, minefields, and underwater listening devices. Allied bombers attacked Rabaul but suffered losses while achieving little success. Before *Guardfish* arrived, submarines had found antisubmarine patrols off Rabaul too strong for them to approach the harbor.

An aggressive skipper, Klakring decided that if ships in Rabaul would not come out, he would go in. What happened is described in his patrol report: "The sea became glassy so we ran deep approaching Blanche Bay. We also ran silent and passed at least three, possibly four, echo ranging patrol vessels off the entrance. An erratic set made it necessary to check our position every quarter hour with sets of bearings taken quickly on account of the patrols around us and numerous planes that were seen each time we raised the periscope. We finally got a good set up on six vessels anchored in the lower reach of Simpson Harbor." Klakring lined up the vessels as an overlapping target and prepared to fire as soon as the torpedoes came within range. With only a mile to go, he reported, "I raised the periscope for a final fix . . . and, as I did, the periscope was zoomed by a small plane and [a] shore battery . . . opened up and fired rapidly. The . . . explosion of the shells were heard close aboard and I observed two patrol vessels head over towards us. At this point the forward torpedo room reported that we had been struck over the wardroom. We abandoned the attack, turned around and went deep."[12]

Klakring twisted *Guardfish* around in the shallow water to escape. Surprisingly, several nearby patrol boats neither closed nor dropped depth charges. After *Guardfish* reached deeper water, the patrol craft converged and began depth-charging, continuing for the rest of the day and into the night. The screws of the patrol boats could be clearly heard inside the submarine along with each of the depth charges.[13]

Klakring continued:

> Only two depth charges were felt that were close enough to cause real concern but the boat was a mess from the heat and sweat of our almost full day of silent running and the several inches of pressure which had accumulated made the atmosphere so oppressive that I decided we were getting nowhere that way, so we surfaced and cleared out on four engines. On surfacing two patrol boats were seen, one on the port bow and one just abaft the port beam about two miles away. It was quite dark and I doubt they saw us for we outdistanced them quickly without being fired on.
>
> Thus we missed our day of glory by just ten or fifteen minutes—a heart breaking experience. . . . The abortive attempt to penetrate Rabaul and its aftermath were distressing physically and mentally.[14]

Only after *Guardfish* arrived in Brisbane did her officers learn that Rabaul Harbor was heavily mined. Inside the harbor the Japanese patrol boats had kept their distance to avoid their own mines. After *Guardfish's* hot reception, no other submarine attempted to enter Rabaul Harbor.

Task Force 42 was still at top strength as 1942 ended. On 1 January 1943 it boasted twenty-five ships including *Fulton, Sperry,* and *Tulsa* in Brisbane, *Holland* in Melbourne repairing a damaged rudder, and twenty-one submarines, nine refitting in Brisbane and twelve on patrol in the Solomons.[15]

Through 1942 Captain Christie's command grew from a single squadron of old S-boats to a major task force playing a vital role at a critical stage of the war. Christie was handling his responsibilities to two supreme commanders skillfully and diplomatically and gaining great satisfaction from controlling a large group of submarines at war. He had also built up his task force and its support structure. This was about to change. Late in November 1942, Christie was ordered to the U.S. Navy's torpedo factory at Newport, Rhode Island.

For several months the shortage of torpedoes had caused great concern. As the year progressed, the torpedo supply fell further behind demand. It was vital that torpedo production be increased so that American submarines, destroyers, and carrier aircraft were not hampered by lacking their main offensive weapon. Christie was involved with torpedo development through much of his career. This background and his knowledge of operations put Christie in a unique position to speed up torpedo supply.

The orders to Newport were a serious blow to Christie, who set about having them reversed. Carpender, his immediate superior, formally asked for the orders to be changed, and Christie himself wrote to several contacts in Washington. His pleas were unavailing. Increasing torpedo production was even more important than his operational responsibilities in Brisbane. After delaying for weeks, Christie relinquished command of Task Force 42 on 22 December 1942.

For his service in Brisbane, Christie was awarded the Legion of Merit by President Roosevelt. He was also well regarded by men at the lowest level of his command. Although he was a strict disciplinarian, "white-hat" sailors appreciated the close, personal, almost fatherly interest he took in their well-being.[16]

8

THE COMPOUND AND THE CITY

"The Creek Street Brawl" was the name one Brisbane policeman gave to the events of Thanksgiving night, 26 November 1942. It was also known to some Americans as the "Thanksgiving Day Riots" or the "Cigarette War." But to most it is the more colorful "Battle of Brisbane," and erupting just seventeen days after their arrival, it affected *Fulton*'s crew.

There are almost as many accounts of the incident as there were participants. It was a brawl, one of many that occurred in wartime Brisbane. Mary K. Browne, observing from her American Red Cross Center across the road, described it as "a riot of about two thousand" that "steadily grew in size and seriousness."[1] The name "Cigarette War" refers to one precipitating factor: the banning of sales of American cigarettes to Australians. Another factor was resentment by Australian troops, after three years of war, at their glamorous, better-paid American counterparts monopolizing the girls and taking over the cities. "Battle" is a little dramatic. An American MP's weapon killed one Australian and wounded some others. But all the remaining injuries incurred that night and the next were from fists and boots. The participation of men from the submarine base was minor, reflecting their small numbers in the total of Brisbane servicemen.

A report of the events appeared in the *Fulton Bow Plane,* an annual survey of the ship's activities exclusively for circulation to the crew. The *Bow Plane*'s 1943 issue referred to the incident in a cryptic style: "Do you remember . . . the Battle of Hush Hush Number Four [Brisbane] [and] . . . shore patrol duty—how fast the sailmakers and carpenters turned out shore patrol gear—how a handful of shore patrol stopped a riot by just holding their ground—the *Tulsa*'s landing force—how the movies cleared out when the call for volunteer shore patrol went over the loud speaker system?"[2]

Chuck Meyer, who had joined *Fulton* nine months before, recalled the incident and the events leading up to it.[3] He noted that American sailors, in their distinctive white uniforms, were rarely harassed when on leave. Most of the friction that occurred was between American and Australian soldiers, easily identified in their different khaki uniforms. Yet in the two weeks between *Fulton*'s arrival and the "Battle of Brisbane," one sailor found with an Australian's wife was "severely beaten," and others began wrapping lead strips in their neckerchiefs to use as defensive weapons. Then, on 25 November, a sailor's body was found floating between *Fulton* and the wharf. Officially the cause of death was "accidental drowning in line of duty."[4] Rumor had it that he had been beaten and thrown into the river.

On the first night of the "battle" the shore patrol rounded up sailors from theaters and dance halls for transport straight to the ship. The next evening, angry Australians were in the streets looking for trouble, and they chased some Americans into the Roma Street police station. As Meyer recalled, "They surrounded the buildings and began throwing missiles at the police, MPs, and shore patrol. . . . It was a very noisy, violent, and disorderly crowd that swelled to thousands in minutes. . . . Calls went out to the U.S. ships (*Fulton* and *Tulsa*) for reinforcements."

Meyer continued: "On the *Fulton,* the word was passed [for two] standby watch sections to muster on the second deck outside the carpenter shop, in our liberty uniform. Forty men were picked, given leggings, duty belts, an SP arm band, and a twenty-four-inch piece of swab handle (because the ship was out of batons) that carpenter mates were sawing off of new swabs as fast as possible. A newly commissioned very young officer, an ensign, was put in charge, and we were rushed down to the dockside and into a waiting truck. With the truck's horn blowing, we passed through the wharf gates even as they were being reinforced with armed extra security personnel." Nearing the Roma Street police station, they saw a crowd of Australians completely surrounding it, blocking access. *Fulton*'s sailors formed ranks to forward march but "stopped abruptly as the Australians confronted us face to face with taunts and warnings to get back in our truck or get hurt."

"We were all scared to death," Meyer admitted. "There were so many of them and so few of us. But this brash young officer in charge and leading us gave the order to 'close ranks,' and we did. . . . With that our gallant ensign (who admitted he was equally as scared as we were) pulled out his

.45-caliber automatic. While attempting to jack a shell into the chamber, . . . a loud bang was heard as his weapon fired into the air." The effect was dramatic: "Those in front of us that had been blocking our way into the police station scattered, and we marched quick-time inside the circling mob." The American sailors formed "a long line, going eyeball to eyeball with these agitated Australians, still shouting for the blood of soldiers . . . in the police station."

Soon afterward a truckload of sailors arrived from the gunboat *Tulsa*: "They all had Thompson submachine guns, and each of them was dressed in full battle dress, with helmets and gas masks. On seeing their way blocked by the mob of Australians, they fired a few rounds from their machine guns, and the crowd immediately opened and the truck . . . drove right to the police station steps." The taunting, pushing, and aggressive behavior of the mob subsided as additional army and civilian police came into the station. "The Australians started backing down and moving away. Groups of them were dispersing . . . as they saw the police move out into the mob and pull a few ringleaders into the station house. . . . Trucks with armed men aboard as escorts drove the servicemen who had sought shelter . . . out through the last remaining stragglers of the mob that was once estimated to be in excess of three thousand people."[5]

The 1943 *Bow Plane* suggested, tongue in cheek, a special campaign ribbon for participants in the Battle of Brisbane, its colors alternating black and blue.[6] Wayne Jemmett from *Fulton* discussed the riots with a brother of his girlfriend, a soldier in the Australian 9th Division, agreeing "what a bad deal we both thought that was. We expressed our regrets over that."[7] Chuck Meyer, who had faced the mob, still declared, "The eleven months I spent in Australia were without doubt the most pleasant time of my whole life. . . . It was an 'eye-opener,' and I fell in love with the country and the people."[8]

For almost a year *Fulton*, beside New Farm Wharf, was the focus of Brisbane's submarine war. There were other installations ashore, but as the city flooded with Allied servicemen, *Fulton* became the hub. In Brisbane, *Fulton* refitted sixty-seven submarines, carried out voyage repairs, and attended other ships. Until a hospital was established ashore, *Fulton's* medical department treated all naval forces in the area. "The best tender in the fleet," "the Silent Partner of the Silent Service," "the Can-Do Ship"— these were some of the titles *Fulton* earned. The hard-worked crew saw it differently: "Send it to the *Fulton*. . . . Steal it from the *Fulton*. . . . Blame it on the *Fulton*. . . . Make it on the *Fulton*—ash trays to French commodes."[9]

New Farm Wharf from the main gate showing upperworks of
Fulton (*right*) and *Sperry* (*distant*).
Official U.S. Navy photograph, in collection of *Bowfin*
Submarine Museum and Park, Honolulu

Although navy numbers in Brisbane did not peak until mid-1944, the
two months before *Sperry* sailed were the submariners' busiest. But there
was time for lighter activities. At Christmas 1942, each tender hosted a
party including games, gifts, and Christmas dinner for 150 children. It was
a mouth-watering feast for the needy children of rationed Brisbane.
Beginning with apples and tomato soup, it progressed to ham and turkey
with salad, vegetables, and cranberry sauce, followed by fruitcake, lemonade, and ice cream for anyone who still had room. The Brisbane weekly
newspaper *Truth* explained the party's background. In a navywide custom,
enlisted men took up a collection among themselves to give a party for the
poor children of whatever port they were in at Christmastime. *Sperry* and
Fulton's men collected £500 (US$1,600 at the 1943 exchange rate) and
gave Brisbane's children a day to remember. The thoughtful gifts included
cricket bats and practical items. Each child also received a pair of shoes,
with a new dress for each girl and a suit for each boy.[10]

The crews did not forget to treat themselves. *Sperry*'s men welcomed
the New Year with a dance at Cantwell's Hall, and both tenders hosted an
outdoor "smoker" for Task Force 42. The sixteen vaudeville acts, the best
in Brisbane, were well received. The song-and-dance items were inter-

Brisbane children enjoy Christmas dinner aboard the U.S. Navy's
submarine tender *Fulton* in 1942.
Courtesy of Sophia Jordan

spersed with "sensational acrobatics," a performance by Evie Hayes ("the
girl from Seattle"), Doris Whimp and the Cremorne Ballet, and four
"spots of nonsense" by the well-known Australian comedian Roy ("Mo")
Rene. What the chaplains thought of Mo's "Flo's Letter" sketch ("One
Yank and They're Down") is not recorded.[11]

The city saw little of the activity that went on within the tightly guarded
compound on New Farm Wharf. Guards were stationed not only on the
perimeter but also inside the wool sheds across Macquarie Street. Boredom was a problem for *Fulton*'s craftsmen. No matter where the ship was,
they slept in the same mess, kept the same schedule, and worked in the
same workshop. On submarines there was constant rotation of personnel.
Experienced men returned home as the nucleus of crews for new boats or,
for respite from the strain of patrols, transferred to relief crews ashore. A
20 percent crew turnover after each patrol was typical, as authorities
aimed at restricting men to five patrols. Though some sailors made more
patrols, New Farm saw a constant stream of arrivals and departures.

In mid-1944 the Submarine Repair Unit and crews in port comprised a third of the peak U.S. Navy total of sixty-five hundred men. Compared with the tens of thousands of Allied troops straining the city's resources and the 14 percent rise in civilian population, the submariners' numbers were small. The strain was most obvious in transport. With gasoline rationing forcing private cars off the road, a rising flood of civilians and servicemen swamped the trams. Between 1940–41 and 1944–45, tram journeys increased by more than 60 percent. With a tram terminus at New Farm Wharf, submariners contributed to these numbers, paying their two-pence servicemen's concession fare into the city.[12]

The Brisbane City Council was not the only entity that had trouble coping with the influx of servicemen. Christie's sailors had eagerly accepted the Tattersalls Club's offer of honorary membership. In a month, bar profits soared by 50 percent, but most of the increase came from the sale of bottled spirits, and the cellar was running dry at a time when replenishment was well nigh impossible. Bottled spirits were accordingly rationed to full members only, and by July 1942, honorary membership was restricted to officers.[13]

Fulton's 1943 *Bow Plane* provides a record of her eleven months in Brisbane. Reports of the return of the battered *Growler* and visits by Admiral Halsey, the undersecretary of war, and Mrs. Eleanor Roosevelt are mixed with entries regarding other significant events. Hotels including the Bellevue, Embassy, Royal, Lennons, and even the temperance Canberra were remembered with affection. Other venues mentioned were the Coconut Grove, Trocadero, Cremorne, Cantwell's Ritz Ballroom, and the Chungking Chinese restaurant in the Valley. One cryptic entry was, "GQ [general quarters] when the *Fulton* fired the only two shots fired in the 'Battle of Hush Hush Number Four'—another job for the ship's carpenters." Apparently a regular GQ exercise ended this time with a gun firing. Resultant damage to a suburban building was quickly and quietly repaired.

The *Bow Plane's* account of Eleanor Roosevelt's visit ("America's First Lady, Mrs. Franklin D. Roosevelt, honored us with a visit and a very inspiring speech") is economical with detail. Her visit was more lavishly reported in the *Courier-Mail*. The newspaper did not mention a visit to New Farm. However, in her "My Day" column inside the First Lady wrote, "We visited a navy group, including a visit to their sick bay, where I was told of appendix operations done at sea by pharmacists mates, who used kitchen knives and spoons for instruments and still not one of these operations had

In her American Red Cross uniform, Mrs. Eleanor Roosevelt, wife of President
Franklin D. Roosevelt, inspects drivers of the Australian Women's National
Emergency Legion at New Farm Wharf on 13 September 1943.

Official U.S. Navy photo, U.S. National Archives, Record Group 80-G, 89586

caused a death."[14] Mrs. Roosevelt's visit was not universally welcomed. Her
earlier remark that American sailors "had to beat off the Australian girls
with a big stick" angered the sailors who had romantic attachments in Brisbane, and it angered their girlfriends even more. Many incensed sailors

said they did not intend to be in the audience, so all leave was stopped to ensure their attendance.

The *Bow Plane* recorded the interactions between task force sailors and Brisbane girls in its usual lighthearted style:

On Women's National Emergency Legion drivers: "Yes all day and No all night."

"The local gal driving her Yank sailor back after thirty-two days over leave."

"Please sir, may I be transferred to the dock? You see, sir, I got a gal over on the beach."

The affection sometimes went deeper: "How quickly the applications for marriage poured in." Many *Fulton,* submarine, and wharf sailors went through the six-month approval-of-marriage process. *Bow Plane* recorded the story of one "machinist mate who almost missed his own marriage ceremony because his early liberty chit was disapproved when all of his guests had approved liberty chits."

When *Fulton* steamed toward New Farm Wharf, Yvonne Verrall, a young member of the WRENS (Women's Royal Emergency Naval Service), put her signaling training to use. Les Cottman told the story in 1999:

Soon after arriving, I was on the signal bridge looking at the sights, when a launch appeared from upstream with some young women in uniform on deck. One began sending with semaphore flags, and, as I could read and send semaphore, I found a pair of flags and asked her for her telephone number, which she gave before the launch passed on downstream.

To make a long story short, that girl, Yvonne Verrall, has been my wife for fifty-five years. We were married . . . at Fremantle, Western Australia, in September of 1944.[15]

David Peto of *Greenling* remembered, "Two crew members had brides that came to the U.S. after the war, and these marriages endured over the years." Peto was himself smitten by an attractive Brisbane lass, "but she preferred another."[16] William Turbeville (*Silversides*) also experienced disappointment in love: "I [might] have married had I not been transferred back to the U.S."[17]

But there was a dark side. Peto continued: "Another crew member introduced his Aussie bride to me in Brisbane, and then a few months

Les and Yvonne Cottman at their wedding in Fremantle on 4 September 1944.
Courtesy of Les and Yvonne Cottman

later, introduced his American bride to me in San Francisco."[18] Wayne Jemmett remembered the *Sperry* sailor who had no intention of telling his Australian date that he was already married.[19] Les Cottman recalled his chief, who returned drunk from liberty "bragging about two sisters he was having sex with who did not know they were dating the same man." Having told his superior what he thought of this, Les received no advancement in rating while that chief petty officer was in charge.[20]

Warm friendships outnumbered romances. In August 1942, Corwin Mendenhall (*Sculpin*) enjoyed generous hospitality. Next refit, he added trips to the Gold Coast for tennis and picnics. A final gesture of hospitality arrived just before *Sculpin* cast off on 18 November to patrol home when a new friend, Chris Christopherson, managing director of Peters, sent twenty gallons of ice cream to the submarine. The friendship, like many others, endured. Mendenhall returned to Brisbane on *Pintado* in 1945, and again Chris Christopherson delivered twenty gallons of ice cream to the wharf.[21]

On the official level, there was some friction. During the war Queensland law prohibited alcohol at dances, but a ship's party without alcohol was unthinkable. Differences between police and the navy escalated until a compromise was reached. A terse two-paragraph letter to Police Commissioner Carroll illustrates the system. The opening paragraph announces two upcoming parties at Cantwell's, the first only three days later. The second paragraph reads, "Beer will be served and no outsiders other than female guests of men attending will be admitted. The time is 8pm till midnight and U.S. Navy Shore Patrol will be present throughout."[22] Commissioner Carroll scrawled below the text, "Caller informed verbally." Relations might have been cool, but the problem was defused.

Other submarine activities figure in the Police Control Centre log, including:

"Preliminary advice of rocket firing from a ship at New Farm Wharf."

"A large floating object sighted five to six miles out to sea which suddenly disappeared."

"Notification of an Australian minesweeper, aircraft and U.S. submarines carrying out full caliber firing in Moreton Bay."

"Investigation of a 3am flare from the river and another from Wickham Park coinciding with a flashing light from a top floor of the [nearby] Canberra Hotel. The matter was closed when enquiries revealed the Canberra's second top floor was occupied by sailors."[23]

Most contacts with police were handled quickly and quietly. A Coolangatta sergeant responded to a complaint about drinking on the beach. Finding "a number of submarine sailors with prostitutes" drinking beer from the Pacific Hotel, "which hotel the sailors have taken over as residential quarters," he contacted the hotel's chief petty officer. Together they cleared the beach and closed the case.[24]

Gold Coast police and residents generally took a tolerant view of the often exuberant submariners. Such pranks as sailors ranging the streets in outlandish clothes and drinking beer from chamber pots were met with smiles. The sailors also cooperated with the sergeant, with his country khaki uniform and large hat, whom they called "Sheriff."[25]

Marie Doyle's father was a police detective assigned to Coolangatta's sister town Tweed Heads late in 1942. Marie later remembered how her father, off duty, went about the hotels teaching the Americans the value of Australian money. He also invited some sailors home for a meal, and the family went on picnics up the coast, taking some of them fishing, surfing, and roller-skating.[26]

A long *Sunday Mail* article on 13 February 1944 by war correspondent Osmar White, headed "Rowdyism and Vice Mar City Nights," centered on the base's suburb of New Farm. Reporting rowdy servicemen, drunkenness, and unseemly behavior in the park, White finished with, "During the whole of this time I did not see either a civilian or military policeman on duty." New Farm's police sergeant responded that White was "imagining a lot of things."[27]

Brisbane, for most submariners, had no equal as a leave port. *Fulton's* men and relief crews also appreciated their luck. They were performing vital work in a comfortable, friendly city. Their base had grown to provide much for their off-duty hours. The ship's library, "the Temple of Enlightenment," was crammed with sixteen hundred hard-cover books as well as five thousand of the special servicemen's pocket editions. Other facilities included a theater, beer hall, and hamburger stand. Flourishing inter-unit sporting competitions provided more diversions. Between January and October 1943, *Fulton's* basketball team won fifty-two of its sixty games, amassing a number of trophies including the Army-Navy Southwest Pacific Cup. New Farm was a good posting.

9
A NEW LEADER

Appointed to succeed Christie was Capt. James Fife, Jr. A dedicated officer with twenty years' submarine experience, including command of *Nautilus* and two years in charge of the Submarine School, Fife had more wartime experience than most U.S. officers.

Sent to Great Britain in August 1940, Fife observed for eight months the British Commonwealth's lone battle against Germany and Italy. He suffered German bombing in London, the Midlands, and Malta, and sailed on patrols in three British submarines. He was impressed by the "warrior spirit" of the British, a quality he felt was deficient among U.S. Navy officers early in the war.[1] On his return, after completing a lecture tour on his war experiences, Fife went to command Submarine Squadron 2 in the Philippines. Arriving just before the Japanese attack, he endured enemy bombing and was swept back with the Asiatic Fleet submarines' retreat. At Albany he was in charge of tests proving that American submarine torpedoes were running below their set depth. Then, when his squadron transferred to Brisbane, he was assigned as naval liaison officer to General MacArthur, working closely with him at Port Moresby in November and December 1942.

Fife gained and held the respect of General MacArthur, as well as his naval bosses, Vice Admiral Carpender and Rear Admiral Lockwood. He was well suited to handle the conflicting lines of responsibility between his army and navy superiors in the same diplomatic way as Captain Christie. However, the transfer did not go smoothly. Fife arrived halfway through December, but Christie's delays meant that Fife did not take over

Capt. James Fife (*center*) with Vice Admiral Carpender behind, at the award of
a Presidential Unit Citation to USS *Guardfish* in Brisbane on 10 August 1943.

Official U.S. Navy photo, U.S. National Archives, Record Group 80-G, 394388

until 22 December 1942. Furthermore, Fife and Christie differed on com-
manding-officer appointments. Believing that Christie assigned commands "on a sort of friendship basis," Fife immediately set up "an impar-
tial commanding officers' list."[2] This caused resentment among officers
promised a command by Christie.

Fife's leadership style was strong and uncompromising. One of his early
captains, Lieutenant Commander Klakring of *Guardfish*, many years later
described his approach: "Jimmy Fife was . . . very intensive and feisty and
productive. . . . He was not tolerating in the interference or changes in his
plans, but he was . . . in many respects a very great guy."[3]

Fife drew two lessons from his wartime experience that influenced his
command style. The first was the importance of encouraging the "warrior
spirit" that had so impressed him in Britain's war. He wanted his captains
to be aggressive and determined in carrying the battle to enemy shipping.
Captains not sufficiently aggressive or productive would be relieved.[4] The

other was the value of using decrypted enemy radio messages to determine enemy dispositions and movements, as he had first seen done while working with MacArthur in Port Moresby.[5]

The Allies recognized that enemy radio traffic was a valuable source of intelligence. All radio messages were coded, and the codes were changed periodically, but the Allies worked intently to break enemy codes and decipher their messages. In the first half of 1942 the Japanese naval code had been sufficiently broken to provide enough information to win the battles of the Coral Sea and Midway.

In the Southwest Pacific, the army's Central Bureau decrypting enemy radio messages reported to General MacArthur. For the navy, the best information came from their networks at Washington and Honolulu and the joint U.S. and Australian Fleet Radio Unit at Melbourne (FRUMel). FRUMel briefed Capt. A. McCollum, head of fleet intelligence in Carpender's headquarters, and data on specific enemy ships was passed to Task Force 42's commander. If the message was processed quickly enough, an interception at sea was possible.

Fife believed that he should use this information to direct submarines to attack positions. Accordingly, he adopted a more directive control over his submarines than Christie had done, ordering specific submarines by nightly radio to more promising areas. Interceptions derived from radio decryption were communicated by separate messages headed "ultra secret." These "ultra" messages could be decoded only by the communications officer and read by the captain. In Fife's view, this better perspective would help improve his submarines' results.

Within days of taking over, Fife withdrew his boats from the unproductive Buna–Huon Gulf area and concentrated them against Rabaul–Kavieng traffic. Roving patrols permitted "full latitude in the employment of submarines with regard to their location and with the main mission to sink enemy shipping entering and operating within the area."[6] His policy was explained in patrol operation orders: "The situation in the SOLOMONS–BIS-MARCKS AREA, as regards submarine operations, is changing frequently. The number of our submarines now on patrol is inadequate for constant coverage of all shipping routes. Their operations must be controlled almost entirely by dispatch . . . in order that the areas and routes indicated as being extensively used by the enemy at any given time may be covered."[7] To his staff Fife described this as "playing checkers" with submarines.[8]

Fife took over a strong force of more than twenty modern submarines patrolling the Solomon Islands and Bismarck Archipelago and more open seas north of New Guinea. Results had been lackluster throughout 1942, although December brought an increase in success from submarines coming from Pearl Harbor. This improvement continued in January 1943, giving early promise for Fife's directive strategy. He positioned three submarines east of Bougainville on the convoy route from Truk to Shortland Island, a Japanese advanced base for Guadalcanal operations. Although this move left other areas unguarded, the three submarines sank four ships here in three weeks.[9]

But the greatest successes in January 1943 were achieved by two submarines on patrols from Brisbane. In the difficult battle being fought, these patrols gave the submarine force a much needed shot in the arm.

The first Pearl Harbor submarine to patrol Brisbane was *Silversides* (Lt. Comdr. C. C. Burlingame). Burlingame was "as aggressive as they come,"[10] and his shore leaves were legendary. During three weeks in Brisbane, *Silversides* crew soaked up Australian culture, relishing the local beer. Casting off before a big audience of well-wishers on 17 December 1942, the officers and many crewmen wore Australian military slouch hats, and her executive officer, Lieutenant Davenport, gave a spirited rendition of "Waltzing Matilda" on a battered trombone.

After five days at sea, off Bougainville, Fireman G. Platter collapsed with stomach pains. Pharmacist's Mate T. Moore diagnosed a burst appendix requiring immediate attention. Although Moore's training had been confined to first aid, he decided that an operation was essential to prevent fatal peritonitis. Accordingly, Burlingame took *Silversides* deep and steady while Moore operated with other crewmen assisting. After a grueling five hours Platter was laid in his bunk, and he duly recovered.

The operation over, *Silversides* surfaced to charge her batteries. As the hatch opened, a vessel was sighted. Two torpedoes were fired, but one exploded just after leaving its tube, blowing "our stern out of the water and us out of our wits."[11] The enemy vessel, a destroyer, immediately forced *Silversides* deep. Later Burlingame attempted again to surface, but once more the submarine was shaken by a cracking explosion. An aircraft had joined the destroyer and dropped three bombs directly over the submarine. The explosion burst light bulbs and jammed the bow planes into a dive, sending *Silversides* plunging for the bottom. She was brought under control just before reaching crush depth. With the destroyer overhead, *Silversides* waited throughout the day. Then, with air foul and batteries drained, she finally surfaced. It was Christmas Eve, and her crew looked forward to the following day of peace and goodwill.

More than three weeks had passed when, off Truk, *Silversides* sighted

the 10,000-ton tanker *Toei Maru*. Burlingame dodged her escort and hit the
tanker with two torpedoes. The big ship erupted into a ball of flame, broke
up, and sank. The next day a seaplane suddenly bombed the submerged
Silversides. The mystified crew wondered how they had been detected.
When they next surfaced they saw leaking oil trailing behind them. The
leak was plugged, but the crew then spent all day making repairs from an
engine-room fire.

That same day Burlingame received an "ultra" about a convoy carrying
reinforcements to Rabaul. First sighting a column of destroyers, Burlingame then saw a convoy's smoke and mastheads. Surfacing out of sight,
Silversides sped to an ambush position ahead. Known as an "end-around,"
this maneuver allowed follow-up attacks after the initial interception. That
evening, *Silversides* was well placed as the convoy of four freighters and two
escorts approached. Burlingame avoided a patrol boat and fired six torpedoes at three freighters forming an overlapping target. Five hits were heard,
followed by breaking-up noises, but with escorts close by, Burlingame
could not risk a periscope confirmation.

As the enemy charged overhead, *Silversides* sagged, bow-heavy, and
trim was restored only after some effort. The cause was identified as the
sixth torpedo protruding from its tube. Every crewman knew the danger a
loose torpedo posed to safety, but an alerted enemy and glassy calm conditions meant that nothing could be done for the time being. After dark, *Silversides* surfaced, and the torpedo was safely ejected. But the submarine
was again leaking a trail of air bubbles and oil, so it was time to "head for
the barn."

This patrol was an epic of endurance. Every success was followed by
setbacks. Nevertheless, through skill and determination, *Silversides* overcame these setbacks, arriving triumphantly at Pearl Harbor on 31 January
1943, her crew proudly wearing their Australian hats.

Burlingame's patrol report was reviewed and *Silversides* credited with
sinking the tanker off Truk and damaging two vessels from the convoy. In
fact, all five torpedoes fired at the convoy hit their marks, and all three
freighters were sunk. With American torpedoes frequently failing at this
stage, it was a remarkable achievement. Four ships totaling 27,798 tons
were sunk, a record for an American patrol up to that time.

A month behind *Silversides*, *Wahoo* sailed for Pearl Harbor. *Wahoo* had
been reborn during her three weeks in Brisbane. After two undistinguished
patrols, morale was low. Fife relieved *Wahoo*'s captain and appointed Lt.
Comdr. D. W. Morton. Morton's friendly and informal manner masked

Lt. Comdr. D. W. Morton displays the improvised map he used
for *Wahoo*'s attack on Wewak Harbor.

Official U.S. Navy photo, U.S. National Archives, Record Group 80-G, 35733

unswerving determination to get results. The radical changes that he introduced in Brisbane kindled a new spirit on *Wahoo*.

Stories of Japanese atrocities in the islands and the memory of the
treacherous attack on Pearl Harbor strengthened Morton's determination

to give no quarter to the enemy. Posters were installed in each compartment exhorting the crew to "shoot the sons of bitches."[12]

Morton also radically changed the procedure for torpedo attacks.
Established procedure saw the submarine captain making all periscope
observations in directing the attack. Morton, believing that this placed too
much pressure on the captain, assigned periscope observations and the
ordering of torpedo firing to his executive officer, Lt. R. H. O'Kane. This
freed the captain to assess information from periscope, sonar, and TDC,
and allowed better decisions in the attack and ship-handling. For Morton
and O'Kane it was an unqualified success.[13]

On her passage north *Wahoo* was ordered to reconnoiter Wewak, on
New Guinea's north coast. Wewak was a staging post for convoys, and
Allied aircraft had reported shipping there. Morton's American charts
showed only a ragged coastline, but no "Wewak." Morton's patrol report
described his unconventional solution to the problem: "The position of
WEWAK HARBOR was determined . . . through the interest of D. C. KEETER,
MMı́c U.S. Navy who had purchased an Australian 'two-bit' school atlas
of the area. . . . By making an accurate tracing slide [of Wewak], and using
[a] camera and a signal light as a projector, a large scale chart was constructed of the whole harbor."[14]

Although "reconnoiter" usually meant "observe and report," Morton
pressed in as far as possible. Before dawn on 24 January 1943, *Wahoo* dived
off Wewak to penetrate the harbor, avoiding antisubmarine patrols.

At 1:18 PM a destroyer was sighted, and for more than an hour Morton
maneuvered for a torpedo attack. Three torpedoes fired at the now moving
enemy missed astern, as did a fourth. Tension rose as the destroyer rushed
at *Wahoo* from less than a mile. Morton had practiced this scenario with
the escort after leaving Brisbane. But steely nerves were needed to face
down a real enemy. Morton waited until the range fell to twelve hundred
yards before firing "down the throat." The torpedo missed, and *Wahoo* had
just one bow torpedo left. It needed eight hundred yards to arm.

Adjusting, O'Kane fired at minimum range, and *Wahoo* dived deep as
her crew braced for depth charges. The sound of propellers roared
through the hull. Then "a mighty roar and cracking" shook *Wahoo,* followed by the sound of the destroyer's boilers belching steam into the sea.
"Never was apprehension and despair changed to elation more abruptly."[15]

The crippled destroyer *Harusame* limped toward shore to subside onto
the bottom. Several periscope photographs showed her low in the water
near jungle and her crew crowding her upper-works. (Despite appearances, this was not the end. She was refloated and rejoined the fleet, only

to be sunk in June 1944.) Wewak's defenses were now stirred up, and shore guns and aircraft fought to pin *Wahoo* down while patrol boats searched. Not daring to raise *Wahoo*'s periscope, Morton conned her nine miles out of Wewak Harbor to the open sea by dead reckoning and listening to wave sounds.

For more than a year submarine commanders had complained that the Mark 14 torpedo's magnetic exploder was defective. The torpedoing of *Harusame,* which saved *Wahoo* so dramatically, convinced Morton of its effectiveness, and he became its vocal advocate.

Well out to sea the next morning, *Wahoo* sighted a native fishing boat whose crew had run out of food. Three had died, and another three were very ill. After giving them food and water, *Wahoo* continued toward Palau. That evening *Wahoo* crossed the Equator, and despite the heavy fighting the day before in enemy waters, Morton led a crossing-the-line ceremony. This was a pleasant surprise, as "en route south, no one had dreamed of suggesting ceremonies on crossing the Equator."[16]

Around 8 AM the next day, 26 January, smoke was sighted developing into the mastheads of two ships. *Wahoo* dived and prepared to attack. Using her stern torpedo tubes, *Wahoo* hit both vessels. Morton then swung to fire bow torpedoes. One ship was listing and sinking by the stern. The other, apparently damaged, was heading directly for *Wahoo*. To his surprise, O'Kane saw a third Japanese ship, previously obscured behind the others. Three torpedoes were fired at this large transport. Two hit.

The damaged vessel was close to ramming *Wahoo*. For the second time in three days Morton ordered a "down-the-throat" shot. Again, one torpedo hit, followed by a series of explosions as *Wahoo* dived deep. Returning to periscope depth, O'Kane saw that their first target, *Fukuei Maru No. 2,* had sunk, the transport *Buyo Maru* was stopped, and the attempted rammer was moving with difficulty. Two more torpedoes fired at *Buyo Maru* and caused an explosion that "blew her midships section higher than a kite. Troops commenced jumping over the side like ants off a hot plate. Her stern went up and she headed for the bottom."[17]

Morton then turned to the rammer, which had survived two apparent hits. The freighter *Pacific Maru* was escaping too quickly for the submerged *Wahoo*. Then a fourth Japanese ship appeared on the horizon. This was a tanker, and the two made their way north together.

Morton wrote in his patrol report, "Decided to let these two ships get over the horizon while we surfaced to charge batteries and destroy the estimated twenty troop boats now in the water. . . . At 1135 made battle surface and manned all guns. Fired 4" gun at largest scow loaded with troops.

Although all troops in this boat apparently jumped in the water our fire was returned by small caliber machine guns. We then opened fire with everything that we had. Then set course . . . at flank speed to overtake the cripple and tanker."[18]

John Clary, a sailor aboard *Wahoo*, wrote in his diary:

> We figured that there was about 7,000 troops in lifeboats & swimming around off the transport so we got word to surface battle. . . . Between shells I glanced out over the sea & saw thousands of Japs swimming around & some in lifeboats, but after 1/2 hour of 4" shells, 20mm, 50cal & 30cal firing we just about cleared the sea of Japs. It was like swatting flies. One Jap floated to about 12' from the Sub & we could tell he was playing possum. We wanted to get him alive but the Capt. said, "Shoot the Sonza bitch" so a Tommy gun put him out of action.[19]

The gunning down of survivors of the transport showed Morton at his most ruthless. His decision remains controversial. On the one hand, survivors of the sinking were protected under the 1929 Geneva Convention. On the other, Morton had his orders to destroy enemy air, land, or sea forces encountered. Morton considered the difficult fighting in New Guinea and believed that it was better to destroy troops at sea than allow them to join the battle. Allied commanders made a similar decision five weeks later in the same area after a Japanese convoy was sunk in the Battle of the Bismarck Sea. For days, Allied ships and aircraft gunned down enemy survivors in the water.

Sadly, the matter was further complicated. Of 1,126 people on *Buyo Maru*, 491 were Indian prisoners of war being transported to Rabaul. These prisoners came under the same fire as the Japanese. James DeRose quoted eyewitness accounts in his book *Unrestricted Warfare:* "Captain A. K. Dawe, a British doctor from the 40th IGH, remembered that the 'boats were destroyed by the submarine.' Sepoy Ghulam Mohd, of the 5/2 (Punjab) swore that '. . . the submarine . . . opened fire on us. We shouted and said we were Indian POWs but with no result.'" The next day, Japanese ships rescued the survivors. Altogether, 87 Japanese and 195 Indians died in the incident.[20]

After fifteen to twenty minutes of firing, *Wahoo* resumed chasing the two fleeing vessels. It was almost sunset when *Wahoo* caught up and submerged for another attack. However, the two vessels were zigzagging, and more than an hour later Morton fired three torpedoes at the undamaged tanker for one hit. Darkness fell with both Japanese vessels still able to maneuver and *Wahoo* with only four torpedoes left in her stern tubes. This forced *Wahoo* to chase the enemy, then turn to bring her stern tubes to bear. After two hours of chasing and twisting, *Wahoo* fired two torpedoes at the tanker, and Morton believed that she sank.

Only *Pacific Maru* remained, apparently damaged but still moving freely and firing. Her accurate gunfire forced *Wahoo* to dive. Surfacing soon afterward, *Wahoo* saw a warship's searchlight beam sweeping toward them from over the horizon. Morton fired his last two torpedoes at *Pacific Maru* at long range. "They both hit. . . . Fifteen minutes after firing the freighter sank leaving only the destroyer's search-light sweeping a clear horizon. It had required four hits from three separate attacks to sink this ship."[21]

With all the convoy sunk and all torpedoes expended, *Wahoo* turned away. Reflecting on their accomplishments, Morton told O'Kane the secret of his success: "Tenacity, Dick. Stay with 'em till they're on the bottom!"[22] It would be a winning formula for both, as O'Kane and Morton ended the war as the two most successful American submarine commanders in numbers of confirmed ships sunk.

The next morning a second convoy was sighted. For Morton there was no question but to attack, but without torpedoes the means were limited. After close observation the nearest vessel, a tanker, was selected to be sunk by gunfire. *Wahoo* surfaced ahead of the convoy and raced toward the tanker to cut her off. The ships turned away, and some opened fire. As Morton closed on the now isolated tanker, unexpectedly from beyond the convoy there appeared heavy smoke and the mast of a warship, first identified as an "antiquated coal-burning corvette."[23]

Morton turned at top speed to draw the escort away. The "corvette," in fact a modern destroyer, chased, then turned and fired controlled broadsides at the submarine. *Wahoo* hurriedly dived, and the destroyer raced to her position and dropped a pattern of very close depth charges. Clary confided in his diary, "We didn't make a sound & it was sure hot. The sweat ran off us by the bucket full."[24] The destroyer returned immediately to guarding her convoy. That night Morton radioed the day's events: "Another running gun battle today. Destroyer gunning, *Wahoo* running."[25]

The following day *Wahoo* reached Fais Island to shell the phosphate works, but an armed naval auxiliary prevented this. *Wahoo* had expended all her torpedoes. She had not yet reached her patrol position off Palau, but it was time to go home.

A photo used to report *Wahoo*'s spectacular third patrol
in Brisbane's morning paper, seven weeks afterward.
No hint was given that the patrol commenced from Brisbane.
Naval Historical Center, NH 42275

Wahoo reached Pearl Harbor on 7 February 1943, three weeks after
leaving Brisbane. Morton had tied a broom to the periscope shears, indicating a "clean sweep" of the convoy. Small flags fluttered for each ship
sunk by *Wahoo*, and a long pennant proclaimed "SHOT THE SUNZA-
BITCHES." It was the first time an American submarine had destroyed a
complete convoy, and a large welcoming party was on the dock for *Wahoo*'s
arrival. *Wahoo* was awarded a Presidential Unit Citation, and Morton
received a Navy Cross. Vice Admiral Lockwood called *Wahoo* "the One-
Boat Wolf Pack."[26]

Amid grim wartime news this achievement was worth celebrating, and
the "Silent Service" relaxed its secrecy. The press were introduced. Morton became an instant hero and *Wahoo* a legend. Six weeks later the
Courier-Mail featured pictures from the patrol, but nothing suggested
that *Wahoo* had any connection with Brisbane.[27]

Morton had demonstrated the "warrior spirit" that Captain Fife felt his officers so badly needed. Morton's pursuit of the convoy to destruction and his determined penetration of Wewak were an inspiration. He was regarded as the outstanding submarine commander of the time, and his reputation grew in the following months.

In some respects Morton had been lucky. In her first three days *Wahoo* found two enemy convoys. Other submarines spent weeks without sighting a convoy, or only glimpsing one in the distance. Further, it was rare for Brisbane submarines to find an unescorted convoy. However, in this Morton made his own luck. The convoy's assigned escort was *Harusame,* which *Wahoo* torpedoed at Wewak. Without an escort, the convoy was an easy target.

Morton openly reported his controversial gunning of *Buyo Maru's* survivors. His superior's endorsement of his report tacitly approved his actions: "The judgement and decisions displayed by the Commanding Officer were sound."[28] However, few U.S. captains followed Morton's example.

Although the convoy's destruction boosted morale at the time, postwar research confirmed only *Fukuei Maru No.* 2 and *Buyo Maru* as sunk. The tanker has never been conclusively identified but was credited to *Wahoo* in 1947 as "unknown maru." *Pacific Maru* was not sunk, as Morton believed, but survived with only light damage.[29] Maybe her escape was deserved, as she had survived two torpedo attacks and bravely attempted to ram *Wahoo* before escaping over the horizon. That night her evasive movements and accurate gunfire kept *Wahoo* at bay for several hours before Morton thought he sank her in the final torpedo attack. In fact, she returned the next day to help rescue survivors.

It seems that *Wahoo's* reported hits were actually premature explosions too far from the ship to cause damage. This was a common experience at the time, a result of the torpedo's faulty magnetic exploder. Morton had yet to recognize his torpedoes' shortcomings. His dramatic success over the destroyer convinced him of the magnetic exploder's worth. His attitude changed three patrols later when he returned with *Wahoo* empty-handed and frustrated by repeated torpedo failures.

Morton led *Wahoo* on four more spectacular patrols, but time was running out. Nine months later, *Wahoo* and Commander Morton were reported overdue and formally posted as missing in action. Many of those participating in her spectacular Brisbane patrol had left her before then, including O'Kane. He was appointed captain of *Tang,* aboard which he sank twenty-four enemy ships, more than any other American submarine commander.

10
HARD TIMES

The year 1942 had been a challenging and active one for Brisbane's submarines. They had seen front-line fighting, but success had proved elusive. Nevertheless, the only loss was *S39*, and all her crew had been saved. Early in 1943 the fortunes of Brisbane's submarines turned dramatically.

Argonaut was America's largest wartime submarine and the only one built primarily for minelaying. By 1943, slow and cumbersome, she was approaching old age. Minelaying did not suit American wartime submarine strategy, and in September 1942 *Argonaut* was overhauled and converted into a transport. Her size was an advantage here, as she could accommodate 120 troops. Furthermore, in avoiding rather than seeking out the enemy, her handling shortcomings would be less exposed. By December 1942 she was assigned to the Southwest Pacific to undertake special missions in the Solomons, Bismarck Archipelago, and Philippines.

Captain Fife had been Task Force 42 commander for five days when *Argonaut* (Lt. Comdr. J. R. Pierce) came under his control on her way to Brisbane. Keen to make more impact on the Solomons battle, he ordered *Argonaut* to divert and patrol the southern approaches to Rabaul. These were the enemy's most heavily guarded seas in the entire Southwest Pacific. *Argonaut*'s deficiencies increased her danger. *Wahoo*'s O'Kane, who served four years in *Argonaut*, described her fighting capacity: "If a fleet boat were stripped of one battery, two engines, six torpedo tubes, and could use no more than 15 degrees of rudder, she would still have greater torpedo attack and evasion ability than *Argonaut*."[1]

Intelligence revealed movements of a convoy from Lae to Rabaul, and Fife directed *Argonaut* to intercept. The big submarine contacted the convoy on 10 January 1943 and commenced a torpedo attack. By chance, a passing U.S. aircraft witnessed the battle below. The bomber crew saw one destroyer torpedoed and damaged. They also saw other destroyers dropping depth charges and water boiling with their explosions. Then, to their horror, they saw the submarine's bow break the surface at a steep angle, hang there with destroyers pouring gunfire into it, then slip back under water. They had dropped their bombs earlier and were powerless to intervene.[2]

Confirmation of the sinking soon came from Japanese radio. For a week Task Force 42 tried to contact *Argonaut*, but without response. *Argonaut* and 105 crewmen were lost. She was the first Brisbane loss to enemy action and the first involving fatalities. Her sinking was felt widely, as many submariners knew a friend on the boat. The impact of *Argonaut*'s loss was nowhere greater than on Chief Quartermaster G. S. Jenkins's family of twelve children. Missing American servicemen's wives received their pay for a year, but after that a small monthly allowance replaced it. However, a friendly Pearl Harbor supply officer saw to it that Mrs. Jenkins and her children never went hungry, and groceries were delivered every week.[3]

Beyond its personal impact, *Argonaut*'s loss affected Task Force 42's operations. Sent to carry out special missions, her absence meant that these missions must now be assigned to operational submarines. Immediate plans to land thirty Australian commandos and five tons of stores on Bougainville were hurriedly revised, and *Gato*, which took over this assignment, had to divide the mission into two trips. The demands of special missions remained heavy throughout 1943, engaging six of Brisbane's front-line submarines for varying periods.

While the loss of *Argonaut* was a blow, within a month Task Force 42 was mourning further loss of life in an action that became legendary.

Growler (Comdr. Howard W. Gilmore), a modern submarine sent from Pearl Harbor late in 1942, sailed from Brisbane on New Year's Day 1943 to patrol the Bismarck Archipelago. Gilmore was experienced and fearless. In three war patrols he had sunk five ships, including sinking one destroyer and damaging two others in Kiska Harbor on 4 July 1942.

Over the next four weeks Fife's nightly radio directions moved *Growler* about. She fought six battles involving depth-charge, gunfire, or bomb counterattacks. In the first, on 16 January, *Growler* sank the 5,857-ton *Chifuku Maru*. On 5 February, attempting another attack before dawn, *Growler* was heavily depth-charged, rupturing a gasket into the forward main ballast tank and causing a steady leak. Repairs reduced the leak.

Resuming her patrol, *Growler* was on the surface in the early hours of 7 February when a ship's shadow was sighted through the darkness.

Gilmore drew away to give room for a surface torpedo attack. At two thousand yards the Japanese vessel turned to ram *Growler*. In poor visibility, this was not immediately recognized. By the time evasive action commenced, the range was too close to fire.

What happened next is described in the patrol report: "Bridge gave order 'Left full rudder' and sounded the collision alarm. *Growler* hit enemy vessel head on, swinging with left rudder, at 17 knots. . . . The impact was terrific, knocking everyone down; *Growler* heeled over about 50 degrees."[4]

Motor Machinist's Mate Ed Packwood, who married a Brisbane girl and later retired there, was in the after engine room and recalled, "Five or six minutes after coming on our new course we felt a sharp port turn and a minute later we hit! Diving and collision alarms went off together. I heard machine gun fire and smelled gun smoke. . . . By then I was hanging in the ladder with my right arm, standing on the #4 engine. The boat had violently rolled over and when we righted, I looked forward and could see no one standing in either engine room."[5]

Following the impact, the enemy vessel opened fire, sweeping *Growler*'s bridge at point-blank range with .50-caliber machine guns. Ens. W. W. Williams and lookout Fireman W. F. Kelley fell dead while another two lookouts were wounded. Gilmore, wounded on the bridge, called, "Take her down." The two uninjured crewmen helped the lookouts below. Gilmore did not follow.

Executive Officer Lt. Comdr. Arnold F. Schade hesitated in following his captain's order. Years later Schade recalled these terrible moments:

> I was in the conning tower . . . for torpedo firing. . . . About this time they opened fire on us and all hell broke loose. . . . That's when Gilmore said, "Take her down, Arnie," and I said, "OK. Clear the bridge." So we cleared the bridge and got them all down there. . . . The lieutenant of the afterpart was killed and so was Gilmore and they were up on deck and were just blown over the side. Both of them. I went up myself. I stuck my head through the hatch and yelled. There was nobody there but the two sailors who were wounded and we were dragging them down. So, by this time we had already had the word to "take her down." . . . I turned . . . and said, "Sound the diving alarm." And that's when we went down.[6]

Diving brought *Growler* only momentary relief. Submerged, the damage became apparent. Water poured in through a bullet hole in the conning tower hatch and other smaller holes. Flooded electrical circuits

Growler's bow bent at right angles to port at New Farm Wharf.
Official U.S. Navy photo, U.S. National Archives, Record Group 19-N, 52453

grounded out. Flooding increased. Little regard was given to two depth charges as the crew struggled to save the boat.

After half an hour Schade surfaced to fight it out. There was no sign of Commander Gilmore, the two other crewmen, or the enemy. Their adversary, the naval store-ship *Hayasaki,* had not been sunk, as believed, but had disappeared into the gloom. She became one of the few Japanese warships to survive the war.

The crew now saw the full extent of the damage. *Growler's* bow was bent eighteen feet at right angles to port. Gunfire had wrecked the bridge, punched a number of holes in the conning tower, and disabled both periscopes. *Growler's* speed was reduced to eight knots, and holes needed plugging before she could dive. In addition, two armed torpedoes protruding from the damaged bow tubes could explode at any moment.

By dawn, repairs enabled *Growler* to submerge, and further repairs made one periscope serviceable. The leaks were controlled, but underwater handling proved difficult. That night Schade advised Fife of *Growler's* predicament while his crew set about bringing the crippled submarine two thousand miles home from hostile waters. Air cover was provided through dangerous narrows, and after ten slow days, pushing her battered bow through the sea, *Growler* entered Moreton Bay, her crew exhausted.

Before entering the river the crew disarmed the dangling torpedoes, and on 17 February, Schade brought *Growler* in under her own power. *Fulton* lowered her colors in honor of the dead as *Growler* berthed alongside. It was a solemn occasion, and the sight of *Growler* was one *Fulton*'s men would never forget.

Growler's crew members also carried lifelong memories. Ed Packwood remembered, "The fold-down seat where the skipper died was nothing but splinters. . . . My watch oiler had gone up for lookout just before battle stations. His name was Kelley—he didn't come home with us."[7]

But Gilmore's ordering *Growler* to dive at the cost of his own life was a story to stir the heart. His final words, "Take her down," became a symbol of courage and self-sacrifice inspiring the nation at a time of gloom. Howard Gilmore's heroism was recognized by the posthumous award of the Congressional Medal of Honor, the United States' highest decoration for courage—the first ever awarded to a submariner in battle.

In the three weeks before *Growler* returned, four submarines sailed from Brisbane on war patrol. Only one returned. The remaining three, *Amberjack* (Lt. Comdr. J. A. Bole), *Grampus* (Lt. Comdr. J. R. Craig), and *Triton* (Lt. Comdr. G. K. MacKenzie), all manned by veteran crews, went missing and were presumed lost with all hands.

Captain Fife had brought a sense of urgency to Task Force 42's operations. *Amberjack*'s rest period was reduced, and she sailed only twelve days after her previous patrol. Fife exercised tight control over his submarines at sea, directing them to new areas and intercept positions from the latest available intelligence. *Amberjack* received ten different position changes from Brisbane during this patrol, and *Grampus* received almost as many redirections. *Triton*'s patrol took her through the Rabaul–Shortland Islands area, then north to the Equator on the Rabaul–Truk convoy route.

First news came from *Amberjack*, which sent three messages in early February. She had sunk a schooner by gunfire and claimed an ammunition ship sunk at night, but this ship swept *Amberjack* with machine-gun fire, killing Chief Pharmacist's Mate A. C. Beeman and wounding an officer. Her final message on 14 February 1943 reported rescuing a Japanese airman and the submarine being forced down.[8]

MacKenzie, newly commanding *Triton*, also sent several messages. *Triton* located a convoy north of Manus Island on 6 March and reported sinking two ships in her first attack. Over the following day and two nights *Tri-*

ton pursued the convoy, making further attacks. MacKenzie believed that *Triton* hit three ships, but he was not able to observe results. Halsey did not wait for confirmation and credited *Triton* with four ships, radioing, "MacKenzie—You are doing extremely well for a beginner. . . . It is definitely Morton's next move and *Triton's* blitz will make *Wahoo* green with envy."[9]

In fact *Triton's* first attack sank *Kiriha Maru* and damaged *Mito Maru*, but counterattacks over the next two days, coupled with poorly performing American torpedoes, apparently prevented further sinkings. *Triton* soon found another convoy, reporting on 11 March, "Two groups of smokes, five or more ships each, plus escorts. . . . Am chasing." It was her final message.[10]

In stark contrast to *Amberjack* and *Triton*, nothing was heard from *Grampus*. *Grampus* sailed on 11 February 1943 and exercised with her surface escort off the Queensland coast. They parted the next day, and *Grampus* was never seen or heard from again.

As the submarines' patrol periods expired, headquarters staff became concerned when no reports came from submarines of their expected return. Concern for *Grampus* first arose on 7 March 1943, when nothing had been heard from her in almost a month. Further concern arose three days later when *Amberjack* failed to report her estimated time of arrival. Both were repeatedly ordered to report immediately, but no answer was received. Both *Amberjack* and *Grampus* were declared missing, presumed lost on 22 March 1943.

On 25 March 1943, *Triton* was ordered to return home, but no acknowledgment came. She too was ordered to reply, but there was only silence. When she failed to arrive in Brisbane, she was declared overdue, presumed lost on 10 April 1943. *Triton's* loss was a hard blow, as she was the first American submarine to fire torpedoes in the Pacific, and she was one of the navy's most successful submarines.

During the next fortnight the families of the 219 missing crewmen each received a grim telegram telling of their loved one's sacrifice. Twelve months later, with no indication of survivors, each crewman was officially presumed killed in action and a Purple Heart awarded.

Knowledge that a submarine was overdue was confined to those who needed to know. Security was paramount. Crews of other submarines were not informed. Their own submarine was their world, and they did not have regular contact with crews of other boats. Civilians were told nothing. Crews of each submarine were strictly ordered to tell no one outside where they had been or what they had seen. Submarine crews associated with civilians while on liberty but were forbidden to tell them anything. As a result, submarines became the "Silent Service," and little was known of their accomplishments.

Losses were officially announced some months later. News of the loss of *Amberjack* and *Grampus* was not released by Washington until 13 June 1943, almost three months after the boats had been declared missing, presumed lost.[11]

David Peto, who was communications officer on *Greenling* when these three submarines were posted missing, later wrote:

> I had a good friend in *Triton*. I recall the messages we received addressed to *Triton* ... [urging] *Triton* to respond to previous messages. We all assumed that *Triton* was beyond response. The authorities may have briefed the COs on losses ... but the rest of us were "out of the loop," for security reasons, I presume. ... [My friend] had been befriended by a family of Aussies in Surfers Paradise, Southport. When next I got to the Surfers Paradise Hotel I was asked by one of them if I'd heard from him. He had given them a bottle of Scotch whiskey to share upon his return. I wanted to tell them not to wait for him any longer but resisted—again, for security reasons.[12]

Some also recall the unanswered questions that arose when an expected submarine failed to arrive at New Farm Wharf. As usual, a welcoming party had assembled. Some sailors remember that, after waiting some time, they were dismissed and the food returned to store. Some, including *Triton* crewmen Willard Devling and William Turbeville, have clear memories of Captain Fife's distressed announcement that the submarine would not be arriving, and they later heard that she had been sunk close to home.[13] Searches of available official records have not substantiated this event.

Tragically, all these submarines were lost with all hands, 324 men. There were no survivors from almost three-quarters of the fifty-two American submarines lost during the war. Submariners accepted this fact, that they either came back whole or not at all. During the war 3,620 submariners' lives were lost, about 22 percent of all who served. This was the highest casualty rate of any branch of the American armed services.

Despite these high losses, American submariners gave little thought to the possibility of being sunk and just went on with the job. In fact, many were eager to stay with the boat and not be left behind. Robert Brown recalled being injured in a fall off a horse while on liberty at Lismore.

Despite his pain, he declined treatment in case he was removed from *Greenling*. He sailed on the next patrol and years later discovered that he had broken his collarbone in this fall.[14]

Although they discounted the risks to themselves, submariners were, and remain, deeply conscious of their missing comrades.

Brisbane's losses in the first three months of 1943 were unprecedented in the U.S. submarine service. In thirteen months of war, only three submarines were posted missing in action in all theaters. Now four submarines had been lost from a single command in only three months. Furthermore, the losses immediately followed Fife's taking command in Brisbane.

Fife, a man of steel will, believed that he was on the right course. He wrote to Lockwood, in charge of Pearl Harbor submarines, "They can't get Japs without taking chances. . . . [Don't] think the time has arrived to inject caution into the system because it is too difficult to overcome again."[15] Nevertheless, these losses moved him because, as he put it, "I knew all of these people so well personally." He offered his resignation, but Carpender refused to accept it, telling Fife, "If you go under, I'll go with you." Fife was impressed by Carpender's loyalty downward, a great encouragement to him in his adversity.[16]

The style of Fife's leadership was more demanding than Christie's, and he exercised more direct control over submarines at sea. However, except for *Argonaut,* there were few clues as to the cause of the losses. Nevertheless, these losses needed investigation and lessons learned. Accordingly, an independent officer, Capt. A. R. McCann, was appointed to investigate. After collecting available evidence, McCann reported to Carpender. The report was kept secret, even from task force commanders in Pearl Harbor and Fremantle. However, long afterward McCann reportedly said, "I exonerated Fife completely. The losses were in no way his fault. The boats may have been sunk by our own aircraft. There was no way to tell."[17]

One of the issues examined was Fife's redirection of submarines at sea, which seemed to some excessive. Christie was particularly critical, writing to Fife, "Radio despatches concerning *Grampus* and *Amberjack* totalled 106. Forty-six of these were reports of positions of submarines for higher command. Many of these despatches gave specific names, locations, and times."[18] Fife answered Christie's criticisms in detail, stating that movements requested were generally short and locations were along traffic routes rather than specific positions.[19] Fife continued to direct submarines at sea, but radio security was tightened and the scale of instructions reduced.

Undoubtedly Fife felt responsible for these losses, and he responded in a characteristically energetic and fearless manner by making a series of flights over enemy territory to seek answers and locate targets. Altogether Fife made six flights in April and May, two of which were attacked. These located a few targets but turned up no clues to explain the loss of his submarines.

However, returning submarines reported clear evidence that enemy antisubmarine measures were becoming more effective. Each patrol report included a section dealing with this subject. Although there were some weaknesses in Japanese equipment and technique, their shipping in the area was almost always escorted, and escorts were alert and well prepared. Improvements included combined air and surface hunts, destroyer radar, heavier depth charges with deeper settings, and detectors for submarines' radar.

Improved Japanese depth charges early in 1943 were indeed a concern. Initially Japanese depth charges exploded at relatively shallow settings, and submarines could escape by diving below this depth. This contributed to the submarines' comparatively light losses in 1942. The deeper, more powerful depth charges were cited with causing the loss of six submarines, including Fife's four, in the first four months of 1943.

Long after the war, Fife could look more objectively at the reason for his losses: "During the heat of this Solomons campaign, all the submarine captains I had out there had responded extremely well, and they were very anxious to inflict damage on the Japs, working down the Slot in the Solomons, and they may have gone over the other way, where they had abandoned caution."[20] The antisubmarine battle had become more deadly in the first half of 1943.

Immediately after the war, strong efforts were made to identify losses using Japanese records. The results were published in 1946 in the Commander of the Submarine Force's *U.S. Submarine Losses, World War II*.

Amberjack's loss was matched with an antisubmarine attack south of Rabaul on 16 February 1943 by aircraft and the escorts *Hiyodori* and *Submarine Chaser No. 18*. *Triton* was listed as sunk by three destroyers north of Manus Island on 15 March 1943. However, for *Grampus* only shadowy assumptions could be made about her movements after leaving her surface escort. These assumptions led to her being presumed sunk in the northern Solomons on 5 March 1943 by a pair of destroyers that were themselves sunk later that same night.[21]

However, by the very nature of submarine warfare, where the submarine remains unseen and evidence of destruction may be lacking or deceptive, doubts remain. Families with loved ones on "eternal patrol" long for answers so that they can find peace in their loss and gain some certainty to help resolve their grief. Frequently this closure cannot come until they find their loved one's actual resting place and understand the truth about what happened. For *Amberjack, Grampus,* and *Triton,* the evidence for each of their losses remains speculative. Furthermore, later research and the persistence of wartime memories cast doubt on the reliability of some official explanations. For example, academic research published in 1998 could not confirm the attack on *Triton* or identify the three destroyers credited with her sinking on 15 March 1943.[22] *Submarine Chaser No. 24* attacked a submarine that day in *Triton*'s general area, but evidence is conflicting as to whether her victim was sunk.[23]

Sixty years later, it is unlikely that the true cause of these losses will ever be determined. Nevertheless, each officer and sailor who died is still remembered by his family. All are remembered and commemorated by fellow submariners who survived to see peace return.

After four submarines were lost early in 1943, a fifth Brisbane boat luckily escaped a similar fate. *Gato* (Lt. Comdr. R. J. Foley) departed Brisbane on 19 March 1943 on her fifth war patrol. She carried coastwatchers for Bougainville in the special mission originally planned for *Argonaut.* The mission was completed ten days later with *Gato* evacuating a record fifty-one passengers to safety. Then she returned to the war against shipping.

At 3 AM on 4 April 1943, *Gato* was cruising off New Ireland in rain squalls and haze when a large freighter appeared two miles away. An escort emerged, and Foley circled away and submerged for a torpedo attack. Through the second periscope Foley's executive officer, Lt. Comdr. N. G. Ward, saw the escort heading straight for *Gato,* and he yelled, "Take her down! All ahead full." Two minutes later, three depth charges exploded. "The first one was practically a direct hit. The shock was violent and the vessel seemed to jump an appreciable distance. . . . The most important immediate result was the loss of all power."[24]

Ward later had no doubts about just how close it had been: "What had happened, he'd dropped [the depth charge] right under our stern. If we hadn't kicked all ahead full when we did, he would have dropped it under the hull, and I would not be talking to you now."[25]

Gato plunged to 380 feet, 80 feet below her operating depth, before being steadied. Leaks continued, and the boat sat at a dramatic up angle with no power. The stricken submarine was surfaced to restore power. Fortunately the escort had disappeared, and the crew made running repairs. *Gato* submerged at dawn.

Through that day Foley weighed up the boat's chances of being able to continue. *Gato* could fire her forward torpedoes and dive quickly, but the aft trim tank was open to the sea, and two more tanks were flooded because of leaks. Compensation forward to keep the submarine level meant that *Gato* had scarcely enough buoyancy to stay afloat. That evening Foley advised Brisbane that he was returning for repairs.[26]

Gato's severe damage stretched Brisbane's repair facilities. *Growler* had entered South Brisbane Dry Dock on 3 April for an estimated four weeks to repair her damaged bow. With *Gato* due in Brisbane on the eleventh, *Growler* was undocked so that *Gato* could be assessed. *Gato* entered the dock on 12 April, and her damaged tanks were made tight, two rear torpedo tubes were made serviceable, and steel plates strengthened her hull. Permanent repairs could not be performed in Brisbane. Sailing on 20 April, *Gato* resumed her patrol, which ended with two months in dock in California where her four aft torpedo tubes were replaced. Then *Gato* returned to Brisbane.

Early April 1943 saw the lowest point in Brisbane's submarine war. In three months, four submarines had been sunk and another two badly damaged, reducing the task force to half its strength. Worse than the loss of boats was the death of 327 sailors. Hard lessons were learned. There would be further losses, but from here on the successes mounted, and Brisbane's submarines made an increasing contribution to victory.

11
FURTHER OPERATIONS

As 1943 commenced, the war in the Southwest Pacific was turning in the Allies' favor. The battle for Guadalcanal was won, and all Japanese had gone by 7 February. In New Guinea the Buna campaign was successful, and Japanese resistance in Papua ended on 23 January.

A decisive victory followed early in March 1943 in the Battle of the Bismarck Sea when aircraft destroyed a troop reinforcement convoy to Lae. After this battle, the only Japanese shipping venturing south of Rabaul were submarines, fast destroyer runs, and nighttime barge traffic to Japanese garrisons. No enemy ship was sunk by submarines to the south of Rabaul after 1 March 1943.

However, the hard fighting of 1942 had worn down both sides. Time was needed to consolidate, restore the strength of troops weakened by disease and battle, and build up for the next move. As a result, near stalemate rested over the Bismarcks and Solomons through the first half of 1943.

The U.S. Navy quickly recognized this strategic improvement, and the concentration of submarines in Brisbane was wound back. Submarine transfers from Pearl Harbor ceased in December 1942. In the future this would occur only in rotating fresh submarines to Brisbane to replace those being rested. *Sperry* sailed for Pearl Harbor on 17 January. Task Force 42's strength dropped that month from three tenders and twenty-one submarines to just one tender and fourteen submarines.

Fulton remained in Brisbane with twelve boats of Squadron 8. Heavy losses in February and March further reduced submarine numbers. Although these losses were quickly replaced, task force strength was only ten submarines by 1 June 1943.[1]

Soon after *Sperry's* departure came a tragedy that had far-reaching effects on American submarine leadership. *Sperry's* commander in Brisbane was Capt. R. H. Smith, an experienced submariner who doubled as task force personnel officer. Four days before *Sperry* sailed he was relieved by Comdr. R. E. Blue and flew to Pearl Harbor. On 20 January 1943 he boarded a flying boat with Rear Adm. R. H. English, commander of Pearl Harbor submarines, and other staff officers to fly to San Francisco. They never arrived. In bad weather over California the aircraft crashed into a mountain, killing all aboard.

Rear Admiral English's death left a leadership gap in the Pacific Fleet Pearl Harbor submarines. The need to replace him was urgent. Rear Admiral Lockwood from Fremantle was chosen, receiving orders on 5 February 1943 appointing him vice admiral in command of Pacific Fleet submarines. He was replaced in Fremantle as commander of Southwest Pacific submarines and of Task Force 51 by none other than Ralph Christie, recently commander of Task Force 42, now promoted to rear admiral.

Despite its reduction in strength, Task Force 42 boasted twelve submarines in February 1943, compared with only eight in Fremantle. In September 1942 Lockwood had unsuccessfully argued that as Southwest Pacific submarines commander he should be moved to Brisbane to directly command the bulk of the area's submarines. Despite Lockwood's efforts, Christie remained Brisbane's task force commander. Now, by an ironic twist, Christie was on the opposite side of the argument from which he had prospered barely six months previously.

Transiting Brisbane, Christie approached Carpender to have the command positions reversed. Fife takes up the story: "He went up [to Admiral Carpender] and got his ears pinned back and that was that. He went on over to Western Australia, and from then on, he kept trying to absorb my command into his."[2] Over much of the war, relations between the two Southwest Pacific submarine force commanders were cool.

While enjoying Carpender's support in controlling Task Force 42's operations, Fife came under Christie's command in implementing policy. In this, one issue above all else caused increasing disquiet among submarine crews: torpedoes.

Although torpedo shortages concerned all commands, a greater issue to submarine crews was their poor performance. Defects had appeared in the first month of the war. Initially, command blamed low success on poor marksmanship or incorrect handling. However, Lockwood and Fife's tests in Albany during July 1942 showed that torpedoes ran more than eleven feet below their set depth, often passing well under their targets. Remedial instructions were issued, and corrective kits began to be distributed late in 1942. They were slow in reaching Brisbane, and it was not until March 1943 that all submarines carried torpedoes converted to correct depth performance. Despite these efforts, results did not improve, and submarine crews began to notice further defects.

The standard torpedo used by fleet-submarines was the Mark 14, developed between the wars by the U.S. Navy's Bureau of Ordnance. It was a complex steam-propelled weapon with high- and low-speed settings, gyro course control, and two different devices for exploding its warhead: a conventional contact trigger and a state-of-the-art magnetic exploder to set off the warhead by means of the target's own magnetic field. The magnetic trigger was particularly designed to attack a battleship by striking below her armored belt and exploding under the unprotected keel, breaking the ship's back.

Such a sophisticated weapon was also expensive. At around $10,000, it was as costly in 1940 as a fighter aircraft airframe. After just one successful trial it was considered too expensive for more live tests, so nonexplosive trials were carried out, then the exploders were locked away for when war came. When Pearl Harbor was attacked, they were little more than a rumor to most submariners.

Christie was closely associated with development of the Mark 14 torpedo and its magnetic pistol during his recurring postings to the Naval Torpedo Station, including one as officer in charge. He was convinced of the magnetic trigger's efficacy and believed that it provided a significant advantage over the enemy.

Submarine captains' faith in the magnetic exploder was shaken when they found torpedoes exploding a short distance after firing or just short of their targets. This usually alerted the enemy vessel, which escaped, and more quickly revealed the submarine for counterattack. Seeing a difficult attack fail and then suffering a pounding shook morale. Later at base, commanders would be criticized for lack of results and poor torpedo handling. For many months the Bureau of Ordnance ignored any criticism of the torpedoes and thereafter pursued modifications to keep them in use.

Christie also discounted any criticism of magnetic exploders when he was Task Force 42 commander, blaming poor maintenance, inadequate training, and improper firing settings. Now, returned to Australia, he was determined that his submarine crews would continue to use Mark 14s as designed. Fife was obliged to follow orders.

It was difficult to determine the extent to which torpedo defects caused the poor results of Brisbane submarines, as alert escorts often made it impossible to observe results. But evidence was mounting, such as the experience of *Drum* (Lt. Comdr. B. McMahon) when she met the unescorted freighter *Nisshun Maru* on 18 April 1943. Out of eight torpedoes fired to sink her, three exploded prematurely.[3]

Too often submarines returned to port having fired most of their torpedoes with little to show for it. *Grayback* (Lt. Comdr. E. C. Stephan) fired forty-four torpedoes in two patrols but sank nothing confirmed in postwar reckoning. In her first 1943 patrol *Albacore* (Lieutenant Commander Lake) fired twenty-one torpedoes. Lake reported one premature explosion and only three hits, two later believed to have been premature explosions close to the target.

Wahoo's brilliant patrol during January 1943 was cited as proof of the magnetic exploder's effectiveness, as it had been used on all torpedoes fired. Morton claimed that the torpedo's magnetic function had saved *Wahoo* in her showdown with *Harusame* at Wewak. So use of the magnetic exploder on Mark 14 torpedoes continued.

Another shortcoming of American torpedoes was their comparatively small warhead—at 500 pounds of TNT, lighter than other major powers' torpedoes. Consequently, effective hits might do no more than merely damage the target. Destroyers, being relatively small, with narrow beam, large compartments, and high-pressure boilers, were vulnerable to torpedoes. However, of the five destroyers torpedoed by Brisbane submarines in the first half of 1943, only two sank. This deficiency was remedied later in 1943 by increasing the warhead's weight to 650 pounds of a more powerful explosive, Torpex.

A more frightening defect was the occasional faulty torpedo whose rudder malfunctioned, sending it on a circular run back toward the submarine that had fired it. *Triton* was forced to avoid being struck by one of her own torpedoes on 6 March 1943, and *Grouper* had a similar narrow escape on 13 July.

The predominant objective of every submarine was to sink enemy ships. Fife repeatedly referred to this in his patrol report endorsements:

> The percentage [of torpedo hits] is . . . unsatisfactory not so much from the point of view of torpedo expenditure as from the number of valuable targets that got away.[4]

> Torpedo performance again resulted in an enemy ship escaping damage after being hit.[5]

Submarine Combat Pin.
Official U.S. Navy design

A patrol was declared successful when enemy shipping was sunk. A combat pin worn on the uniform recognized a successful patrol. A star was added for each additional successful patrol.

In four patrols *Greenling* sank eleven enemy vessels, and each patrol was judged successful. Her fifth patrol, commencing on 21 February 1943 with a new captain, Lt. Comdr. J. D. Grant, was different. Her first assignment was a special mission landing coastwatchers on New Britain, and this was successfully accomplished. Intercepting an important convoy two weeks later, Grant conned *Greenling* under the escort screen and fired torpedoes at close range. None exploded. Two escorts quickly administered an accurate depth-charge attack. After four hours *Greenling* escaped unscathed then moved to the convoy routes north of New Guinea for more than a month of rain and heavy seas without sighting one suitable target. She returned to Brisbane after two months with no sinkings. Despite the special mission and savage battle with the escorts, the patrol was deemed unsuccessful, and no combat insignia was awarded.

The official view focused on results, and little sympathy was lost on any hardships suffered. Submarine crews held a different view. To them, any patrol you returned from was a success. Crews promoted success in their own way in the form of the battle flag, stitched at sea and flown from the periscope on return from patrol. Every enemy ship claimed as sunk or damaged was on the flag. Usually a small Japanese flag denoted each success, a plain rising sun for a merchant ship or the naval ensign's radiating rays for a warship. In the war's early stages the flag was usually black with a piratical skull and crossbones, like those flown by the Royal Navy's submarines. Designs varied as the war progressed, often centering on a cartoon representation of the submarine's name and including other achievements like medals awarded and rescues effected.

Drum crew members in Brisbane on 13 May 1943 after their fifth war patrol.
Then–Lt. M. H. Rindskopf, *Drum*'s executive officer,
is in the back row, second from the left.

Official U.S. Navy photo, U.S. National Archives, Record Group 80-G, 51071

Rabaul was supplied by convoys from Palau to the northwest and Truk to the north. It was a Palau convoy that *Wahoo* intercepted in January, and *Triton* was operating against these convoys when she was lost. By March 1943, Allied intelligence had established the general route of these convoys.

The route from Palau led southeast to the Equator, then eastward until it turned to Kavieng. The route from Truk went southward to Kavieng. Shipping moved on to Rabaul when the opportunity looked favorable. The Equator was the demarcation between Fife's jurisdiction and Lockwood's area, and the two commanders resolved that Fife's submarines would cover this section of the route.

About this time, American intelligence broke the Japanese convoy code, referred to as the "maru code." This gave much information on convoy routes and schedules, including each day's noon positions. It also allowed signals about convoy diversions or attacks to be read. This information enabled Fife to send "ultra" messages to position submarines to attack convoys.

Armed with this knowledge, Fife now concentrated his submarines north of New Guinea around the Equator. This area of wide ocean spaces, free of reefs and narrow straits, gave submarine captains freedom of movement to better plan their attacks and race ahead for a second strike. Being more remote from enemy air bases, submarines cruised on the surface during the day, extending their field of vision and utilizing their high surface speed. Still, a vigilant lookout was maintained against air attack.

Fife deployed his submarines in adjoining patrol areas along the estimated convoy route and directed more than one submarine to attack the same convoy. Concentrating his submarines increased the chance of success and reduced risk by dividing the convoy's escorts.

An early success with this new tactic occurred late in March 1943 when *Guardfish* located a convoy north of Manus Island. As frequently occurred, alert escorts detected *Guardfish* before she could attack and depth-charged her. However, *Tuna* (Lt. Comdr. A. Holtz) was directed to the same convoy, sinking *Kurohime Maru* and damaging another vessel.

Despite promising prospects, results were slow in coming. Alert and active Japanese escorts frustrated many attacks, as they had in the Solomons. However, the main reason success remained elusive was the general contraction in Japanese shipping. As strategic activity declined from March 1943, enemy shipping movements also receded, and there were fewer targets. *Grouper* (Lt. Comdr. M. Hottel) had no opportunity to fire any torpedoes on her patrol in April and May 1943, and *Guardfish*, with high-scoring Lieutenant Commander Klakring in command, came home from her fourth patrol in April empty-handed because of a lack of enemy contacts.

Finding targets for his submarines was one reason driving Fife to make flights over enemy territory in April and May 1943. They were helpful in finding some targets, but not very many.[6] Throughout the month of May, Fife's boats sank only three ships. The drought would continue for several months yet.

The essential link between Fife and his boats was the nightly radio "Fox" schedule. Submarines were informed of enemy movements and changes to patrol areas for both themselves and other submarines. Messages from submarines were restricted to enemy reports, but coded reports of weather in enemy waters were included where possible.

Radio provided a reassuring link for submarines a long way from home. *Drum*'s crew appreciated the historical allusion of their task force commander's signals, "Fife to *Drum*."[7] And when a submarine struck trouble, support across the airwaves was prompt. Lieutenant Commander Ramage was impressed when he reported to Pearl Harbor that *Trout* had been damaged in October 1942: "Almost immediately . . . I got a dispatch back from Admiral Halsey. It said, 'Give me your route points.' So I fired off a dispatch giving my route points at A, B, C. . . . And he came back with D, E, F, right into Brisbane. . . . You never had such confidence. . . . I mean, everybody was right with you every place you went."[8]

In patrol areas, submarines followed a standard routine. David Peto, *Greenling*'s communications officer, described a four-hour watch:

> Submerged, the more experienced officers stood periscope watches in the conning tower, and the others acted as the diving officer in the control room below. They were responsible for maintaining the proper depth . . . and for keeping the boat properly ballasted and trimmed. . . . Also in the conning tower were the helmsman, the quartermaster, and the sonar operator. Usually we operated at 100 feet depth, rising two or three times an hour to periscope depth (60 to 56 feet) . . . to search for targets. It was during these hours at quiet times that the conning tower personnel had the opportunity to converse. As we were all young with different backgrounds, we had a lot to talk about.[9]

With targets scarce, two-month patrols became an ordeal of routine and boredom. Off-duty hours dragged by, and Charles Schechter *(Drum)* summed them up thus: "We ate, slept, read books, and listened to music."[10] For novices there was the serious business of studying to qualify in submarines. This involved learning all the compartments, as well as the different equipment and how it worked, and having their knowledge tested by an officer in a walk through the boat. Every man aboard should be able to take his place on watch in any role required, and act quickly and without instruction in an emergency. Qualifying on submarines entitled the sailor to wear the coveted submariner's dolphins.

Two veterans have described off-duty hours on these quiet patrols:

> To ease the boredom we played many games . . . we played poker, chess, checkers (draughts), cribbage, and acey-deucy, which is the

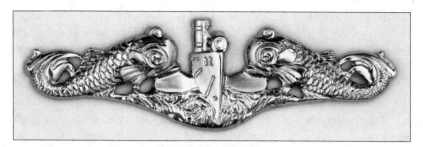

Submariner's Dolphins.
Official U.S. Navy design

Navy version of backgammon. At the start of the patrol tournaments would be organised. Nearly everyone on the ship, officers included, joined in. We also read a lot. The fore-runners of today's paperback books were supplied to us free of charge. . . . Some of the books which bordered on spicy were passed from hand to hand until they were falling apart.[11]

Our crew's mess (the after battery) was the social center of the submarine. It was here we listened to Tokyo Rose and the radio. We played the record player, we played poker or other card and dice games, and wrote letters there. We gossiped about each other and the war and the submarine officers. . . . We had an open-galley policy, which meant that anyone could make themselves a sandwich during the night hours.[12]

Teasing a shipmate, called "pinging" aboard submarines, helped to ease the tension. This was usually good-natured, but there was a limit as to what could be tolerated in a submarine's close confines. The cook, commonly known as the "stewburner," came in for more than his fair share of this attention.

Creative cooks were absolutely essential to maintaining crew morale. Not only did cooks need to make meals palatable and attractive, but they also had to work with the food available. Moldy yeast needed to be reactivated, weevils needed to be sifted out of the flour, and canned food, stacked tightly in corners, needed to be accessible in sufficient variety to ensure balanced and varied meals. Ordinary cooks' bread tended to be indifferent, so a baker was added to the crew to improve this staple. A side product was pastries, desserts, and birthday cakes. Overriding all else was the need for a healthy diet. Seamen from the days of sail knew the danger of scurvy caused by vitamin C deficiency. The risk remained, and when *Saury* ended her fifth patrol commencing from Brisbane, most of her crew were suffering the sore, bleeding gums and loose teeth of scurvy.[13]

Serious injuries and illnesses were few, but when a boat sailed, one of the crew usually brought a common cold on board that spread like wildfire. Gastric upsets were also common, as was toothache, wisdom teeth often causing problems for crewmen just out of their teens. These were dealt with by the pharmacist's mate, who had special first-aid training for detached service.[14]

Emergencies occurred from time to time, and appendicitis needed immediate treatment. Pharmacist's mates were instructed to put the patient to bed packed in ice and kept on a liquid diet until reaching port. However, where an appendix threatened to rupture, more urgent measures were taken. Emergency appendectomies were performed at sea on Brisbane's *Grayback* and *Silversides* in December 1942 by pharmacist's mates using makeshift implements, working from a medical book and without surgical training.

Although Japanese ships may have been hard to find, the enemy's voice was readily heard in the smooth, seductive tones of Tokyo Rose. When running on the surface at night, many submarines listened to Tokyo Rose as she broadcast the latest American music and news. Her propaganda may have been laughable, but her messages were designed to sow doubt in the minds of submarine sailors. Her music evoked images of home—first to make the sailors homesick, then to suggest that their sweethearts were sharing the music, and maybe their affections, with others. Her messages aimed to create division—between sailors and civilians at home, between Aussies and Yanks, or between different services.

The news from Tokyo Rose that most interested American submarine crews was any mention of their own submarine. Occasionally the submarine was declared sunk, but more frequently it was a warning that Japanese forces were ready to sink them. Paul Snyder remembered Tokyo Rose identifying *Guardfish*: "When we left Brisbane it was likely a night or two after we left, but we were named and told how they were waiting for us."[15]

Another enemy contact was sighting Japanese hospital ships. Frank Medina remembered *Guardfish* meeting one early in 1943: "I was on lookout when out of the black night came this neon-lit ship. It was a plump target for our torpedo tubes, but it turned out to be a huge Japanese hospital ship."[16] Hospital ships were protected by the Geneva Convention and recognized in the task force's operation orders. Under this convention they were to be painted white overall, with large red crosses and a broad green band around the hull. Those sighted by Brisbane submarines were correctly marked and were allowed free passage.

Hospital ships could be a distracting presence, as *Drum* discovered on 7/8 July 1943. During the day, *Drum* (Lieutenant Commander McMahon) had sighted a large tanker but was unable to close the range to attack. Her sister *Peto* (Lt. Comdr. W. Nelson) was more fortunate and torpedoed and damaged the tanker. *Drum* surfaced at dusk and chased, hoping to complete the sinking. A glow was sighted, believed to be the burning tanker. *Drum* prepared to attack. Then the glow was recognized as the light of a hospital ship, and the attack was canceled. The tanker escaped into the night.[17]

Sometimes hospital ships appeared to be the only enemy shipping at sea. *Greenling* (Lieutenant Commander Grant) sighted only two vessels in the course of one month, both of them hospital ships. Not all submarine captains were satisfied that hospital ships deserved the protection of international convention. On 15 December 1942, *Seadragon* (Lt. Comdr. W. E. Ferrall) sighted *Hikawa Maru* (11,625 tons) correctly painted and registered as a hospital ship. However, she was following a zigzag course and was under escort, raising questions in Ferrall's mind. Despite his doubts, he let the big liner proceed.[18]

Following the Bismarck Sea battle, Japan diverted submarines to run supplies from Rabaul to its army in Lae. Consequently, enemy submarines assumed greater importance in Fife's planning. Australian coastwatchers at Cape Orford, New Britain, reported shipping movements, and, aided by radio intelligence, Fife attempted to trap these supply submarines. *Guardfish* waited off the cape for five days early in June without sighting the enemy.

Later that month *Greenling* took up the ambush, and David Peto recalled, "We sighted one sub but were unable to close to firing range, and another the following day with equal lack of success. We were hopeful of results but were ordered out of that area to another area before we could capitalize on the information."[19]

Results of the Cape Orford ambush were disappointing, but the Brisbane task force achieved success in a submarine duel on 27 July 1943. *Scamp* (Lt. Comdr. W. G. Ebert) was patrolling west of New Hanover that evening when noise from a high-speed engine was heard, and Ebert sighted a surfaced submarine. Drawing closer, *Scamp*'s sonar operator heard the sound of torpedoes approaching, and *Scamp* dived deep to avoid. The torpedoes having passed, Ebert brought *Scamp* to periscope depth to find the submarine still surfaced with a Japanese flag on its conning tower.

Torpedoes were fired, and one was heard to hit, followed by the sound of tearing metal. A tall smoke pillar and diesel oil on the sea confirmed the destruction of *I-168*, just eight minutes after the first sighting. This was a significant success, as *I-168* had sunk the American aircraft carrier *Yorktown* at the Battle of Midway.

In early 1943, Japanese submarines remained a threat off eastern Australia. Enemy sightings off Brisbane dictated that American submarines exercise caution as soon as they met the open sea off Caloundra. On 4 June 1943, *Drum* sailed on patrol but was recalled when the transport *Edward Chambers* was shelled by a submarine twenty miles east of Cape Moreton. The area was used for exercises and routing into Brisbane, so bombing restrictions applied. Now the bombing restrictions were temporarily revoked, and *Drum's* departure was postponed a day. Not realized at the time, the submarine *I-174* moved away after this action and was the last Japanese submarine to operate off eastern Australia.

Despite their withdrawal from the Queensland coast, Japanese submarines continued to threaten American submarines in their operational areas. Although locations of enemy submarines revealed by radio intelligence were advised in the "Fox" bulletins, the only sure defense was a vigilant lookout and immediate response.

In the light of combat experience and technological advance, various improvements were introduced into American submarines.

One unpleasant discovery was how visible fleet-submarines were at night. Their large, bulky, enclosed bridges could frequently be seen by sharp-eyed Japanese lookouts. On her heroic fourth patrol from Brisbane, *Growler* attempted three separate night surface attacks, and each time she was sighted, prompting Fife to write, "The patrol had several instances . . . wherein *Growler* paid the usual penalty for excessive silhouette which has occurred so many times since the war began. . . . As a result of this condition many valuable enemy ships are still afloat and operating instead of being on the bottom."[20] Fife might well have mentioned the extra danger to survival of a silhouette so easily seen. Some adjustments to bridge structures were made in Brisbane, but more extensive work installing smaller bridges of new design was carried out as fleet-submarines returned for dockyard overhaul in the United States.

Another modification in early 1943 was fitting a 20mm antiaircraft gun.

Submarines refitting alongside *Fulton* in the Brisbane River.
A torpedo is being loaded onto one, and bridge modifications
to reduce silhouette are in progress on another.
Official U.S. Navy photo, U.S. National Archives, Record Group 80-G, 51804

This was a major advance on the lighter machine guns carried and would
also assist in surface actions. Initially the 20mm gun was mounted on the
"cigarette deck" at the rear of the bridge, but in early 1943 a platform
added forward of the bridge carried another 20mm gun.

The major technological advance of early 1943 was fitting SJ surface-
search radar, supplementing the primitive SD air-warning radar. SJ sets
rotated, projecting a directional beam from which a contact's range could
be read. This new radar promised to improve attack capability. Attacks
could now be initiated against an unseen target. Furthermore, shallow
submerged attacks could be made with the radar just above the waves giving an accurate range. From this time on, captains used the new radar
whenever they could.

SJ radar was on fleet-submarines coming from Pearl Harbor in December 1942. Boats already in Brisbane also received it as they refitted at New
Farm. *Grayback*'s SJ radar was installed in Brisbane early in February 1943

A fleet-submarine, probably USS *Grouper*, returning to Brisbane on
29 May 1943, is welcomed by a band, fresh food, and mail.
Official U.S. Navy photo, U.S. National Archives, Record Group 80-G, 51795

before her sixth patrol. Unfortunately, promise was not always matched by
reality. *Grayback* returned disappointed with the new radar, finding that it
failed to operate long enough to be useful. *Gato* was another that found
her SJ radar erratic around the same period.

The disappointment was not surprising, as sets needed refining and
operators needed experience. Ira King, communications officer of *Darter*,
put the state of electronics at that time into perspective: "Tubes were in all
electronic equipment. Transistors had not been invented. The equipment
was bulky and hot and subject to failure at any time."[21]

Nevertheless, SJ radar offered great improvement in a submarine's
attack capability. *Guardfish* (Lieutenant Commander Klakring) provided
an early demonstration of its potential when radar located a destroyer in
heavy rain off New Hanover late on 12 January 1943. To avoid detection,
Guardfish made a submerged approach at a depth of forty feet with her
radar just above the surface. Torpedoes fired on the radar bearing sank
Patrol Boat No. 1 (ex–destroyer *Shimakaze*). Klakring reported that at no
stage could he see the destroyer through the periscope.

Although SJ radar opened up new possibilities, submarine captains found that their elementary SD air-warning radar had become a liability. Introduced early in 1942, SD warned lookouts of approaching aircraft. However, SD radar gave off powerful radiation that was detected and tracked by enemy radio direction-finding equipment. SD radar would then attract enemy aircraft, homing in along the radar's transmissions. On 14 May 1943 Fife discouraged further use of SD radar. Submarines would rely on visual lookouts to warn of possible air attack.

Another new item arriving from the United States was the target bearing transmitter (TBT). This incorporated a powerful pair of binoculars mounted on the bridge as an aiming device for surface attacks, particularly at night. For submarine officers from the Asiatic Fleet or S-boats, SJ radar and the TBT opened up possibilities they could only have dreamed of previously.

Following their defeats in Guadalcanal and Papua, the Japanese strengthened their positions at Munda and Vila in the Solomons and at Lae and Salamaua in New Guinea. Allied leaders were also considering their next strategic move. Vice Admiral Halsey visited Brisbane to confer with General MacArthur and plan the next offensive. While in Brisbane, on 16 April 1943, Halsey paid an unofficial visit to the submarine task force, which by this time had a new name.

In a navywide restructuring, the Southwest Pacific Naval Force was renamed the Seventh Fleet on 15 March 1943. The Seventh Fleet remained under Carpender, with all task forces renumbered in the 70 series. Brisbane's submarines, formerly Task Force 42, became Task Force 72, while Fremantle's Task Force 51 became Task Force 71. With only a small surface striking force centered on three cruisers, HMAS *Australia, Hobart,* and USS *Phoenix,* Carpender's force hardly deserved to be called a fleet. Submarines remained its main offensive force.

12

SUPPORTING THE COASTWATCHERS

The events of 1942 had demonstrated the submarine's versatility in performing covert activities like reconnaissance, rescue, and support of shore parties. These activities developed further during 1943 with *Nautilus*'s rescue of civilians on New Year's Day. That week *Grayback* (Lt. Comdr. E. Stephan) rescued six B26 crewmen and acted as a navigation beacon for cruisers bombarding Munda airfield.

Missions of mercy continued, but most Brisbane special missions supported coastwatchers. Australian "Ferdinand" parties on Japanese-held islands in the western Solomons had been crucial in the Guadalcanal victory. Brisbane submarines provided vital support. The bond between submariners and coastwatchers grew in 1943.

With Guadalcanal secured, Allied leaders needed to extend coastwatcher reporting areas. In addition, coastwatchers' tasks gradually changed from long-term surveillance to preinvasion surveys. The first move involved landing a coastwatching team at Cape Orford to monitor Japanese traffic south of Rabaul.

Malcolm Wright, who had landed from *S42* on New Britain in July 1942, returned to Cape Orford. With Capt. Peter Figgis and Lt. Les Williams, he boarded *Greenling* at New Farm Wharf just before dawn on 21 February 1943. Four New Guinea team members, including Sergeant Simogun, had joined earlier in American uniforms.[1] David Peto, *Greenling*'s communications officer, remembered: "They came aboard after midnight on the morning of departure—all very hush hush. Only the skipper [Lieutenant Commander Grant] and [the executive officer] knew about it. The rest of us were surprised to greet our new shipmates after we got under way."[2] The

Australians quickly changed out of their uniforms, and they stayed out of sight as the boat departed. But they had not anticipated the pilot coming below to the wardroom. To his friendly greeting, Williams drawled a non-committal answer as his jaws worked on imaginary gum. The unsuspecting pilot moved on.

The eight-day transit was generally smooth. The New Guineans repaid the crew's hospitality with mini "sing-sings." But there were some prank-sters among the crew who enjoyed getting a rise out of their guests with such practical jokes as suddenly starting the below-deck auxiliary engine just as the New Guineans were passing through. Not all the pranks were well received. Putting a bottle of hot Tabasco sauce to his lips, a torpedo-man mimed swallowing and satisfaction while carefully blocking the bot-tle's neck. Then he passed it to his victim. After a hearty swig, the irate New Guinean had to be restrained from using his machete on the joker, who hid until his victim cooled down. In general the party enjoyed the crew's hospitality, although the New Guineans, to the sailors' surprise, turned down ice water and ice cream.

On the night of 1 March, Wright and three others checked the landing area. The next night, the rest of the party and all the supplies landed. A power boat provided by Admiral Carpender speeded the unloading.

Almost seven months later, on the night of 28/29 September, *Grouper* (Lt. Comdr. M. Hottel) delivered a further forty-three coastwatchers and three thousand pounds of supplies to Wright on New Britain. It was the largest party to land from one submarine. Wright moved the party, too big and noisy for his taste, off the beach before dawn, and the arrivals dis-persed to support the Allied advance. *Grouper* took back Capt. A. L. Post, a shot-down pilot who had been Wright's guest.

The Japanese keenly appreciated the damage done by the coastwatchers and made a major effort to destroy the Australian network. Read and Mason, the "saviors" of Guadalcanal, were particularly targeted. Mason was located above important Buin anchorage. Read sent details of enemy movements from Kavieng and Buka. Their air-raid warnings, urgently broadcast in plain language, were equally clear to Japanese monitors.

Recognizing the coastwatchers' effect on the battle, the Japanese mounted campaigns against them, starting with Mason in the south. The coastal islanders were turned against him, forcing him to retreat inland. When two hundred Japanese converged on his camp in January, Mason began a bush trek of one hundred miles through the mountains to join Read in the north. There were problems too in the north, from Japanese pressure and civilian refugees. As well, Lt. J. H. Mackie requested relief for his twenty-five Independent Company soldiers, who had now spent a year operating behind enemy lines with Read.

Four submarine missions resolved the situation. On 19 March 1943, Lieutenant Commander Foley headed *Gato* north out of Moreton Bay. His orders included "to land Lieutenant Keenan RANVR and party with their supplies on Bougainville, and to evacuate twelve commandos and twelve civilians from the same point."[3] Keenan had returned from five months on Vella Lavella late in February before becoming involved in the "Bougainville venture." Plans for landing thirty men and ten thousand pounds of stores in a single trip had to be amended when the U.S. Navy advised that, "Owing to certain circumstances, a smaller submarine was to be used."[4] The "circumstances" were the loss of *Argonaut* seven weeks before.

Early on 19 March, Keenan, three Bougainvilleans, Lieutenant Bedkober, and eleven AIF (Australian Imperial Force) replacements secretly boarded *Gato*. HMAS *Gympie* escorted the submarine to sea, exercising with her throughout the next day. Keenan with his *Grampus* experience felt at home, but, he recalled, "When I went along to the aft torpedo room to see how [the Bougainvilleans] were making out they were wishing such ships had never been invented." However, as "the officers and crew extended every hospitality possible" and calmer seas ensued, "most of the lads . . . commenced to enjoy the trip."[5]

Meanwhile on Bougainville, Read assembled the party for the planned evacuation on 28 March. That afternoon a small Japanese vessel anchored right off the embarkation point, forcing Read to postpone the operation.

Deciding on a submerged day entry, Foley was in the harbor by mid-afternoon. Studying the vessel, he found no activity anywhere and left. Around 8 PM two bonfires were sighted, and *Gato* returned. In midchannel, Foley received from Brisbane Read's postponement message. Unable to turn, he coolly reentered the harbor, silently turned, and left. The next morning, so did the unsuspecting Japanese.

That evening Foley picked up the signal fire. About 8:30, *Gato* stopped close to the beach. Read surprised Foley with the news that the evacuees numbered fifty-one, not twenty-four. Foley replied that he could take them all. The dinghy, rubber boats, and local canoes loaded and unloaded the submarine. By 9:47 *Gato* had, in pitch black, sailed with twelve AIF commandos, three Belgian nuns, nine mothers, twenty-seven children, and cargo. Read had also dispatched the Kieta and Buka Passage financial records. They were duly delivered to Canberra—the only such records to reach there.[6]

Foley recorded his packed vessel's voyage: "Ran eastwards at four engine speed, getting our passengers settled. All were 'troupers' and were quickly adopted by the ship's company. The adoption was reciprocal. . . . One ten months old child would sleep nowhere but in the arms of a bearded torpe-doman." He described *Gato*'s varied complement: . . . "(a) The children; . . . a cycle of awe, apprehension, mischief, raucousness, and unwilling sleep. (b) The mothers; distraught, then trustful. (c) The nuns; benign, and patient. (d) The soldiers; 'Haven't you got some dirty jobs we can help you with?' and 'Is there any beer in Brisbane?' (e) The *Gato* crew; clumsy but enthusiastic volunteer nursemaids."[7]

It was a dangerous passage through poorly charted shoals, and the presence of fifty-one extra bodies rapidly degraded the submerged air quality. Forty-eight crowded hours later, the evacuees boarded a surface vessel off Florida Island. *Gato*'s crew had risen magnificently to the challenge. Eric Feldt summed it up: "It was typical of the U.S. submarine service where nothing was too onerous, nothing was too dangerous, the worst job a part of the day's work."[8]

Soon after transferring her passengers, *Gato* was damaged in action and had to limp back to Brisbane for repairs. She resumed her interrupted patrol on 20 April. On board for Bougainville were Capt. Eric "Wobbie" Robinson, Lt. George Stevenson, and the remaining fourteen AIF replacements, arriving off Teop Harbor on 28 April.[9] Enemy activity forced the landing south to Teopasino Plantation in a particularly poorly charted area. After dusk on 29 April, Foley "gritted teeth and followed direction" to run blind through the gap in the reef.

As before, a fleet of canoes augmented the rubber boats in the task of loading and unloading, and *Gato* departed half an hour after midnight. Clear of the reef, Foley set course to rendezvous with sub chaser SC504. The next evening north of Florida Island, *Gato* transferred her passengers and some letters, then resumed her patrol.

Compared with the previous load, *Gato* had traveled light, with only twenty-three passengers. In addition to Lieutenant Mackie and his last twelve AIF men there were Thomas Wade, bishop of Bougainville, six priests, two brothers, and one civilian male. The missionaries were in bad shape but responded well to the treatment and food received on board.

Mission accomplished, Foley summed up the submariners' aversion to special missions: "In addition to the time taken from their stations and the possible loss from rocks, shoals, and enemy traps, submarines diverted for this work are thereafter greatly restricted in their movements for the duration of the patrol."

Gato spent sixteen days without a single contact, then Foley reconnoitered Greenwich Island, Numa Numa on Bougainville, Ocean Island, and Tarawa before completing the eventful, interrupted fifth patrol at Pearl Harbor on 6 June.

Just six weeks after Robinson's landing, he and Read lost all but their lives in an attack on their camp. Five days later Lieutenant Bedkober and two others were killed. Then, on 26 June, Lieutenant Stevenson was shot dead in his camp. That day Read radioed, "Reluctantly urge immediate evacuation."

The call was answered by sending *Guardfish* (Lt. Comdr. N. G. Ward), which on 24 July sighted first the coastwatchers' white cloth signal, then, after dark, their signal fire. Lt. Ken Curtis and four men took a rubber boat ashore while the submarine closed the breakers and launched seven other boats.

Ward was not a novice at this work; he had been Foley's executive officer at Teop. He had been given command of *Guardfish* the day before *Gato* sailed to resume her interrupted patrol. Now he surpassed Foley's fifty-one passengers by taking aboard sixty-two. In addition to Mason and Keenan, there were twenty-two AIF soldiers, two survivors of a crashed Catalina aircraft, nine police, thirteen Bougainvillean scouts, seven Chinese, one Fijian, four wives, and two children.

A crowded day and a half later the passengers transferred to a patrol craft off Savo Island. Then *Guardfish* returned about thirty miles north of the first beach for a second evacuation. Here, on 28 July, Read and Robinson brought aboard their two Fijian right-hand men, ten police, seven scouts, and a scout's wife and child. Two days later the group transferred to a sub chaser off Rendova, and *Guardfish* set course for Brisbane.

Curtis recalled that most of the policemen's .303 rifles "were held together with baling wire." For safety's sake, *Guardfish* crew disposed of the coastwatchers' hand grenades as they boarded, so Curtis was shocked when on a midnight inspection he found one rolling on the deck. The next morning, after he came upon an AIF commando disarming a grenade, a more thorough sweep for explosives was initiated.[10] As always, the children came in for special treatment as the crew emptied their lockers of hoarded candy.

Mason and Read had been forced off Bougainville. *Guardfish* had saved the saviors of Guadalcanal. Yet it would not be long before other submarines returned with coastwatchers to Bougainville.

As the Americans switched to the offensive, the coastwatchers' task changed. A week before Mason left Bougainville, Josselyn and Firth on Vella Lavella guided a marine reconnaissance party for planned August landings. Other such missions followed.

On 19 September 1943 *Guardfish* joined *Gato* at Tulagi before both boats embarked parties to reconnoiter landing beaches on west and east Bougainville respectively. Ward landed his marines and local scouts at Empress Augusta Bay, recovering them a week later. A month later, just days before the marines' 1 November assault, *Guardfish* put two coastwatcher parties ashore north of the Torokina landing beach. In these groups John Keenan and "Wobbie" Robinson returned to Bougainville.

During the landing Ward noted discrepancies in his charts and surveyed the bay, verifying the earliest edition and also discovering three previously unknown coral pinnacles in the landing area. In *Gato* and *Guardfish,* Ward completed four special missions and five visits to Bougainville in 1943, having been hand-picked by Halsey for the last two missions on the strength of his prior experience and success.

Short insertions to support the advance continued. On the night of 30/31 October 1943, *Scamp* (Commander Ebert) landed four Australians and nine New Guineans under Capt. Harry Murray on New Ireland to report on Japanese shipping.

Murray, awarded the Distinguished Conduct Medal during World War I, had, after the Japanese advance, made a four-month trek from his New Ireland plantation to join the coastwatchers. At Tabragalba, south of Brisbane, he established a camp for coastwatcher training and recuperation. By August 1943 he commanded more than three hundred Australians and New Guineans. Following his lead, the Americans had seven hundred Americans, Filipinos, and Indonesians in an adjoining camp.

Murray then obtained this field assignment. His party of Australians and New Guineans flew to board *Scamp* at Guadalcanal. New to submarines, Murray carefully followed the instructions he was given about using the head. But he had not anticipated the submariners' sense of humor. When he "got his own back" and laughter erupted outside, he took his initiation in good part and headed for a shower. On 30 October the party landed, and *Scamp* resumed her patrol. A successful mission ended when a PT boat then returned the party to Guadalcanal.[11]

Detached to the Americans, Murray was ordered on Christmas Eve to reconnoiter sites on New Britain and Boang Island with ten inexperienced American technical specialists under marine Capt. Clifford Quilici. Unhappy with the plan and the novice party, Murray objected forcefully. Some changes were made, but his request for radios was denied.

On 26 December, *Peto* (Comdr. W. Nelson) left Guadalcanal with the ten Americans, two Australians, and four New Guineans. At Boang Island Murray took two New Guineans and four Americans ashore as scouts. The lack of radios was felt immediately: their visual "all clear" was misinterpreted, and the others stayed aboard. The depleted party pressed on with intelligence gathering.

Then, in the afternoon, the survey complete, islanders warned Murray that the Japanese were hunting them. Murray set an ambush, but, with the specialists' poor marksmanship, four of the seven enemy escaped. To avoid retaliation, the party paddled off early in gale-force winds to await *Peto* at sea. Murray kept his seasick men afloat until the agreed time. Then he grabbed the flashlight to give the agreed red signal, but the red mask was gone. Knowing that *Peto* would respond only to red, he desperately flashed white. He flashed for ninety minutes until *Peto*, risking herself by responding to incorrect signals, retrieved them.[12]

The mission was terminated, and *Peto* returned to Guadalcanal where Quilici reported, "Strongly recommend that patrols in the future be specially trained . . . and . . . heavily armed." He concluded, "This patrol is indebted to Captain Murray and Captain Nelson for our lives."[13]

A Military Cross and Silver Star were awarded in recognition of Murray's actions. But an earlier honor moved him more. At Tulagi, Commander Nelson addressed the party and *Peto*'s crew. After praising the Allied cooperation, the coastwatchers, Quilici, and Murray, he turned to the Australian. Removing his own dolphins, Nelson continued, "I have the honor to bestow on you membership of the United States submarine corps." Murray's wife later wrote, "Murray was very mindful of the rare honor. . . . Nothing had ever touched him so profoundly."[14]

Submariners and coastwatchers developed a deep mutual admiration. These men from opposite sides of the Pacific found that they had a lot in common. They were members of elite, unorthodox, and motivated forces. They operated far behind enemy lines. Cut off from support, they relied completely on their comrades. Their achievements were out of all proportion to their small forces, and if things went wrong, they made the ultimate sacrifice in lonely obscurity.

Capt. H. Murray (*right*) wears the submariner's dolphins
presented to him by Comdr. W. T. Nelson (*left*), captain
of *Peto*, following the hazardous survey of Boang Island.

Wisconsin Maritime Museum, Manitowoc, collection

One of the last big Brisbane operations is a case in point. *Dace* (Lt.
Comdr. B. D. Claggett) sailed from the Brisbane outpost of Milne Bay on
16 March 1944 with a coastwatcher party under Capt. G. C. Harris to reconnoiter for landings at Tanahmerah Bay. A week later, eleven landed.

Capt. G. C. Harris (third from right, standing) with his
coastwatcher party aboard *Dace* in March 1944.

Official U.S. Navy photo, U.S. National Archives, Record Group 80-G, 343626

Villagers reported the party, and they were ambushed on their second
morning ashore. Two were killed in the ambush, and Harris was executed
after capture. Six members of the party eventually linked up with Allied
forces.

"Blue" Harris and his mates are remembered among the thirty-six
coastwatchers who died at their lonely posts. Others in the Philippines
and the then Dutch East Indies suffered the same fate.

The submarines that landed, supplied, and sometimes retrieved these
agents also lived with danger. The two forces had a common bond. Eric
Feldt, the coastwatchers' founder, paid tribute to the submariners: "The
U.S. submarines had early come to our help, a help ungrudgingly given,
with grave risks cheerfully accepted."[15]

13
BUILDUP IN BRISBANE

"The base they're building is going to make Sub Base Pearl look like a farmer's garage," wrote a Fremantle staff officer in December 1942 after visiting Brisbane.[1] Two tenders lay alongside New Farm Wharf, which was busy with workshops, barracks, and storage servicing two submarine squadrons. Working parties "on the beach" with labor from the civilian Australian Works Council had set up a base in the wharf's sheds supplementing the tenders.

Captain Fife said in a postwar interview, "As soon as I took over . . . in Brisbane, I continued what had been started before me . . . but . . . hadn't gotten very far. . . . I knew the time was coming when I'd want to put a tender up in New Guinea . . . and still keep a repair facility back there in Brisbane. So I scouted all over Australia and got all the machine tools that I could commandeer . . . and I had set up quite an ingenious little repair base . . . on New Farm Wharf."[2]

"Ingenious" described the base well. By August 1943 the workshops could complete 70 percent of a submarine's overhaul. Soon after, with the arrival of gyro, radio, sound, and battery equipment and their operators, the base's capability reached 100 percent. When, on 20 April 1945, the U.S. Navy returned it, $41,000 of navy funds and $1.7 million of reciprocal lend-lease money had transformed the site. The final bill included $109,686.56 for rent and $39,814.96 to settle damages claims.[3]

In this narrow, 1,089-foot-long space, four large sheds and dockmaster's and customs buildings were transformed as new buildings rose around them. New floors and partitions converted simple sheds into multilevel storage areas, workshops, and barracks. Elevated walkways connected the buildings.

The main entrance of the self-contained Submarine Repair Unit, Navy 134, was off Macquarie Street at the wharf's upstream end. A one-way traffic pattern had vehicles pass between the two rows of buildings and then curve around the downstream end to return along the wharf. Behind the gate were number 1 barracks, housing eighty men and stores buildings, while number 2 barracks faced the river with the sick bay at its upstream end and the post office at the other. The two-story medical building had twenty-eight beds and provided both dental and medical care.

The buildings along Macquarie Street served the personnel. Near the gate were the duty office, fire station, laundry, and officers club. Running along Macquarie Street to the old brick public-works building was a large multipurpose building housing number 3 barracks, a movie theater, library, a beer hall, and other facilities. Underneath was a large air-raid shelter.

Farther downstream above another air-raid shelter were the duty officer's and chief petty officers' quarters adjoining the mess hall, galley, garage, and armory. Past the lower Macquarie Street gate was the attack teacher. At the far end were the blacksmith and pipe-turner shops, the ice plant, and diving and paint lockers. Along the short northern boundary were quarters for eighty officers.

Along the wharf toward the gate were workshops and storage areas of the ship and boat repair section. In the sheds were all the shops to completely overhaul up to seven submarines a month. The addition most obvious to Brisbane's citizens was the visual station. In a "control tower" on the river shed's roof, it communicated with vessels in the river by two thirty-foot signal masts and two twelve-inch searchlights.[4]

On 15 January 1943 Rear Adm. Daniel E. Barbey established his Amphibious Force, Southwest Pacific, headquarters in Brisbane. Fife later recalled, "He saw what I had at New Farm Wharf, and he went up and asked Admiral Carpender if he couldn't take it away from me. Barbey was senior to me. [This] was another case where Admiral Carpender was wonderful. He pinned Barbey's ears back, and I didn't have any more trouble from that source after that."[5]

Beyond the New Farm compound, the submarine base took over a corner of the Windsor State School's grounds for the Submarine Supply Center. After acquisition in February 1943, the Allied Works Council quickly built the center, which received, stored, and distributed submarine spare parts to tenders and bases. Four officers, fifty-three enlisted men, and seventeen civilians, mainly young Brisbane women office workers, staffed this separate unit.

One civilian, Elfrida George, later recalled that the office staff moved to Windsor from temporary quarters in the front window of a furniture store. Her six-day week in the large warehouse was mainly spent checking invoices of incoming parts and marking their numbers on the bins. Young American storemen then stocked them. The center extended along Lutwyche Road in a combined sleeping quarters and office building and ancillary units. Elfrida remembered the first commanding officer, Lt. C. W. Harvey, as a workaholic who expected and obtained high standards of accuracy, continually stressing the vital importance of precision. Lt. C. B. Sprott, Harvey's successor, maintained the standard in a more relaxed manner. And it wasn't easy. Many companies did not adhere strictly to designation codes. The executive officer spent hours comparing catalogues and parts from different manufacturers. When he found a match, an exultant shout echoed through the warehouse: "Same damned thing!"[6]

A high security fence separated the base from the school, and the headmaster forbade any student to approach the base. But children and sailors found ways around the edict, and "candy and goodies from the canteen were passed to the kids."[7]

If school property was not exempt from acquisition, neither was church property. On 2 September 1942, Australian Army Hirings took over the Benedict Stone Factory from "His Grace, Reverend Archbishop, James Duhig." Until the Americans vacated it on 6 April 1945, it was the U.S. Navy Torpedo Repair Shop. The factory in Bowen Hills had been set up to manufacture the artificial Benedict Stone for Archbishop Duhig's grandest project, a huge cathedral. It never advanced beyond the foundations. The navy turned the long-derelict factory, a basic building, into an efficient facility. Torpedoes for all U.S. aircraft and ships smaller than destroyers in Australia were received, overhauled, and issued there.[8] One Australian officer was impressed when he visited in April 1943, reporting on the "extremely well-equipped" and "almost completely self-contained" facility with almost two hundred torpedoes in store.[9]

The submarines shared other base facilities. One was the U.S. Naval Magazine at Mount Coot-tha. Established on 1 August 1942, the magazine grew to store all types of ammunition and explosives for all U.S. Navy activities and ships in the Brisbane area. Final cost was $300,000 in navy funds and $35,162.60 from reverse lend-lease. There was also $900.54 rent.

Staff of the Submarine Supply Center, Windsor.
The commanding officer, Lt. C. B. Sprott, is in the front row, center,
and Elfrida George is in the back row on the left.
Courtesy of Elfrida George

The magazine's 196 personnel occupied huts and tents on the mountain side of Sir Samuel Griffith Drive. The magazine huts were spaced all along the drive and in offshoots up the valley of East Ithaca Creek and to Simpson Falls. The first magazines constructed under the trees after the undergrowth had been cleared were of wood covered in fibrolite. Later the Allied Works Council and U.S. Navy construction battalions erected prefabricated ARMCO steel magazines shipped from the United States. Most storage buildings were covered with earth.[10]

Another vital installation was South Brisbane Dry Dock. From 29 April 1942 to 19 February 1945, fifty-one submarines made eighty-five entries. The support ships *Tulsa* and *Coucal* also used the dock. Over that period submarine entries were second only to the merchant vessel total.[11]

The dock did not come under the task force's control but remained under the Queensland Department of Harbours and Marine. The Seventh Fleet commander commented, "Submarine Repair Unit schedules submarines docking and pays drydock fee. Labor is furnished in the form of working parties by the Submarine Repair Unit and Relief Crews."[12]

At the beginning of the Pacific war it was recognized that this small dry dock would be inadequate. In 1942 the Queensland and Australian governments began Brisbane Graving Dock (Cairncross Dock), which could accommodate small aircraft carriers and 25,000-ton ocean liners. Admitting its first ships on 22 June 1944, Cairncross relieved the docking pressure for the war's last fifteen months.

But in crisis time, South Brisbane had to meet demand. Conflict was inevitable. Although the Seventh Fleet commander had unwritten priority on use of the dock, there were times when he did not get it. Letters requesting Brisbane's naval officer in charge (NOIC) be given control received tardy professions of cooperation from Queensland's premier and did not solve the problem. Commander Seventh Fleet's message of 4 August 1944 to the Australian Navy Board read, "Docking of a dredge barge on 1 August without prior reference to NOIC has eliminated an urgently needed submarine . . . docking. . . . Consider essential priority control be firmly vested in NOIC Brisbane."[13]

The other side had a case. In 1945 the Queensland Marine Department's chief engineer reported, "Overhaul of the Department's ships has again been rather irregular, . . . naval vessels at all times being given preference."[14] The department's main vessels were dredges—essential to maintain depth in the ports. Cooperation eased the situation. In that year,

Flying Fish in South Brisbane Dry Dock in July 1944.

Original watercolor painting presented to her captain, Lt. Comdr. R. D. Risser,
who issued copies to all crew members. Reproduction courtesy of R. D. Martin, *Flying Fish.*

when nineteen dredges and twenty-three submarines used South Brisbane Dry Dock, the submarine *Narwhal* shared Cairncross with the dredge *Maryborough* and *Nautilus* with two hopper barges.

The shipbuilding and engineering firm of Evans Deakin coordinated repair work. Skilled staff were transferred to the South Brisbane Ship Repair Yard, which spread over a neighboring timber yard. Often working around the clock, the Evans Deakin men joined recalled retired Australian and American tradesmen, seamen from the submarines, relief crews, and repair unit sailors. The diverse staff performed maintenance, voyage, and battle damage repairs on all types of American submarines.

Dry-dock worker Luke Curtis remembered ice cream, scarce in wartime Brisbane, being freely available on deck and "Nugget" Dixon becoming a specialist in maintaining the submarines' toilet valves. Later in Cairncross, Curtis helped ease the stiffness of *Nautilus*'s diving planes. One innovation ingeniously solved a serious problem on boats with hollow propeller shafts. As they turned, any particles inside tumbled, making noise that would be detectable by enemy sonar. The solution was to fill the shafts with fine, dry sand, producing a solid, silent shaft. *Dace*'s shafts were filled at South Brisbane in August 1944. Curtis described these dockworkers: "The tradesmen were excellent, and, with the usual Australian manner, could improvise and overcome most, if not all, obstacles." He also applauded the subcontractors for their reliable, high-quality work, often performed at short notice and at all hours.[15]

Subcontractors included Peters Slip at Kangaroo Point, Sargeants Engineering, and Carriers and Warren Joseph, who worked on refrigerators and air conditioners. The Electrical Repair Company contracted electrical work, while Greenfields, Synchrome, and Hirga maintained and repaired timepieces.

Evans Deakin and the Ipswich Railway Workshops handled heavy engineering. The former's Rocklea workshops made shafts and bronze propellers. One job of the Ipswich workshops was "the machining, polishing, and static balancing of thirty 28 by 28 inch and 28 by 29 inch propellers for U.S. Naval craft . . . no grinding, scratches, or file marks were permissible."[16]

Sometimes the pressure was extreme. Bryan Gormley, a plumber with Watson Brothers, was sent to reinstate the battle-damaged lead sheeting around a submarine's batteries. The impatient captain astonished Bryan by ordering the submarine's "hard patch" cut open so that whole sheets could be passed down. The hull was then rewelded as Bryan redoubled his efforts. The young plumber's next shock was more personal. As he was finishing the job, the boat cast off. The idea of sailing to confront the Japanese navy concentrated his mind as they transited Moreton Bay. Bryan finished the job in time to join the pilot in his launch as the boat sped northward.[17]

Other U.S. Navy units in Brisbane had less direct but still important contact with the submarine task force. The fleet commander in the AMP Building's room 519, two floors below General MacArthur, worked through the base headquarters near New Farm Park. A large receiving barracks was constructed at New Farm Park, and the naval officers club still survives, riverside in Merthyr Park. Service Force was at Victoria Park, and warehouses at Perry Park, Newmarket, Windsor, and Toombul housed supplies.

Surrounding the Camp Hill Hotel was Mobile Fleet Hospital 109. On its elevated site it treated sick and wounded sailors and marines from the whole Southwest Pacific. Established in July 1943 for 500 patients, its capacity rose to 2,000 beds and a staff of 859 housed in mainly prefabricated buildings.

At its peak, the base could accommodate 6,464 shore-based officers and men. The highest numbers attained were 685 officers in June 1944 and 5,682 enlisted men during the next month. The submarine task force was always a major component. However, the number of U.S. Navy personnel was insignificant compared with the total U.S. Army ground and air forces, which comprised the bulk of the seventy-five thousand Americans in southeast Queensland in December 1943.

Navy personnel could be made, at times, to feel like second-class citizens in MacArthur's capital as two submarine captains, Slade Cutter of *Seahorse* and Bladen Claggett of *Dace,* found when looking for a good night out in May 1944. Slade Cutter told the story later: "Lennons Hotel is where MacArthur's headquarters was located. . . . [The Army] took it over, and they had a nightclub down below. . . . Naval officers were barred, couldn't get in. . . . We decided to go to the Lennons Hotel, we didn't know about this barring of Naval officers. . . . [There] were two MPs. One of them said, 'You can't go in, only army personnel, unless you are the guest of an army officer.'" Happily, help was at hand: "This captain or first lieutenant came up and heard it, and he said, 'These gentlemen are my guests,' and with that he took us in—we had two girls—and left us. But we were in, and we had a great time and felt real good about beating the system." The favor was returned when the army officer and some nurses were guests aboard *Seahorse* on Moreton Bay.[18]

The submarine base, like its craft, tried to maintain a low profile, but it was a futile exercise. Residents and visitors on the opposite riverbank had fine views of New Farm Wharf. Boats in South Brisbane Dry Dock were similarly visible. The hill at Memorial Park overlooked the site, and homeward-bound commuters had grandstand seats as their trams ground up Stanley Street.

Brisbane residents may have looked, but they could not talk, as Herbert Peachey discovered. On a tram in January 1943 a companion asked Peachey whether there was anything worth seeing in the river. He replied, "Yes, there is a mother ship, four submarines, five torpedo boats, and a landing barge at New Farm Wharf." Overhearing the conversation, a zealous naval auxiliary officer marched Peachey to the Valley police station. There he was charged with a breach of national security regulations, prosecuted, and later fined.[19]

"Rammed. Bow and Tubes wrecked. Bullet hole[s] conn. tower patched. Dead are Gilmore, Williams, Kelley Fireman Third." This stark message transmitted on 7 February 1943 to Brisbane followed *Growler's* collision with *Hayasaki.*

Fife made full use of *Growler*'s transit time. Alerting Evans Deakin, he had plans flown out so that "they'd started fabricating from plans before she got in."[20] Yet he had reservations as to whether the firm could handle the job. These persisted after *Growler*'s arrival, when he endorsed the patrol report, "Extensive repairs will be necessary to fit *Growler* for next patrol. Whether they can be accomplished locally will not be determined until survey is completed."[21] After detailed examination beside the tender, it was decided to repair *Growler* in Brisbane.

On 21 February pilot Jack Ahern delivered the battered boat to a wharf upstream of the dry dock. After HMAS *Tongkol* left, *Growler* entered on the twenty-third. But events at sea intervened. The next day HMAS *Moreton* requested approval "to dock and repair US submarine *Gardfish* [*sic*]." Another message the same day sought permission to repair "US submarine *Gato*."[22] So Captain Ahern returned *Growler* to New Farm and brought *Guardfish* to replace her. Then *Gato* spent 11 to 13 March in the dock before her fifth war patrol.

On 2 March another teleprinter message went to the Navy Board: "Decision is to prefabricate new bow in sections. Anticipate second docking about 1 April for about twenty-eight days. In case of other emergencies during that time period vessel can be undocked with about twenty-four hours' notice."[23]

On 3 April HMAS *Swan* left the dock and *Growler* entered. After five days the submarine left. *Gato* had been badly damaged and almost sunk by depth charge on 4 April and was returning to Brisbane for repairs. From 12 to 15 April, *Gato*'s men, *Fulton*'s repair crew, and the dockworkers restored her seaworthiness.

When *Gato* left, *Growler* entered for the third time. Over the next two weeks the new bow, made at Evans Deakin's Rocklea works, was attached. After welding was completed, Capt. H. L. Ball, Queensland manager of the electro-medical firm Watson Victor, used radioactive cobalt from the United States to x-ray the welds. They turned out to be first class.[24]

Growler's men got to know the dockworkers. Arthur Ullrich remembered them as "rugged men, experts in their several crafts, meticulous in their performance, and great after-hours beer drinkers." Ullrich went on: "These men took great pride in their work, rightfully so. They gave us a better bow than the boat was built with. At the conclusion of the repair work they requested permission to weld a small steel silhouette cutout of a kangaroo on both sides of the bow."[25]

Other submarines also wore this emblem. A kangaroo decorated the

Photo of a painting of *Growler* by McClelland Barclay.
Reproduction courtesy of the Queensland Maritime Museum, Brisbane

patch on *Guardfish* after her December 1943 collision, and another appeared on *Tuna* after she docked in August 1943 to repair bomb damage from a "friendly" aircraft.

The leaping kangaroos were highlighted in port and painted over on patrol, earning *Growler* her nickname, "Kangaroo Express." One features prominently in the framed photograph Captain Downes, the base's materiel officer, presented to Evans Deakin in appreciation of their work.

The work on *Gato* and *Growler* was possibly the most spectacular carried out in Brisbane, but much more repair and maintenance was done. Most tender and relief crews' work was first class, like South Brisbane's. But when *Dace* returned from patrol in May 1944, her enginemen's complaints suggested that the work done before they had sailed from Milne Bay in March had fallen below *Fulton's* usual standards, and they forcefully made their feelings known.

The subsequent repairs in Brisbane gave better satisfaction. One piece of equipment was too large to pass through a hatch, so *Dace's* hard patch was removed. Harry Caldwell observed these repairs: "It became time to reinstall the hard patch and so close the hole in the submarine's hull. This was accomplished by a team of lean, muscular Australians who wielded heavy sledgehammers. I had seen riveting done before with an air-powered riveting gun, but never anything like this. When the job was done we tested it by . . . diving to three hundred plus feet. Neither the hard patch nor any of the rivets leaked a drop. We were all impressed."[26]

Another, more pleasant occasion during some refits was the presentation of awards. Vice Admiral Carpender himself officiated at the ceremony on *Growler* in South Brisbane Dry Dock on 27 February 1943 when fourteen men were honored. Eleven were from *Growler,* including Lieutenant Commander Schade, who received the Silver Star and Navy Cross.

Work in the docks was not without hazards, and fatalities occurred. Motor Machinist's Mate Robert Gould of the relief crew was electrocuted aboard *Darter* on 9 March 1944 at South Brisbane. He was working in a head when his arm touched a live connection, and he received a fatal electric shock.[27] The *Courier-Mail* of 1 December 1944 reported "the first fatal accident" at Cairncross dock. Sailors working on *Narwhal* were trucked back to the base for meals. With two others seated beside the driver, Motor Machinist's Mate C. G. Fields clambered onto the truck bed. Through an error on the driver's part, the truck crashed fifty feet to the dock floor. Thrown out, Fields was killed instantly.[28]

Submarine crews received invaluable support from the Brisbane and Coast and Torres Strait pilots. These master mariners were the unsung heroes of the Queensland maritime effort. They were stretched to the limit. One, signing himself "Ad Unum Omnes" [All for One], pleaded in a letter to the *Courier-Mail* "for time off so we can enjoy our homes as other people can."[29] It was a futile appeal, and they continued answering calls at all hours.

Brisbane pilots guided ships across Moreton Bay and in the river. Further afield, the Coast and Torres Strait captains ranged from Caloundra to New Guinea's eastern tip and the western entrance to Torres Strait. The job was not only taxing but sometimes exciting. The fear that Captain Thompson felt when his submarine was attacked was succeeded by anger when he learned that the aircraft was "friendly." Capt. Eric McWilliam, piloting *S46*, reported striking a submerged object northeast of Townsville in mid-1942. Mines had been sown in the area. They were lucky. Farther afield, pilots guided submarines through Torres Strait's Great North East Channel throughout 1944 and 1945.

Some of the pilots' experiences became prized after-dinner stories. The steep downward angle of Capt. Gerry Bruce's first dive and the steward's alarm made him later seek out the captain, who confessed that it had been not a prank but the result of a miscalculation. Capt. Bill Cain took the pilots' record for longest time under water when he spent the whole submerged transit in *Carp* from China Strait to the Reef in the wardroom. He went to work after the boat surfaced to transit the Reef. Bill also became the deepest pilot when *Rasher* took him down to six hundred feet.[30]

14
LEAVE IN QUEENSLAND

"You can tell the crew that we are going to Brisbane, Australia."

Hearing this, Jim Sterling recalled, "I barely checked the impulse to shout."[1] His reaction was not unusual. Brisbane was already a famous leave port when *Wahoo* ended her second patrol in December 1942.

Sterling, the ship's yeoman, recorded a typical crew's leave in Brisbane between patrols. At 3 AM on 26 December, land appeared on the radar. The messroom was already crowded with excited men. Soon the bridge watch were feasting on the sight and smell of trees. Off Caloundra, *Wahoo* made her recognition signal, and a slightly built civilian stepped from a boat and climbed to the bridge. The pilot's relaxed attitude and such informal commands as "right a spoke" initially disconcerted the officers. But as they negotiated the winding approach, plots confirmed that they were precisely on track.

The crew drank in the sights, especially on this steamy Boxing Day holiday, of girls in bathing suits waving from riverside pools. Around noon a band was heard as they approached New Farm Wharf. An unfamiliar tune following the "Beer Barrel Polka" turned out to be the popular British song "Bless 'Em All," amended by Australia-based submariners to "Sink 'Em All." Within a year, the song had spread throughout the service.

Wahoo eased alongside *Sperry.* In forty-five minutes the crew left for the temperance Canberra Hotel with their mail, fresh fruit, and bulging wallets. A beer party, with bottles smuggled in wrapped in newspaper, ended a long day.

The next morning, to escape the heat, Sterling joined the line in front of an air-conditioned theater. Conversation with the attractive young woman behind him led to dinner, dancing, and a two-week romance. Maureen tutored him in Australian English, the best restaurants, dances, and bars. Sterling quickly adapted to saying "serviettes" (napkins), standing for both "God Save the King" and "The Star-Spangled Banner" before films, and joining community singing at dances.

On his dates with Maureen, Sterling regularly used the same charcoal-burner-powered taxi. "Matey," the driver, impressed the wary Asiatic Fleet veteran of many ports with his honesty. As he gave the large amount of change for the first fare, "Matey" commented, "You don't have to worry about an Australian shortchanging you." The couple drove to the country for walks and horseback riding and once to the fun fair in Fortitude Valley.

Two weeks' leave ended with *Wahoo*'s ship's dance. Sterling and Maureen's long talk that night concluded in an agreement that there would be no promises between them. They never saw one another again.[2]

Richard O'Kane, *Wahoo*'s executive officer, recalled the two weeks from an officer's perspective.[3] Captains on leave were assigned a house with a cook and steward. The other officers were accommodated in apartments and hotels. O'Kane's group were driven to an apartment block where, noting the mosquitoes and unscreened windows, he chose an upstairs unit. The first real relaxation in two months began with "a dozen cold tall bottles of Australian ale."

After drinks, food was the next imperative. The officers, tired and hungry, piled into a cab and headed for a restaurant. O'Kane described it as "old world . . . with deep mahogany paneling [and] generous tablecloths." A printed card explained that no food order could exceed the value of three shillings and sixpence. However, the bar was not restricted and prices were low, so the officers continued to quench their longstanding thirsts. O'Kane was pleasantly surprised at how well he ate, putting away a large plate of fried oysters, salad, and vegetables, followed by dessert, for what he calculated as ninety cents.

For the officers, it was generally a quiet leave of long walks, time at the beach, and preparations for the next patrol. A memorable New Year's Eve party with new Australian friends was a notable exception. Many of the meals that they prepared themselves were enhanced with "depth charge medicine" (brandy) in the sauces.[4]

After only a couple of days, George Grider and three others followed up word of a cottage at "Paradise Beach" [sic], and they ended up spending "the healthiest rest period any of us had during the whole war." Grider and his friends spent most of their time in the water off the "wonderful" beach.[5]

Comedian Joe E. Brown impersonates Adolph Hitler
on New Farm Wharf in September 1943.
Official U.S. Navy photo, U.S. National Archives, Record Group 80-G, 81217

Although O'Kane left a restrained account of his liberty in Brisbane, others admitted to a more lively two weeks. Lt. Comdr. Slade Cutter (*Seahorse*) described how he and fellow officers at Harwood House set fire to the chest hair of two sleeping colleagues. "Looking back on it," Cutter continued, "how [could] reasonably mature people in their early thirties do such a thing?" After two weeks of hard drinking and letting off steam, "we got completely unwound, and then you got ready for sea, and it was all business then. You were checking all your equipment, and everybody was very serious; all the foolishness stopped."[6]

With four patrols from Brisbane, *Growler*'s crew had many experiences ashore. Arthur Ullrich, an electrician's mate, recalled that *Growler*'s crew were dispersed among a number of hotels for one leave. His hotel was "in a small but picturesque suburb . . . out of town . . . with a stream that ran through it." Walking past the kitchen on his first morning, he encountered "a very pleasant woman [with] a manner that indicated she would brook no refusal" who asked if he would like steak and eggs. Arthur, who had never heard of the dish and usually started the day with a cup of coffee and a cigarette, agreed. "It was superb. I've been a breakfast eater from that day on." After each of the succeeding three patrols, he returned to that same hotel.[7]

Leonard Greenwood's assigned hotel was the top-of-the-line Lennons, home to General MacArthur. However, his most significant meeting there was with a one-armed Australian World War I veteran. An invitation home to tea led to a correspondence of many years' duration between the Brisbane family and Greenwood's parents.[8]

Paul Toper, who sailed on four of *Growler*'s patrols, spent one leave in Casino in northern New South Wales with the family of his future wife. Five *Growler* crew married local girls.[9] Milton Weymouth, a *Growler* "plank owner," met his wife-to-be on a blind date after the fourth patrol. Audrey was a trainee nurse living at Brisbane General Hospital. When she worked the 3 to 11 PM shift, Weymouth caught two trams to the hospital. When the nurses' curfew ended the visit well after the last tram, Weymouth made the hourlong trek on foot through deserted streets back to his bed. Audrey later accepted his marriage proposal, and they were married in Brisbane on 26 December 1944, after he had transferred from *Growler*.[10] *Growler* had been lost with all hands on 8 November, in the South China Sea.

Greenling first arrived in Brisbane on 31 January 1943. Clutching their pay, with the lowest denomination being a £5 note, some of the crew joined sailors from the base on an old tram. David Peto remembered that the conductress, swamped with £5 notes for the two-penny fare, gave up and granted a free Sunday ride to the city. Turning to a spruce sailor whom he assumed was from the base, Peto asked, "How far have we got to go?" "Damned if I know," Stan Larsen replied. "I've been with you on *Greenling*." It was amazing how a shave and best uniform could change a man.[11]

Despite the scarcity of accommodations in Brisbane, Larry Hall (*Guardfish*) and a shipmate always stayed for their two weeks between patrols at Mrs. George Hall's roominghouse. A rapport had formed because Mrs. Hall's husband had exactly the same name as Larry's father. When they were at sea the rooms were rented out, but they were always available on their return.[12]

Many of the submariners have lingering recollections of food, freedom, and fair company on leave in Brisbane. Ira King (*Darter*) remembered, "We ate, we drank, and we took long showers. Water is such a scarcity on submarines. We used to go down to the Valley and have Chinese food. . . . Our commissary carried such rare wartime things as butter and pork

Tom Parks (*center*) and shipmates from USS *Sailfish*
at Coolangatta in November 1942.
Courtesy of Tom Parks

chops. It wasn't very difficult to invite some young lady to come up to the
flat for dinner."[13]

Tom Parks (*Sailfish*) recalled, "Dances were held in the town hall every
weekend, and we had a chance to meet some very nice Australian girls.
. . . The National Hotel was our favorite restaurant for dinner. They served
a sirloin steak or two that must have weighed four pounds. It was all two
hungry Yanks could do to eat it all."[14]

Both Australians and Americans appreciated steak, but certain other
American favorites had to be explained to their hosts. Robert Griffiths
(*Narwhal*) recalled, "Stopping at a soda fountain . . . we asked for a banana
split. They didn't know what we were talking about. So we went to a
nearby store to buy bananas, came back, and told the clerk how to make
them."[15]

Two *Guardfish* sailors remembered evenings when sailors in pressed
white uniforms swarmed to favored hotels for dinner, then, on a Friday or
Saturday, to the Trocadero. Dancing in the cavernous hall would end with
the band playing "Goodnight Ladies." Some submariners, their dates, and
friends then adjourned to continue partying at a four-bedroom house they
had rented nearby. These late-night parties, fueled with ample beer, wine,
and spirits, prompted the neighbors to dub the house "Maniac Manor."[16]

An American sailor home for dinner with a family in Toowoomba.
Official U.S. Navy photo, U.S. National Archives, Record Group 80-G, 257117

Nonwhite soldiers were in segregated units, and the separation continued off duty. Black U.S. men and women had their own Carver Club in
Grey Street, South Brisbane. Most submarines had at least two black or
Filipino stewards. Segregation was impossible within such tight confines,
and, with all crew members in a submarine being required to exercise a
multiplicity of skills, "The black sailors were very much an integral part of
a highly skilled happy outfit, both on and off patrol."[17] On *Wahoo,* Mess
Attendants Jayson and Manalesay, from the Philippines and Guam, were
highly regarded. The integration on board continued in the Toowoomba
and Gold Coast rest camps.

For country boys there was nothing better than to get out of the city to a
small town or farm. Willard Devling (*Triton*) and a friend saw at the Red
Cross Center an invitation to a farm owned by a retired Irish sea captain
near Gympie, one hundred miles north of Brisbane. It was "just a modest
home, but a place that made you feel like you were 'back home.'" The two
sailors helped with the farm work, fencing, and fruit picking. "About the

third day we were invited to a neighbor's house for an evening of friendly gathering of all the people in the neighborhood. Tea, cake, pie, and biscuits, also someone would play the piano and everyone joining in singing." The work was hard and tiring, but it gave the two sailors a good feeling, and when the farmer wanted to pay them, "No way would we accept it."[18]

Transferred to *Albacore*, Devling spent later liberties at a small hotel just west of Brisbane near a river: "The place was operated by a wonderful family. Their name was O'Rouke, they had two children, and Mr. O'Rouke's mother lived at the hotel with them. . . . She had many interesting stories to relate . . . For me it was a pleasure to know such wonderful people."[19]

Four of *Darter*'s crew enjoyed their leave in "Yank-free Bundaberg." On the way they kept open house on the overnight train ride, sharing their issue of alcohol.

A group from *Greenling* spent her second refit at Green's Hotel in Lismore, northern New South Wales, and Bob Brown, petty officer in charge of the group, retains a painful memory. Trying to break them out of their daily routine of "steauk and auggs" followed by valiant attempts to drink their way through all of Lismore's bars, he arranged a morning horseback ride.

The next day, twenty horses awaited the group. Brown was uneasy when he saw that all had unfamiliar "English" saddles. However, it didn't daunt his men. They chose mounts and, with the luck and confidence of novices, were away while he was still eyeing the saddle. Realizing that he was already well behind his troop, he threw caution to the wind and mounted.

His haste proved his undoing. Kicks to his mare's ribs had her careening down the road. At the first corner, loose gravel brought her down. Trapped in the stirrups, Brown could not kick free, and she rolled over him. The unruly posse returned to find their leader streaming blood and nursing his elbow and shoulder. Brown limped back to the hotel. Fearing that the injury would bar him from the next patrol, Brown had the pharmacist's mate tape him up, and he treated the pain himself with an unorthodox combination of steak and eggs and boilermakers (whiskey and beer). Years later an x-ray revealed an old fracture of the left collarbone. Brown's only wound from the war had come from a horse in friendly Lismore.[20]

Submariners ranged far on leave. Bill Webb *(Darter)* remembered Brisbane's people as friendly but, with the large numbers of servicemen swamping the city, not as welcoming as residents of other cities that weren't so "invaded." Fremantle and Perth were such towns with "few Americans, other than submariners, . . . and we were welcomed with open

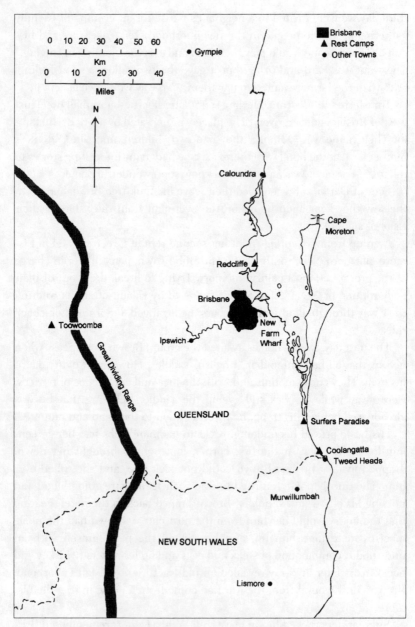

Submarine Crew Rest Areas in Southeast Queensland
and Northern New South Wales.

arms." While *Darter* refitted in Brisbane, Webb and his friends "chose to visit Sydney, where we dated Aussie girls, U.S. Army nurses, and American Red Cross girls."[21]

Arriving in Brisbane in June 1944, Ens. Hugh Story (*Bluegill*) was given a choice of leave venues: "an attractive apartment in the suburbs, Surfers Paradise, or Sydney." Summing up Brisbane as "an army town," Hugh and three friends hitched a ride by flying boat to Rose Bay in Sydney. There they enjoyed a bungalow at Pott's Point and "great nights at Christies, Romanos, the Roosevelt Club, and the races at Randwick."[22]

Sailors on New Farm Wharf advised some of *Dace's* crew, "Don't go on liberty in Brisbane. Get the train and go to Sydney." Half the crew took the advice for "a great liberty . . . in that great city [with] a few sailors, but hardly any soldiers or marines."[23]

The value of liberty after a grueling war patrol is best summed up by an independent observer. Robert J. Casey, in his *Battle Below*, written in 1943 but not released until 1945, described submariners on leave in Honolulu:

> When they came off patrol they were pallid and strained looking and tired. All of them were thin. . . . In a matter of some seventy-two hours they would have lost their corpse-like whiteness and with it their grave reserve. I was struck with the extreme youth of the submariners. The skippers were all lieutenant commanders, few of whom seemed to be more than thirty years old. The crewmen, you felt, might average nineteen or twenty. I still wonder at their mental tolerance. . . . [Men] who lived virtually in each other's laps for months on end, ashore, where they had every opportunity to separate and enjoy a few hours of privacy, were seldom out of one another's company.[24]

They were more than shipmates. They were family.

15
THE REST CENTERS

During 1942 the numbers of submariners grew while total servicemen numbers mushroomed. Demand for accommodation soared, and tensions rose as more competed for the city's limited resources. The "free swinging horseplay," as Clay Blair put it, of cashed-up young submariners on leave "worried Chips Carpender and Jimmy Fife. . . . Carpender had believed the solution was to get the submariners out of town into remote rest camps, and when Fife took command he began construction of two major submarine rest and recuperation centers."[1]

Fife described the arrangements: "We wanted to keep our own submarine men separate, and we set up these rest camps of our own, and the other services were very resentful of that, that provision that we'd made for our men. In Brisbane, we made two. One was down on the beach . . . south of Brisbane, and that was merely a case of getting in there and renting some facilities that already existed. The other one was up in the mountains at Toowoomba. . . . [We] just turned to, with Australian labor, and built them. . . . [Crews] were given an option, whether they wanted to go to the seashore or up into the mountains to rest." As a by-product, Fife found, "As soon as we had our own rest camp set up . . . our security, amongst submarine people out there in Australia, was extremely satisfactory all through the war."[2]

As sailors' recollections show, the men's leave options were not restricted to the official camps. Still, the Toowoomba and Coolangatta camps did not lack customers from their openings in June and July 1943 respectively.

Toowoomba

Toowoomba had two camps: Newtown Park for 150 men, and Laurel Bank Park for 100. The sailors had individual rooms in twenty-five "guesthouses" among croquet lawns, flower beds, and tennis and basketball courts. Larger buildings housed recreation and mess halls, sick bays, and offices.[3]

An official report stated, "Toowoomba was an ideal place for the enlisted personnel. . . . Local golf courses, tennis courts, horseback riding academies, etc., were used by the men. . . . Most . . . were off submarines. . . . The U.S. sailors were very popular with the residents of Toowoomba."[4] *Bluegill's* crew were "bused up. . . . Reports were all hands had a jolly good time, all came back alive, and Toowoomba was still standing."[5] David Peto found Toowoomba pleasant but a big advantage was "a U.S. Army medical facility—nurses!—nearby."[6]

Arnie Banzhaf of *Darter* later remembered it as a beautiful town. Days were spent playing softball or golf or riding horses. Evenings were filled with cards, walking, or movies. The food was outstanding, and the beer was "good Australian beer." But Banzhaf added the rider, "Most of us were not booze drinkers. We were just kids then." The dances too were not wholly satisfactory: "The gals would dance with you, but that was it. . . . The girls didn't want to go out with us because it was a very small place, and they knew that their boyfriends would be coming back from the war someday."[7]

Redcliffe

Closer to Brisbane, the Seabrae Guesthouse at Redcliffe, accommodating 160 guests, and the adjoining Masonic Hall were acquired in June 1943 and relinquished in January 1945. Redcliffe, on Moreton Bay twenty miles from Brisbane's center, was a popular beach resort until the postwar rise in car ownership made the surf beaches of the North and South Coasts more accessible. Seabrae, on a prime bayside site, was a large two-storied guesthouse.

Brochures invited sailors to "an American fun spot" for "fun under the sun by the sea." The writer listed ten attractions "you get free" and then added, putting a positive spin on the boardinghouse's shared accommodation, "Because rooms are so large, there are two beds in each of the big airy rooms." Seabrae's pleasures were typical of the rest centers: walking, riding, boating, fishing, and games, as well as dances and swimming in the sheltered bay waters. The exercise and sea air sharpened already healthy young appetites. Local farmer Mrs. Saddler made a tidy profit trying, but never managing, to fill the demand for dressed chickens. Seabrae's finest night was Saturday 4 September 1943, when three hundred guests enjoyed the first performance in Australia of the legendary Artie Shaw Band.[8]

Chuck Meyer remembered the horses, reputed to have come from a racing stable: "Several of the sailors almost killed themselves riding or trying to ride the horses. . . . I knew personally that they were fast, as I rode one on the beach one day, and once was enough for me." Meyer also remembered Margate Theatre with its low canvas seats where Seabrae guests were given free passes.[9]

Coolangatta

Coolangatta was the site of the main enlisted men's rest camps between July 1943 and April 1945. Its success was lauded in an official report: "Coolangatta is perhaps one of the most attractive of Queensland coastal towns, and is located about sixty-five miles south of Brisbane. It was an exceptionally good choice of location for a leave area, and one which met with the approval of all men who visited there."[10]

The main camp was at Kirra Beach, housing 150 men in single rooms in fifteen fibrolite huts. Two other camps, at Marine Parade and on Greenmount Hill, catered to fifty men each in five ten-roomed huts. Each area had its own showers, latrines, and separate recreation and mess halls. Kirra also included a garage, workshop, offices, sick bay, and accommodation for fifty-eight staff.

Each guest room contained a single bed, locker, chair, and writing table. The recreation room had lounge chairs, phones, and a canteen with a well-stocked refrigerator and a wood-burning fireplace for winter evenings. The recreation facilities progressively grew to include a flood-lit tennis court that also served for handball, a boxing ring, a softball diamond, barbecue pits, a punching-bag platform, and "an outdoor animal cage" (contents not specified).[11]

Surfers Paradise

The officers' Leave Area "S" was the leased thirty-six-room Surfers Paradise Hotel at the northern end of a twenty-mile-long sweep of beaches. At its peak, this facility accommodated up to fifty guests at a time. Norvell

Ward, captain of *Guardfish,* remembered, "I went down to Paradise Beach [*sic*]. They had what we called a rest and recuperation hotel, even though there was damn little recuperation, and not much rest. . . . When we returned to the ship we came back to rest, but we'd been revitalized. It was a delightful spot."[12]

Cottages at Surfers Paradise were reserved for submarine officers, some coming with additional comforts, as Slade Cutter, captain of *Seahorse,* discovered when he visited his officers there: "Most of them were still in bed. One of them was in bed with a gal, but the gals were there and these girls stayed there. When one submarine's gang moved out and another moved in, there they were. They kept the house clean, they were lovers, they cooked for them. . . . They were there for the submarine ahead of us, and these girls had been there for several submarines coming in."[13]

American Red Cross Rest Centers

It was the Red Cross that helped the navy become established on the Gold Coast. The Red Cross leased twenty-five rooms at the Surfers Paradise Hotel on 1 August 1942, and on 31 October the organization took possession of the Coolangatta Hotel for enlisted men and Seahaven Guesthouse at Surfers Paradise for officers. These facilities were augmented in November when Greenmount Surfing Pavilion became accommodation for forty more men.

Wanting to control its own premises, the Red Cross transferred its lease on the Surfers Paradise Hotel to the navy in December. The Red Cross further assisted the navy late in 1942 by leasing the Pacifique Hotel at Tweed Heads and the Grande at Coolangatta for enlisted men and officers respectively. Stanley Larsen of *Greenling* recalled "drinking beer, going to dances, a very good beach, and horses to be rented and fall off." Larsen also wooed and later married Margery Jones, a waitress at the Grande.[14]

The Red Cross presence at Surfers Paradise also expanded with convalescent facilities for both the U.S. Army and Navy at Seahaven Guesthouse, Ludoma Guesthouse, and later Sans Souci Private Hotel.[15] By war's end the American Red Cross operated four centers in Brisbane and three on the Gold Coast.

Female American Red Cross workers did much to enhance submariners' leave on the Gold Coast and around Brisbane. The charter of the American Red Cross charged the organization, first, "to furnish volunteer aid to the sick and wounded of armies." In fulfillment of a second charge—"to act in

Greenling crew members celebrate with friends
outside Coolangatta's Hotel Grande.
Courtesy of Peter Winter

matters of voluntary relief and in accord with the military and naval authorities as a medium of communication between the people of the United
States of America and their Army and Navy"—these remarkable women
(and some men) worked tirelessly around Brisbane. These volunteers were
found in camps, leave centers, and Red Cross leave centers.

Eveline Williams and Marian Daniel, "able-bodied recreation workers,"
were stationed at Coolangatta Naval Leave Area in early 1944. Despite
Fife's assertion that the camp was exclusively for submariners, the 303
guests who arrived in February came from aircraft, amphibious, and construction units as well as boats.[16] At Surfers Paradise where there was a
strong army presence, navy and army mingled freely. This increased the
Red Cross workers' load. The army club director reported in November
1943, "In spite of the rumor that 'the navy takes care of its own,' we seem
to get as many navy as army. There are two submarine crews who, though
billeted at Surfers Paradise Hotel, spend all their waking hours with us
when on leave."[17] A year later, little had changed: "Outside of making a
desirable building and pleasant surroundings for their men, the navy does
little else for their amusement. We are supplying them with writing paper,
a ping pong table, Victory books, and magazines, and planning their recre-

ation activities. . . . We also found that the navy uses our recreation equipment exclusively. Most of our dances are held at the navy club, which is much to our advantage."[18]

The Red Cross workers' efforts were appreciated. Corwin Mendenhall of *Pintado*, whose crew, in January 1945, was the last to use the navy's camp, rated Red Cross worker Ellen Rosenberg and her athletics director, Joan Smith, as "great." He admired Surfers Paradise for its "endless" beach, "amazing" surf, and "lush" trees. Away from the beach he enjoyed parties, tennis, picnics, horseback and bike riding, and dances organized by the "good-humored and energetic" Red Cross duo. Many activities were in the company of occupants of the army rest camp and the enlisted men's hotel.[19]

Coolangatta Red Cross worker Eveline Williams's first 1944 report outlines camp life with no reveille, the recreation hall always open, and sailors encouraged to bring girls to meals.[20] Most guests "did the town" and found a holidaying girl on their first day. Some, however, hit the pubs and canteen bar first. "We're very used to seeing them a little drunk. That's when they like to talk most."

Few read, played cards, or wrote letters that would have to be routed to their units for censorship. They could do that "off-duty, up north." The greatest attractions in the library were wall maps of the South Pacific and of the United States with guests' hometowns marked.

Dances were most popular—at the leave area, Jazzland at Coolangatta, and the pavilion opposite the Red Cross Club. Girls came from the women's Australian Air Force camp, the holiday hotels, and the local area. The twice-weekly evening beach hamburger roasts and fish fries also attracted crowds.

Daytime activities included surfing, fishing, tennis, roller-skating, bike riding, horseback riding, golf, boat trips, and picnics. In camp, guests could play volleyball or horseshoes, or just laze around. Army-navy games were keenly contested on the basketball courts.

Many holidaying girls joined in these activities. Away from their homes in Brisbane and beyond, they were not as constrained in their friendships as those in small-town Toowoomba.

The camp returned Coolangatta's hospitality. Beginning on 11 February 1944, three groups of schoolchildren were entertained with tours, ice cream, chocolate cake, pink lemonade, and softball games—though not necessarily in that order. A group of Coolangatta ladies, led by the mayor's wife, helped entertain the children. They extended other assistance to the camp as well, helping Eveline with dances, serving as chaperones for local girls, and finding flowers, musicians, and even, when the leave area's piano went out of tune, a replacement.

But a more basic service deepened affection between the young sailors and Coolangatta's mothers. Each week ladies came to sew curtains and mend and alter the sailors' clothes. Then the Red Cross workers joined them for afternoon tea. Eveline valued these opportunities to get to know these selfless local ladies. But, as she reported, others appreciated them, too: "The boys are getting used to seeing the townswomen around on Tuesdays, and some of them come over and talk, especially to the older women who have sons in the service overseas." Young Americans far from home and Australian mothers with their sons also facing dangers far away had an empathy that transcended age and nationality.[21]

Robert Brown, chief of the boat on *Greenling*, expressed the deep emotional bond that developed: "U.S. Navy submarine personnel had a great admiration for the Australians, . . . those at home and your military forces both at home and abroad. In a way we lived through the agony and heartbreak of relatives of your forces in North Africa. Most of us knew families that lost a son, father, or husband in that part of the war, so it was very real to us, too. Due to our operations very few Americans were in constant touch with those at home in the States, so we related your heartbreak to how our people were suffering at home, too."[22]

Kemper Moore, Red Cross director at Surfers Paradise, also appreciated the local volunteers who provided "infinite help in a variety of ways," and the local farmers, hotel managers, and grocers who rallied to provide chicken, flowers, and corn on the cob to make Thanksgiving special for the visitors. But the simple things touched most deeply. Moore continued: "The most popular thing they can do is invite these men into their homes."[23] So a constant stream went to Gold Coast homes to enjoy family hospitality.

What became the biggest Red Cross Club in the Southwest Pacific had more soldier and marine guests than sailors, a reflection of wartime Brisbane. The club at Terrica House in the city's center was a popular haunt of submariners who, when a period of liberty began, scanned the club's notice board for offers of hospitality.

Mary K. Browne, a former golf star and U.S. national tennis champion, opened the club on 4 July 1942.[24] She and her assistant were two of only fifty Americans available to staff thirty clubs throughout the northern area. With American workers spread so thin, Australian ladies filled the gaps. By the club's second week a Sunday-night show had been added to the two dances a week, giving the men somewhere to go on Brisbane's then funereal Sundays.

The club's official opening on Thanksgiving Day, 26 November 1942, was a major event, with Admiral Carpender and the army's Colonel Wilson giving short speeches. The recreation room was decorated, and a twenty-six-piece band rendered "inspiring music." The opening at 3:30 PM "could not have been more perfect. . . . But the evening was tragic."[25] Paul Snyder, who assisted at the opening, saw from an upstairs window hundreds of Australian and American servicemen clash in the "Battle of Brisbane." When she left Brisbane after eleven busy months, Mary K. passed to her successor a remodeled five-story club.

Although dances and floor shows were their most obvious activities, the American Red Cross workers and their hundreds of Australian volunteers provided many other services. Church services where men could wear fatigue uniforms were held daily, volunteers sewed on buttons and mended clothes, the Bank of New South Wales provided free money exchange services, and dates and home visits were arranged. Seeing an urgent need, the club set up Brisbane's only all-night restaurant, and the state government bowed to pressure and allowed theaters to screen movies on Sundays.

Working with a committee of soldiers, marines, and sailors, the Red Cross arranged children's Halloween and Christmas parties. For Christmas 1942 the club overcame brownout regulations to sponsor a lighted Christmas tree in the Botanic Gardens and a sixty-four-piece marine band playing carols. For the club's 1943 dawn Easter service in Albert Park, the Brisbane City Council erected a fifty-foot cross.

Mary K. appreciated the work her Brisbane staff did amid all the growth and turmoil. Toward the end of 1943, when she was supervisor of canteen services for the Southwest Pacific area, she wrote, "Too much praise cannot be given to the Australian women who volunteered their services. . . . Without their help it would have been impossible to have taken care of the boys. . . . They are an essential part of the club's operations."[26]

16
TESTING AND TRAINING

"Dived in river off New Farm Wharf" and "submerged at Pile Light"—these entries appear in Brisbane pilot Jack Ahern's logbook for March 1943, when he piloted *Peto* to Dalgety's Wharf, then to the Pile Light.[1]

The dives were not unusual in wartime Brisbane. Bay dives off the Pile Light probed a boat's structural readiness for patrol. Part of prepatrol tests, river dives took place in the deep hole near New Farm. Launches with warning flags stood up- and downstream while the testing submarine sat on the bottom.

Lt. Charles P. Trumbull of *Growler* described the procedure: "After finishing refits [in Brisbane] boats were required to submerge in the river . . . and lie on the bottom with the main ballast tank vents open while the division commander in a row boat inspected the surface over the boat for any air bubbles . . . which would indicate a leak somewhere in the high pressure air bottles located in the tanks."[2]

Not all the defects uncovered were in the boats. One newly appointed captain could not see clearly out of the periscope. Returning to the tender, he complained. *Fulton's* periscope officer came aboard. He found no defect. When the captain insisted that he could not see objects in focus through the instrument, the puzzled tender officer suggested that he use his other eye. He did, and "everything was clear as a bell." A subsequent trip to Brisbane's U.S. Army hospital confirmed a "lazy" left eye. Glasses corrected the problem.[3]

Commander Claggett described unforeseen results from *Dace's* tests later in 1944: "I wanted to check *Dace's* water-tightness, so submerged in Brisbane [*sic*] Bay and found her tight at periscope depth, then went to 100 feet, still tight, 150 feet, still tight. So I ordered 250 feet, and she wouldn't move. . . . We were on the bottom. I had wiped off one sound head but proceeded on patrol rather than admit it."[4] The patrol was *Dace's* most successful of the war.

These diving tests had little impact on the people of Brisbane. Not so the testing beside the tender of unmuffled submarine engines. The thunderous roar and flashes of welding were not appreciated by the base's neighbors, especially at night.

Tests sometimes coincided with training. Charles Trumbull recalled one incident that almost ended in tragedy. *Growler's* captain decided to end a river test by practicing "battle surface"—surfacing for a surprise gunnery action. When the order to surface was given, high-pressure air immediately blasted into the ballast tanks to drive out the water. As the upper hatch broke the surface, the captain flung it open and sprang onto the bridge. Then *Growler* began to sink. Nobody had remembered to close the ballast tank vents left open for the inspection. While the boat was under water, air was pumped in faster than it escaped. But once the open vents were out of the water, the air rushed out, water poured in, and *Growler* sank with the captain climbing the periscope shears. Water poured into the conning tower where the deck and gun crews were packed like sardines. With water up to the conning tower men's armpits, the upper hatch was finally secured, the vents closed, and *Growler* rose again to the surface. Gathering on the bridge, they soberly reflected on how close they had come to drowning in the Brisbane River.[5]

Training extended over a large area, refreshing the skills of crews after leave and helping to integrate new members. Many exercises also provided antisubmarine training for surface warships. Local training areas ranged from New Farm Wharf through the Brisbane area to the bay and beyond—in later years as far as New Guinea.

From its wood-framed building at the New Farm sugar refinery, the audiovisual training aids library issued 450 films in an average month. It served all navy units in the area, but the submarine base was the major customer. At New Farm Wharf, officers received eight to ten hours of refresher and indoctrination training on the attack teacher. An average of thirty officers used this facility each month. Another school instructed classes in night-lookout technique.

Informal training never stopped, with officers and men going over the details of their patrols again and again. Reports circulated widely to captains, and officers shared and debated their experiences in conversations at the officers club. Lieutenant Commander Morton, newly appointed to command *Wahoo,* spent hours on long walks and over beers discussing tactics with Richard O'Kane, his executive officer. It was then that Morton introduced to O'Kane his unorthodox plan whereby the executive officer manned the periscope while the captain concentrated on maneuvering the boat.

Preparing for his new responsibilities, O'Kane commissioned a lazy Susan from *Sperry* and put it on the sideboard in *Wahoo's* wardroom. Ship models were then turned to various angles while O'Kane, peering through a reversed binocular lens from the pantry, estimated the angles. When he needed to rest his eyes, he changed places with his assistants, and they vied to better him in calling the angles. Whenever a ship was reported moving in the river, O'Kane moved to the periscope for more realistic practice.[6]

There was other training alongside, *Growler's* captain reporting, "Test firing, using dummy torpedoes, was conducted alongside the tender."[7]

Much testing and training took place in Moreton Bay. Dives in the sheltered waters trimmed the boats and tested watertight integrity. Checking a vessel's sound emissions took advantage of the bay's freedom from surf noise. These maneuvers were carried out quietly, but that was not possible for gunnery trials. Gunnery training using a target hauled by a tug took place in the bay northeastward of the Pile Light with firing directed against a background of Moreton Island's southern sandbanks. Despite a four-hundred-yard towline, these target shoots were frightening for tug crews: "The submarines would surface from nowhere, fire four or five rounds with their guns, and immediately submerge."[8]

To prevent unnecessary alarm, the navy gave civil police prior warning of gunnery practice. Five such notifications of live firing in Moreton Bay were given to Roma Street police station in March and April 1943. Quieter bay training could still cause alarm. At 4 PM on 5 May 1943 the tender *Canberra* was crossing between Cleveland and Dunwich when her skipper saw the trace of a dark object he believed to be a submarine moving underwater. This was reported to police, who followed it up with local air and naval authorities. An hour later the navy issued a statement "that it is OK."[9] In fact it was *Growler,* which fired exercise torpedoes in the bay that day and tested and fired all guns on the next.

Growler (Lt. Comdr. A. Schade) was working up for her fifth war patrol. On 7 May, with the commander of Submarine Division 82 embarked, she again entered Moreton Bay. The next day, about sixty nautical miles seaward from the swept channel, she practiced attacks and counters with the corvette HMAS *Lithgow.* When *Growler* sailed on patrol, *Lithgow* accompanied her in the dual role of escort and exercise partner. After parting company off Fraser Island, *Lithgow*'s captain wrote, "The exercises were of great value to the S.D. [sound detection] operators." He also noted that the liaison officer on board, Commander Kossler, USN, formerly of *Guardfish*, was "very enlightening" in his tips on *Growler*'s likely actions as the corvette and submarine engaged in mock battles.[10]

Escorts were provided whenever possible for submarines early in their outward passage on patrol. In the three months from 24 April 1943, eight Japanese submarine attacks sank four ships to Brisbane's immediate north and south. The Australian *Kowarra* on 24 April was the first. The new submarine *Pompon* was the last attacked when two torpedoes passed ahead of her a few days after she sailed from Brisbane on 10 July.[11] The greatest loss of life happened right on Brisbane's doorstep. At 4:10 AM on 14 May, *I-177* torpedoed the illuminated hospital ship *Centaur* only ten nautical miles east of Cape Moreton. Of 332 aboard, only 64 survived. The risk of enemy attack off Brisbane was real.

But there was a more pressing reason for the escorts: the risk of "friendly" attack. As a young submariner, D. Russell, newly transferred to *Flying Fish*, was bluntly corrected on 1 August 1944 when he suggested that the escort was there to protect them against Japanese submarine attack: "Hell, that's only about 30% of it. That escort's out there to protect us from our own people and from the Aussies. . . . The bastards all want to be heroes so bad they wouldn't even consider the possibility that we're American."[12]

After trim dives and tests in Moreton Bay, submarines joined their escorts. Over the following days and nights most honed their search, attack, and evasion skills.

Grayback (Lt. Comdr. E. Stephan) sailed on 25 April 1943, escorted by the destroyer *Bagley*, but heavy seas limited their training exercises. Further training ceased when *Bagley* was ordered away as the freighter *Kowarra* had just been reported sunk by an enemy submarine in the same area. *Grayback* submerged and began her patrol.

Newly commanding *Wahoo*, Lieutenant Commander Morton took full advantage of exercises with his surface escort, the destroyer *Patterson*, to practice his aggressive plans. In the bay on 16 January 1943, *Patterson* and *Wahoo* tuned their sonar gear, and Morton tried out ideas for increasing *Wahoo*'s speed. On passage, simulated night surface attacks were followed by a packed day of destroyer-submarine exercises. Morton and O'Kane worked on perfecting their unorthodox attack procedure. After lunch, Morton removed all restrictions, instructing *Patterson* to charge *Wahoo*'s

HMAS *Warramunga* photographed through
Flying Fish's periscope during exercises off Brisbane.
Official U.S. Navy photo, U.S. National Archives, Record Group 80-G, 062143

periscope whenever it was sighted. On the last run Morton rehearsed firing
four torpedoes "down the throat." He would use this tactic twice on this
patrol.

Between 29 April and 4 May 1944 the veteran HMAS *Katoomba*, res-
cuer of *S39*'s crew and a sharer in the sinking of Japanese submarine *I-124*,
escorted *Tunny* (Lt. Comdr. J. Scott) from Brisbane to Milne Bay. Both
ships had just received equipment updates and grasped the opportunity
for intensive training. Scott, a veteran of five patrols in command, wrote of
this time, "It is sincerely felt that this form of training is superior to any
previously received by the *Tunny*. . . . The efficiency of the *Katoomba*'s
asdic gear and counter-attacks was most impressive. . . . [Our] thanks and
respect should be transmitted to the Commanding Officer of HMAS
Katoomba."[13]

Exercises with ships had a twofold purpose: they refreshed the submariners' skills and gave realistic training to surface sailors.

Not all escort training was conventional. Two months after *Katoomba*
and *Tunny* sailed from Brisbane, USS *Seahorse* (Lt. Comdr. S. Cutter) and

HMAS *Parkes* followed to Milne Bay. *Parkes,* the last of sixty corvettes built in Australia, was a product of Brisbane's Evans Deakin shipyard. Brisbane reserve officer "Paddy" Vidgen commissioned her in May 1944.

Unlike *Parkes, Seahorse* was a veteran on her fifth war patrol. Cutter ended the war with nineteen ships sunk, sharing with *Wahoo*'s Morton second place in total number of ships sunk. As *Seahorse* and *Parkes* punched northward, the submarine raced ahead to submerge. Vidgen's crew then searched for the "enemy" and dropped a hand grenade to simulate a depth-charge attack.

After two of these exercises, Cutter surfaced. Signaling that the grenades were hard to hear, he requested that next time *Parkes* drop a depth charge. He wanted to give his new crew members "indoctrination into the world of explosives."[14] Vidgen agreed to drop a depth charge set to explode at 150 feet.

After *Seahorse* had again submerged, *Parkes* moved in. A charge rolled off the stern. The new ship's crew watched as the sea boiled and a loud explosion accompanied a jet of water towering into the air. In seconds the submarine shot to the surface. "A man appeared on the conning tower obviously spending some time trying to get a signal lamp to work. Failing to do so, he at last took out a small battery lamp and signaled the result of our attack. 'Didn't feel a thing.'"[15]

Realistic training sometimes led to mishaps. Two incidents off Brisbane in December 1943 involved the Mediterranean veteran HMAS *Stuart* (Lt. Comdr. Neil Mackinnon). On the morning of 17 December, *Stuart* was exercising asdic operators east of Caloundra with *Scamp* (Lieutenant Commander Ebert). More exercises ran through the afternoon and night. Just after midday, Mackinnon reported, "*Stuart*'s port after depth charge thrower was accidentally fired. *Scamp,* who was on my starboard quarter, saw it fire and sheered further away to starboard. Although the charge was set to safe, it detonated after approximately sixty seconds, at a depth of over 600 feet."[16] After this fright, *Scamp* proceeded on patrol.

Mackinnon had reported a more serious incident only two weeks before. In company with HMAS *Cowra, Stuart* rendezvoused with *Guard-fish* (Lieutenant Commander Ward) about sixty nautical miles northeast of Cape Moreton on 3 December 1943. At the exercise area *Guardfish* attacked *Stuart* playing the role of a convoy while *Cowra* acted as escort. After two runs, Mackinnon noted, "The lighter colored paint used by *Guardfish* [applied in her recent Brisbane refit] made her very difficult to sight." Later, at 11:54 PM, *Stuart* sighted flares and a flashing light. *Guard-fish* then signaled that she had collided with a ship and requested *Stuart*'s assistance.[17]

Lieutenant Commander Ward's report reveals how quickly routine exercises could veer toward disaster.[18] Tracking *Stuart*, he ordered "battle stations" at about 11:48 PM. This took two lookouts off the bridge. Ward was controlling the ship from the conning tower, with radar tracking the target and sound equipment, used for an all-round search, ineffective because of the boat's high speed.

At about 11:54 the bridge reported, "Ship on the starboard bow." Seconds later, "Ship close aboard." Ward raced for the bridge, assessed the situation, and ordered, "Right full rudder. All ahead full." The stern began swinging away from the oncoming vessel, but it was too late. The intruder's bow plowed into *Guardfish*'s side aft.

Guardfish listed to starboard and began to settle by the stern. Ward worked fast, ordering that all main ballast tanks be blown, the emergency signal be fired, all compartments report damage, and the searchlight be turned on. To the relief of all, the submarine was still watertight. Her pressure hull was undamaged.

In the poor visibility of light haze and rain, Ward believed the "small tanker . . . did not see us before the collision." The culprit was a U.S. Army fuel barge, *YO-20*, which *Stuart* later sighted off Caloundra with paint missing from her bows.

In dock, *Guardfish*'s damaged outer plating, main induction, and engine were repaired in time for her to sail on 27 December with a kangaroo welded onto her hull. The incident gave the crew an early Christmas present: a week spent in dry dock "right across the street from [the Ship Inn]."[19]

HMAS *Rushcutter*, the Australian antisubmarine school, was established in Sydney in 1939. The quality of the school's graduates quickly became apparent in both the Atlantic and the Pacific. By war's end, *Rushcutter* had trained American, British, Dutch, and French as well as RAN personnel. Much of the sea training took place off Brisbane. The requisitioned merchant ships HMAS *Kybra* and *Yandra* worked off Brisbane, sometimes with *S42* and *S47*, recalled in order to release modern submarines.

Brisbane met S-boats again when New Caledonia–based *S31* arrived on 18 September 1943 for a refit, ten months after the last S-boats had left. Although her main role was training, *S31* made two war patrols. Later, *S38*, *S42*, *S43*, *S45*, and *S47* returned for both training and special missions. When they refitted in Brisbane, surface forces trained with them.

Milne Bay became the base for *S42* and *S47*, and on 22 March 1944 the commander of Task Force 72 notified surface forces of their availability.

The base at New Farm Wharf from HMAS *Deloraine* in 1943.
A fleet-submarine is refitting alongside *Fulton*,
and the training submarine *S31* is astern.
Courtesy of J. H. Lewis-Hughes

He outlined exercises ranging from basic sound and periscope familiariza-
tion to advanced maneuvers of daytime submerged attacks followed by
counterattacks. Captain Haines urged units to first train personnel in the
school vessels USS *Alabaster* and HMAS *Orara*. The task force commander advised that the submarines' operating schedule would always
have at least one boat available. He finally appealed for consideration for
his men: "Any aid or courtesy extended to submarine[s] away from tender
will be appreciated as these ships are small and living conditions are not
the best in tropical waters." His appeal fell on deaf ears. The naval officer
in charge in Brisbane noted, "It now remains for [COs to train] . . . to an
extent which will ensure that the training submarines barely have time to
eat and sleep."[20]

Kybra's course between 10 and 12 August 1944 exercising with *S47* illustrates this type of training. In joint exercises with aircraft, *S47* anchored in
Moreton Bay before dark on 9 August. After each day's exercises the group

returned to this anchorage, getting under way early the following morning. En route for the training area, the ships carried out radar tracking while aircraft simulated attacks on the surfaced submarine.

In the exercise area, S47 was a target for aircraft as she ran submerged showing her periscope, running with conning tower awash, then maneuvering to avoid attack with her decks awash. Finally the submarine ran submerged on various courses and at various speeds while raising and lowering the periscope.

The aircraft could drop smoke bombs when S47 was submerged, but surface vessels kept at a distance exercising their sound operators. For the next half hour *Kybra* and the other vessels tracked the submerged submarine as she maintained a steady course and speed with periscope showing. Then for two hours S47 moved at a depth of ninety feet on a base course while the surface vessels simulated depth-charge attacks. Hearing the attack signal, the submarine marked her position with a smoke bomb or air bubble.

The final exercise, building on previous lessons, was the most testing. With the hunters withdrawn to three miles, S47 dived to ninety feet and took evasive action as they closed to hunt and attack the submarine over one hour.[21]

There was another form of "training" between patrols—possibly the most important. Submariners, rightly, regarded themselves as different. The skull and crossbones on many submarines' battle flags was an appropriate symbol. Like the pirates of old, they ranged the seas alone in constant danger of attack from any vessel they met as they sought to overwhelm ships, often superior in armament, in devastating surprise attacks. Like the pirates too, superior crew morale was a vital factor in the success of small crews whose survival depended on each man living and working in harmony with the others.

In port they tended to keep together. "They socialized only within their own pod [for] two weeks of booze and fun. . . . They had a tendency to take over one bar. . . . They seemed to go together everywhere."[22]

They were an elite. Almost all submariners were hand-picked volunteers. Like navy aviators, their pay was 50 percent higher than that of surface sailors, in recognition of the hardships of their service. Their food was the best in the navy. Many men welcomed the submarine service's greater responsibilities and promotion opportunities.

Navies are traditional and hierarchical, maintaining a gulf between officers and enlisted men. On most surface warships, officers' accommodation is out of bounds to enlisted men. Such physical separation was impossible on a fleet-submarine. Within its length of 312 feet, an average of seventy men—fewer at the war's start, more in 1945—fitted into whatever space remained after machinery, weapons, and stores had been crammed into the 16-foot-diameter hull.

Gudgeon's crew on her first patrol consisted of seven officers and fifty-five enlisted men. The officers bunked forward of the control room and ate in the adjoining wardroom. But there was little privacy. The sailors in the forward torpedo room passed through the officers' area on their way to and from their duties and the crew mess. As the war progressed, both crew numbers and patrol durations increased, resulting in more supplies having to be crammed aboard. Some heads became temporary storerooms, and officers and men shared the remainder. On the primitive S-boats, only 211 feet long, the forty to forty-five officers and men were forced into even greater intimacy.

Officers carried out their duties under the close gaze of sailors. There was no physical "remoteness of command" in the cramped conning tower, where the captain led a team of two other officers and eight enlisted men. His command entailed greater control and responsibility than that of most other captains. In a submerged engagement, his were the only eyes following the enemy's actions. Sonar and radar gave some information, but a submarine commander, more than any other, was the eyes and brain of his vessel. And unlike most surface ship captains, who operated in company under a superior officer, he had the sole responsibility of deciding when and how to join battle. Finally, he had to do this quickly under the eyes of enlisted men whose lives depended on his decisions.

A wartime submarine captain was in a uniquely stressful position. By the end of the war's first year, nearly 30 percent of American captains had been relieved of command, mainly for disappointing results. Capt. W. J. Holmes, acknowledging that captains varied widely in physique and personality, argued that good peacetime and wartime skippers had discernible traits, and not necessarily the same ones. Soundness in tactics and ship-handling was essential. But in the peacetime navy it was the man "sound" in other things as well, the one who closely monitored all activity and erred on the side of caution, who succeeded. In wartime, Holmes argued, such a man "soon wore himself out and failed to develop subordinates capable of independent action. A wartime captain had to learn to use creative leadership to indoctrinate his officers with the principles he expected them to follow, and then delegate responsibility and authority to go with it."[23]

To this requirement could be added a wartime captain's ability to "lead" rather than "drive" his crew, most of whom were not career navy men, like those commanded in peacetime, but critical civilians enlisted for the duration of the war only. Time ashore between patrols provided a golden opportunity for commanding officers to build bonds with their crews. Paul Snyder recalled that Slade Cutter, the successful captain of *Seahorse,* "spent much time with his crew, often going on liberty with them to local bars and hangouts."[24]

Mike Rindskopf sailed on *Drum's* first eleven patrols, the last two in command. Later he wrote, "I was greatly influenced by our first skipper in *Drum,* Lt. Comdr. Bob Rice, who was amongst the older but also amongst the most successful. He was a skillful periscope handler, and a most effective leader of men. . . . By the time I assumed command at age twenty-six, I had shaped my approach to handling officers and men and honed the skills necessary for success so that I was confident without being reckless."[25]

Wahoo's three weeks in Brisbane from 26 December 1942 to 15 January 1943 provides an outstanding example of a commanding officer's "creative leadership" of a crew in port. For her first two patrols *Wahoo's* captain was Lt. Comdr. Marvin Kennedy, a strict disciplinarian, described by one of his officers as a "perfectionist and slave driver."[26] But his caution on these two patrols left Kennedy, who delegated little, exhausted and the crew dispirited. Fife relieved Kennedy of command when *Wahoo* arrived in Brisbane.

The new captain, Lt. Comdr. "Mush" Morton, turned *Wahoo* around during the Brisbane stay. He ordered the silhouettes of Japanese warships on the bulkheads to be replaced with cheesecake photos, and he locked away the captain's mast (charge) book. Moving into his officers' apartment, he informally shared his ideas. At the ship's dance, officers and men mixed freely.

Back aboard, the crew enjoyed the changes—not just the pinups, but also the new personal lockers. Morton introduced a relaxed atmosphere, encouraging junior officers to share opinions, and sailors appreciated the sense of freedom and of being trusted to get the job done.

Just hours before departure, Morton addressed *Wahoo's* crew: "I am glad to have every one of you aboard the *Wahoo* personally. . . . We will take every reasonable precaution, but our mission is to sink enemy shipping. We are going out there on this war patrol to search for Japs. If anyone doesn't want to go along under these conditions, just see the yeoman. I am giving him verbal authority now to transfer anyone who is not a volunteer. . . . Nothing will ever be said about your remaining in Brisbane, but I must know within half an hour who will be leaving, so that I can get replacements."[27]

Morton's frankness and trust transformed a dispirited crew. In the nine months before *Wahoo* went down off Japan, she sank a total of twenty ships. In her brief career she had only two, very different, captains. As Holmes suggested, both styles of leadership contributed to her success.[28] The disciplinarian trainer, Kennedy, produced a skilled crew that the charismatic, relaxed Morton led to greatness. And Morton laid the foundation of his success not on patrol but in Brisbane.

17
PROGRESS

After the uneasy balance of the first half of 1943, the second half saw the Allies move onto the offensive. Halsey's South Pacific forces moved up the Solomons on 30 June by landing at Rendova and New Georgia. Six weeks later his marines invaded Vella Lavella, bypassing Kolombangara in the first stage of the Allies' "island-hopping" strategy. This strategy envisaged Allied forces bypassing Japanese strong points by occupying weakly held positions farther on, leaving the bypassed garrisons to "wither on the vine." This strategy was made possible by the Pacific battleground, where the sea was a highway to all the protagonists' possessions.

In New Guinea, Australian forces occupied Kiriwina and Woodlark Island on 30 June, and an airfield was built at Kiriwina, only three hundred miles from Rabaul. Australian troops captured Lae and Salamaua by the middle of September 1943. Task Force 72 assisted these operations by patrolling approach routes and through special missions supporting reconnaissance parties. However, their prime function remained the war against shipping.

Gradual improvement in the design and equipment of submarines matched growth in crews' confidence and ability. Although basic design remained essentially the same, improvements were continually made in new submarines. *Balao*, which joined Task Force 72 on 10 July 1943, was a major advance, the first of her class, with a pressure hull of stronger, high-tensile steels extending her operational depth by one hundred feet to four hundred feet. This "thick skin" improved the submarine's evasive capability as well as resistance to depth charges.

An apparently insignificant vessel arrived in Brisbane on 23 June 1943 that in fact offered a major advance in tactical flexibility. Resembling a large oceangoing tug, *Coucal* was a submarine rescue vessel with rescue chambers, powerful pumps, air compressors, and deep-sea divers. Never called on to fulfill her designed purpose, *Coucal* was invaluable in many supporting roles. She could perform salvage work as well as act as a target for submarine exercise torpedoes. She also acted as a small tender at advanced bases. But in Brisbane she brought a new mobility and advanced support to submarines as Glen Battershell, a radioman and *Coucal* "plank owner," explained: "[*Coucal*] took on stores and then went out with the submarines. When they got about as far as they could go they would release more stores to the submarines. That way the submarine could stay out just that much longer."[1]

On 21 July 1943 *Coucal* departed Brisbane with *Growler*, *Silversides*, and *Tuna* commencing patrol. For five days the quartet trained as they sailed north until reaching the Louisiades. Here each submarine topped up her fuel and supplies from *Coucal* and proceeded on patrol independently.

Coucal called at Milne Bay a number of times during 1943, but her stays were short, as her storage space was limited. Every two or three weeks *Coucal* accompanied more submarines out, sometimes also meeting a returning submarine to transfer stores. This simple improvement, with submarines extending their patrols in enemy waters, became a regular feature of Task Force 72 operations.

Sinking enemy ships remained difficult, and results were thin as 1943 progressed. Throughout July, August, and September 1943, Task Force 72 sank only five ships. More than half of Brisbane's patrols at this time returned empty-handed. One reason for this was diversion to special missions, but there were others. In many areas few enemy ships were found. *Growler* (Lieutenant Commander Schade) spent several weeks patrolling south of Truk on two patrols in August and October 1943 without finding any ships to attack.

Nevertheless, Task Force 72 held one particular advantage. Information on enemy shipping movements was increasingly available from decrypted radio signals. This information was passed to commanders by highly classified messages. Lt. David Peto, *Greenling*'s communications officer, described this information: "The navy was reading the Japanese navy's coded messages, which revealed the movements of Japanese shipping in the greatest detail. Latitudes and longitudes, times of arrival at these points, courses and speeds, compositions of convoys, escorts, etc."[2] This enabled Fife to pursue his policy of "playing checkers with submarines" with confidence. When sufficient submarines were available, a patrol line was established so that a wide net was cast to cover any enemy route deviations. Fife moved the whole patrol line, or elements within it, to accommodate new information, sometimes nightly.

Fife's "hands-on" policy offered better results and more productive patrols from submarines whose field of vision was limited. Commenting at the end of the war, Vice Admiral Carpender expressed his belief that this shift from area to tactical control contributed greatly to the submarine campaign's success.[3] However, for submarine commanders it was not always easy to comply with "ultra" orders. In addition, the effort involved in following an "ultra" did not always bring results.

Guardfish's Lieutenant Commander Ward described a disappointment that occurred during June 1943: "This was an intelligence intercept that said, 'There is going to be a Japanese transport passing through such-and-such a point at such-and-such a time.' They broke me off . . . and sent me on a high-speed run around New Ireland to get in position. . . . Either the position given was wrong, or the ship didn't make it, or was ahead of schedule. I don't know what went wrong, but no interception here."[4] As one captain receiving these directions, Ward believed that the overmanaging of submarine positioning—what he called a "go-here, go-there" approach— was a major flaw in Fife's command.

Lieutenant Commander Foley *(Gato)* received an "ultra" from Fife on 10 October 1943 directing him to proceed to a position south of New Ireland if he could get there undetected. Foley decided that the distance of six hundred miles was too far to cover in the required time and remained where he was. Fife was not pleased, and he endorsed Foley's patrol report with the remark, "*Gato's* coverage throughout the patrol would have been better accomplished with surface daytime running. . . . The commanding officer will be indoctrinated to this effect for future patrols."[5]

For most of 1943, Task Force 72's most productive area was the open ocean north of New Guinea where expertly escorted Japanese convoys passed between Palau and Kavieng. The battle against these convoys remained the most important activity of Brisbane's submarine war in 1943.

Despite the advantage of reading enemy radio traffic, Fife's submarines found the convoy battle extremely hard. As well as keeping escorts at top efficiency, the Japanese convoy commander was particularly skillful at evading Fife's traps. After the war Fife complimented this officer: "They had an extremely clever convoy commander. . . . We were getting this information, through breaking the codes, on when their convoys were in motion, and we'd have one submarine pick them up. Then I'd surround them with four submarines. Time after time, that fellow would get away."[6]

Fife's submarines rarely sank more than one vessel from a convoy. A convoy battle in June 1943 illustrates both the difficulties Fife and his captains faced and the defensive skill of the Japanese.

A large convoy passing from Palau to New Britain was located by *Greenling* (Lieutenant Commander Grant) early on 18 June. Grant reported the sighting and shadowed, while Fife directed three more submarines, *Growler*, *Guardfish*, and *Silversides*, to the convoy. *Guardfish* (Lieutenant Commander Ward) made a high-speed daylight dash but, upon arriving at the expected location, saw no convoy. That evening a further message from Fife advised that the convoy had changed course, and the three submarines were directed to a new position.

Guardfish and *Silversides* met in bright moonlight early the next morning (19 June) with the convoy in sight, then split up to make separate attacks. At dawn Ward was surprised to see the convoy make a right-angle turn away, completely avoiding *Silversides*. Alert escorts sighted *Guardfish*'s periscope and attacked, staying with her until the convoy had passed.

The third submarine, *Growler* (Lieutenant Commander Schade), had also raced through the night, and as the convoy was escaping from *Guardfish*, those on *Growler* saw its distant smoke moving away. *Growler* was forced to chase on the surface, meeting *Greenling* three hours later, also chasing the convoy.

The chase had begun to appear hopeless when, around noon, the convoy unexpectedly turned toward *Growler*, which submerged. But an hour later the convoy turned 135 degrees away, forcing *Growler* to resume the chase on the surface. After two hours *Growler* submerged, but the convoy's unpredictable zigzag track made planning the attack difficult.

Finally, at 4:15 PM, *Growler* obtained a suitable position and fired torpedoes at two ships, sinking *Miyadono Maru* and damaging another freighter. Three minutes after *Growler* fired, Japanese destroyers began a counterattack that Schade described as "the most severe ever experienced by this vessel."[7]

After *Growler*'s attack, the convoy scattered under a bad weather front. Throughout the following stormy night, the submarines were unable to press home any attacks. *Growler* found her damaged victim immobile and smoking but was kept away by alert escorts. *Guardfish* found another vessel, but she escaped in a rain squall.

By morning on 20 June the battle was over. Despite Fife's knowledge of this convoy's movements and his concentration of four submarines, the result—one ship sunk and another damaged—was disappointing. From Brisbane, Fife reviewed the battle and broadcast his conclusions with some encouragement for his captains and crews at sea: "Tough luck together with weather and moon working for a clever Jap thwarted round up last convoy. . . . Know you all exerted best efforts and experience gained will prevent next one getting away. The old trick of radical changes at dawn and before and after dusk paid him dividends. He continues to work the weather fronts."[8]

Several months would pass before this experience bore fruit. At the end of November 1943 Fife learned through radio decryption about an important reinforcement convoy to Rabaul and directed his submarines to intercept. A brand-new boat, *Raton*, located the convoy of five transports escorted by two destroyers on 28 November. *Raton*'s captain was Lt. Comdr. J. W. Davis, who had taken S47 to sea in April 1942 for the first war patrol from Brisbane.

Davis made a series of attacks, sinking *Hokko Maru* and *Yuri Maru*. With most torpedoes gone, *Raton* surfaced and reported this success to Fife while shadowing the convoy for two more days. Following Fife's directions, two more submarines arrived, *Gato* (Lieutenant Commander Foley) and another new boat, *Ray* (Lt. Comdr. B. Harral). During the night their captains made plans for a joint attack, shouting across the waves as they cruised together.

Waiting ahead of the enemy, *Gato* attacked first, sinking the transport *Columbia Maru*. The convoy made a drastic change of course away from *Ray* while the escorts attacked *Gato*. Witnessing this from his shadowing position astern, Davis surfaced *Raton* in daylight, in full view of the convoy, presenting his submarine as a decoy to draw the escorts off *Gato*.

Denied the opportunity to attack during the day, *Ray* surfaced and chased the convoy, firing her deck gun in an unsuccessful attempt to divert its two remaining ships. The next morning the convoy met the fourth submarine, *Peto*, located farther along its path. *Peto* torpedoed and sank another freighter, *Konei Maru*, making four out of the convoy's five ships sunk by Fife's submarines without damage to themselves.

Six weeks later, Fife achieved another convoy victory. This convoy was three large tankers carrying fuel for the Japanese fleet at Truk. Fife directed three submarines to form a line to intercept. *Albacore* (Lt. Comdr. J. W. Blanchard) attacked the three escorting destroyers, sinking *Sazanami*.

While the remaining destroyers hunted *Albacore, Scamp* (Lieutenant Commander Ebert) fired six torpedoes, sinking the 10,000-ton *Nippon Maru*. Lieutenant Commander Ward in *Guardfish* saw the two remaining tankers approaching unescorted. Five of the six torpedoes he fired hit, sinking *Kenyo Maru*. With two of the three tankers sunk, the remaining destroyers hurried the lone survivor into Truk.

Directing his submarines to these convoys, Fife set up potential for success. His submarine captains' initiative and teamwork realized that potential. Success could not be achieved from Brisbane. Coordination and flexibility were also needed by the commanders on the scene.

In mid-1943 the problem of poor torpedo performance came to a head at Pearl Harbor. Captains and crews had long suspected that the magnetic exploder was unreliable, causing premature explosions or failures. Clear evidence of torpedo failure now appeared in two attacks on aircraft carriers. Apparently good attacks brought about little damage, and American code-breakers confirmed the carriers' safe arrival, indicating that the torpedoes had exploded prematurely. Concurrently, Lieutenant Commander Morton returned from a patrol characterized by repeated torpedo failure, and his previous support for the magnetic exploder turned into angry condemnation. In the face of this evidence, on 24 June 1943 Admiral Nimitz, on Vice Admiral Lockwood's recommendation, ordered the magnetic exploders disconnected on Pacific Fleet submarines.

Despite the deactivation, torpedo failures continued. It was then realized that there were also faults in the contact detonator. This deficiency was highlighted in an attack in which eight torpedoes hitting a damaged tanker failed to explode. After almost two years of war it was revealed that when a torpedo hit at the optimum 90-degree angle, its firing pin deformed before activating the detonator. The pin was strengthened, but firing so that the torpedo would hit at an oblique angle was also recommended. By mid-October 1943 all Pearl Harbor submarines sailed with torpedoes with all faults corrected.

After almost two years, America's Pacific Fleet submarines finally had reliable and effective torpedoes, but this was not the case for the Seventh Fleet in Australia. Rear Admiral Christie, commanding Seventh Fleet submarines, had been intimately involved in the development of the magnetic exploder at the Bureau of Ordnance's Torpedo Section. The Seventh Fleet did not come under Nimitz's control, and Christie did not want to see this technology abandoned. He believed that the problems lay in how the device was being used, and he would continue to refine it and prove its success. He was supported by the navy's Bureau of Ordnance, which also was reluctant to see the magnetic exploder discarded.

Vice Admiral Carpender accepted Christie's advice, and orders were issued on 11 July 1943 that Seventh Fleet submarines must continue to use the magnetic exploder. These instructions included Task Force 72.

The differences between Pearl Harbor's instructions and those in Australia were a recipe for confusion, particularly for submarines transferring between commands. It also created discontent among crews who had witnessed torpedo failures and seen their concerns recognized by Nimitz and Lockwood, but were forced to continue with equipment they did not trust. Christie and Fife rigorously enforced their torpedo policy.

As a result, some crews sought their own solutions. Lt. Comdr. M. P. Hottel (*Grouper*) was convinced that the magnetic exploder was a failure, and when his entreaties to disconnect it failed, he arranged for his torpedomen to make the alteration unofficially. Fife heard of this plan and ordered *Grouper* to delay departure until all magnetic exploders had been reconnected. The following patrol was frustrating. *Grouper* had a premature explosion in her first attack, and in the next all torpedoes passed under the target without exploding. Blame for this was not laid on the magnetic exploder but was attributed to confusion in resetting torpedoes. These particular torpedoes had been omitted through oversight when Fife's reconnection orders were carried out. Fired for a magnetic setting under the target but without this feature connected, they passed harmlessly under.[9]

Blackfish had a similar experience in her first Brisbane patrol in November 1943 when some torpedoes exploded prematurely while others worked. On her return to Brisbane it was found that, unknown to her crew, some magnetic exploders had been disconnected on the tender before issue. Another submarine to suffer from unofficial adjustments ashore in Brisbane was *Silversides*. The magnetic exploders on her sixth patrol in August 1943 were adjusted to a "hair trigger." As a result, this patrol's first four torpedoes exploded prematurely, and premature explosions occurred in both later attacks on this patrol.[10] The Brisbane submarines' rate of premature explosions reached 13.5 percent during the second half of 1943.

Though bound by his superior's orders, Captain Fife was not blind to the mounting evidence of torpedo failure. By October 1943, when *Drum* (Lt. Comdr. B. McMahon) arrived from a successful patrol, Fife was more ready to acknowledge the problems with magnetic exploders: "There was no definite evidence of faulty exploder performance in any of *Drum's* attacks, although the absence of hits on the day attack of 29 August may have been due to a failure of the magnetic feature of a torpedo passing beneath the target's keel."[11]

Fife's submarines still had magnetic exploders connected when they achieved their resounding convoy success at the end of November 1943. But these exploders made only a qualified contribution to this success. *Raton,* which sank the first two ships, had experienced premature torpedo explosions in the patrol's previous attacks. Her captain disconnected the magnetic exploders on the remaining torpedoes, enabling her to achieve these two sinkings.

Final resolution came early in 1944, directly affecting the three submarines that had achieved victory over the tanker convoy described previously. These submarines, *Albacore, Guardfish,* and *Scamp,* sailed from Brisbane late in December 1943 with the latest modification to the magnetic exploders fitted. The first to make an attack was *Scamp,* which on 6 January attacked a small escorted tanker. All her torpedoes exploded shortly after being fired, and after escaping a counterattack, her captain reported the torpedo failures to Fife. Within hours the submarines received urgent orders not to make further attacks until the magnetic exploders were disconnected. Soon afterward, on 14 January, with torpedoes set for contact operation, all three submarines contributed to victory over the tanker convoy.[12]

On 26 November 1943 Vice Adm. T. C. Kinkaid, appointed at MacArthur's request, succeeded Carpender in command of the Seventh Fleet. Kinkaid came from a command in Admiral Nimitz's Pacific area and was not as tolerant as Carpender of Christie's persistence with the magnetic exploder. Christie was forced to admit defeat and, on 20 January 1944, ordered the magnetic exploder deactivated by Seventh Fleet submarines.

With enemy submarines operating off the Australian coast and all submarines looking much the same to an airman, Brisbane submarines faced the possibility of "friendly" aircraft attack. To minimize this risk, a safety lane was declared off southern Queensland, and outbound submarines were escorted.

As Allied forces advanced through New Guinea and the Solomons, Allied aircraft ranged farther into Task Force 72's patrol areas. The risk of friendly attacks grew from a limited danger near home to a constant possibility throughout a patrol.

On the day *Growler* had her collision, *Swordfish* (Lt. Comdr. J. Lewis) radioed that she had been strafed by an American bomber and forced to cut short the patrol. Two submarines had been forced to return on the same day. Fife advised his captains to "treat our long range recco planes as though they are enemy and get under before they arrive."[13]

By July 1943, Allied air strength had increased and the danger of friendly attacks became more serious. In that month two submarines were forced to seek repairs from friendly fire on successive days.

The first was *Tuna* (Lt. Comdr. A. Holtz), about to transit Vitiaz Strait. A crewman, Frank Medina, described what happened: "We never reached our assigned war patrol area as one of our friendly bombers with itchy fingers decided we were their enemy. They dropped three bombs as we were diving to get away. . . . We surfaced severely damaged to port side. . . . [All] we could do was navigate on the surface, through perilous waters, back to Brisbane."[14]

An RAAF Catalina had made the attack out of a dark, overcast night sky, in an area where Japanese supply submarines were expected. The aircraft detected the submarine in an unrestricted area. Breaking through cloud, it dropped a flare followed by four depth charges as the submarine submerged. When the boat surfaced, the pilot began another run but broke off on seeing a "flickering light." Then, when the boat flashed the correct letter and showed the correct color, the attack was abandoned. In his report the pilot pointed out that *Tuna* made no initial attempt to identify herself and was two hundred nautical miles away from the position given at their preflight briefing.[15] Vice Admiral Carpender concluded, "Do not consider anyone at fault. Occurrence result of hazardous routing through waters under dispute of control which must be accepted."[16] *Tuna* remained in Evans Deakin's hands for two and a half weeks for repairs.

The day after the attack on *Tuna*, another Catalina dropped four depth charges on *Grouper* (Lt. Comdr. M. P. Hottel) off Guadalcanal. Extensive damage forced a return to Brisbane for repairs. Here Hottel met the offending pilot and took him to sea for a brief taste of submarine life. Incorrect briefing of pilots on submarine–air recognition signals was the agreed cause of this error. Poor communication and inadequate pilot briefings were a theme that would recur as the war progressed.

Arriving off the Solomons, *Stingray* (Lt. Comdr. O. J. Earle) was damaged about a month later. Signalman A. A. Montague recalled, "We were cruising in very phosphorescent water at night and the bomber must have seen the wake and dropped four bombs which landed in the water on our starboard side. The explosions put several large dents in our outer hull and knocked me out of my bunk."[17] Earle reported the attack to Fife, who,

after investigation, advised him that it had been made by "friendly" aircraft. Earle retorted, "No friend of ours."[18] With limited damage, *Stingray*
continued her patrol.

Right up to the war's end, American submarines were forced to remain
on their guard against attacks by friendly aircraft.

By late 1943, warships of all kinds were joining the fleet to replace losses,
building up superiority that would overwhelm the Japanese. Submarine
construction was a specialized undertaking, and at the commencement of
the war only three American shipyards built them. Their capacity
expanded, and three more yards began submarine construction. One of
these was Manitowoc Shipbuilding Company in Wisconsin, one thousand
miles inland on the shores of Lake Michigan. *Peto* was Manitowoc's first
submarine completed. She arrived in Brisbane on 14 March 1943.

Submarine numbers in the Pacific were growing, and Admiral King
increased Australia's complement from twenty to thirty. The extras made
up a second submarine squadron at Fremantle, Squadron 16, while
Squadron 8 remained alone in Brisbane.

On passage, new Squadron 16 submarines visited Brisbane for voyage
repairs, operational training, and combat indoctrination. The first to arrive
was *Billfish* on 1 August 1943. Altogether ten Squadron 16 submarines
transited Brisbane in August, September, and October 1943.[19] The submarines exercised off Moreton Bay for between one and two weeks. Then
they sailed to Darwin, where they topped up their fuel, received orders,
and sailed on their first patrols under Task Force 71. Their patrols took
them into the waters of the Dutch East Indies and lower Philippines, ter-
minating in Fremantle.

First patrol results were mixed. Two boats set themselves on course to
join the war's most successful American submarines. *Rasher* sank four
ships on her first patrol, while *Bonefish* sank three. On the other hand,
Puffer endured a prolonged depth-charge attack that kept her submerged
for 37 hours, 45 minutes, the longest submerged ordeal of any American
submarine. With the air foul, oxygen almost exhausted, and the temperature up to 125°F, her crew were lucky to survive. The long period under
water had a devastating effect on morale, with some men, believed strong,
going to pieces while others showed unexpected strength. The incident
was subsequently studied for lessons on the psychological effects of prolonged stress underwater.

Two Squadron 16 submarines did not return from their first patrols.
The first, *Cisco* (Comdr. J. W. Coe), arrived in Brisbane on 1 September

1943 and sailed from Darwin on the nineteenth. Nothing more was heard from her, and when she failed to reply to radio signals on 4 and 5 November, she was posted overdue and presumed lost. *Cisco's* loss was a bitter blow, as Coe was one of the navy's ablest commanders, highly regarded by his crews and his peers. He had commanded *S39* and *Skipjack* in six patrols and racked up the Asiatic Fleet's best score of confirmed sinkings on a single patrol. Coe had played a pivotal role in resolving the problem of deep-running torpedoes, and he pioneered the "down-the-throat" torpedo shot into the teeth of an oncoming target.

The last Squadron 16 submarine through Brisbane was *Capelin* (Lt. Comdr. E. E. Marshall), departing Brisbane on 22 October 1943. Seventeen days out from Darwin, *Capelin* returned for minor repairs, sailing again on 17 November. She did not reply to signals on 9 December and was posted missing, presumed lost. A total of 155 lives were lost aboard *Cisco* and *Capelin*.[20]

The unexplained loss of these submarines on their first patrols caused anxiety. *Capelin* (SS 289) and *Cisco* (SS 290) were consecutive products of Portsmouth Navy Yard, and the crews of their squadron mates from the same shipyard production series wondered whether some weakness in construction had caused their loss. Bill Ruhe, a lieutenant aboard *Crevalle* (SS 291), the next submarine off the production line, organized a thorough check for defects, locating significant weaknesses in two vent pipes, potentially fatal if *Crevalle* were depth-charged. *Crevalle's* crew remedied this defect immediately.[21]

A real probability exists that flaws in construction contributed to *Cisco's* loss. Portsmouth Navy Yard had more than doubled its building capacity, from four slipways in December 1941 to nine construction berths in April 1943. There was extensive use of prefabrication, with large sections assembled before the keel was laid. Worker morale was very high, and teams competed to clear slipways as quickly as possible. Three shifts were worked, with workers often putting in voluntary overtime and extra shifts.[22]

Cisco was launched on Christmas Eve 1942, in the middle of a New England winter, in the record time of fifty-six days after keel laying—a record that stood for the whole war. During construction a fuel tank had burst during testing, requiring a new tank to be welded into place from outside after the hull had been completed. An oil leak persisted throughout her trials and working-up period. This concerned Coe, who wrote, "Oil slick caused by lubricating oil discharge with exhaust at all speeds and loads. This is considered a serious liability in wartime operations. Unsuccessful efforts of operating personnel and contractor's representatives to correct these conditions indicate that they may be a fault of design, material, or workmanship."[23] This intractable leak still concerned Coe as late as 6 September 1943.[24]

With *Cisco* on the verge of her first war patrol, Commander Coe found himself in a quandary. On one hand was the intractable oil leak, and on the other was the clean bill of health *Cisco* received after each repair job, nurturing hopes that maybe this time it would hold. Overshadowing all this was the task force commanders' demand for captains to achieve results. Given the newness of his boat and the expectations of his superiors, plus the number of older or damaged boats needing repair, Coe had no choice but to sail. If the leak recurred, he would have to deal with it at sea.

After the war Japanese records revealed an aircraft attack on 28 September 1943 in the Sulu Sea. The report stated, "Found a sub trailing oil. Bombing. Ships co-operated with us. The oil continued to gush out even on tenth of October." No other American submarine was in the area, and it could only have been *Cisco*.[25] It would seem that the oil leak, with her since her construction, proved fatal.

No clues were ever found to account for *Capelin*'s loss. It remains a mystery to this day.

Advances from June to September 1943 established Allied ascendancy in the Solomons and along the New Guinea coast. Later advances aimed to neutralize the Japanese fortress of Rabaul and take the Allies further along the road to victory. Landings were planned for Bougainville, in order to build an airfield from which to attack Rabaul and Kavieng. At the same time, large Japanese forces at Buin-Faisi would be isolated by the Allies' "island-hopping" strategy. Heavy air raids were mounted on Rabaul and Japanese airfields in Bougainville from mid-October until after the assault to neutralize aerial opposition. Further landings by General MacArthur's forces on New Britain would give the Allies control of the Bismarck Sea and Vitiaz Strait.

The Brisbane submarines played an important part in the preparations for the Bougainville landings, and the landings in turn significantly influenced the Brisbane submarines' future. On his reconnaissance flights in May 1943, Fife had been asked by Halsey to locate landing places on Bougainville for survey parties to find airfield sites. Fife identified two sites, one on the west coast, the other on the east.

Engineer survey parties went to both sites in late September 1943. *Gato* landed one party on the east coast while *Guardfish,* specially chosen by

Halsey, landed another on the west. Both submarines retrieved their parties a week later. Torokina, the western site, was chosen for landings on 1 November. Two nights before the Torokina landing, *Scamp* landed coastwatchers on New Ireland to watch for Japanese movements against the Allied assault.

With Rabaul neutralized by air raids and the Bougainville landings, the front line was moving farther from Brisbane. Recognition of the need to move forward preceded these successes. On 3 September 1943 the commander of the Seventh Fleet reported that advanced Allied naval headquarters, Southwest Pacific area, had been established in Port Moresby. Administration remained in Brisbane.

Enemy shipping in the Brisbane task force's areas was becoming scarce as eastern New Guinea and the Solomons became safe bases to support further Allied advances. In view of this improved situation, Vice Admirals Carpender and Halsey decided to alter the submarine balance between Australia's east and west. The proportion that had so irked both Lockwood and Christie at Fremantle—twelve submarines in the east compared with only eight in the west—would now be reversed. As Brisbane submarines completed their rest periods, they would transfer to Fremantle until Task Force 72 had been reduced to eight vessels. By 1 December 1943, Task Force 72's strength was nine submarines.[26]

The improved position in New Guinea led to another change to Task Force 72, with *Fulton* leaving Brisbane for an advanced base. The move came suddenly on 24 October 1943, when the familiar routine stopped and all shore leave was canceled. No calls ashore were permitted, causing consternation among those with attachments to Australian girls.

Wayne Jemmett, a metalsmith aboard *Fulton,* had become engaged to a Brisbane girl. He had ordered an engagement ring, but it was slow in arriving. Late at night on 24 October he returned to *Fulton* after leave to find the ship ablaze with lights and a hive of activity, clearly preparing to sail. He pleaded to be allowed to go and tell his fiancee but was not allowed off the base. Then he found that the engagement ring had arrived in that day's mail. Jemmett thought frantically about how to resolve this problem. The answer came in the morning when he saw on the submarine alongside a friend who knew his fiancee. Calling out, "Give this to Thelma," Jemmett threw the engagement ring across the gap between the ships. His friend caught the ring, and it was safely delivered.[27]

Joyce Barrett, daughter of the Anglican dean of Brisbane, recalled a last-minute attempted transfer ashore. *Fulton*'s chaplain appealed to her father to find a home for the ship's parrot. In spite of the fact that the crew had taught the bird a full, rich vocabulary, no cathedral parishioner would take it. Joyce has no knowledge of the bird's fate. The *Bow Plane*'s reference to the ship's cook "and his stowaway parrot" may be significant.[28]

At 9 AM the next day the lines were taken in, *Fulton*'s screws turned for the first time in almost a year, and she slowly made her way to sea after having been berthed at New Farm Wharf for fifty weeks. Les Cottman recalled that *Fulton* departed "amid a lot of tears," with "a tremendous farewell by scores of ships and craft and many people shouting and cheering from the riverbank."[29]

Leaving Moreton Bay, *Fulton* was joined by her escort and headed north. On passage her crew speculated on their secret destination. The answer came four days later when *Fulton* moored to a buoy at Gili Gili anchorage in Milne Bay, far out from the shore. Just over a year before, Japanese warships had freely cruised these waters and Australian soldiers had repelled an invasion to bring about the Allies' first victory over Japanese land forces. When *Fulton* arrived on 29 October 1943, Milne Bay was being built up as a major base for offensive operations against New Britain. The Allies were pushing further forward, and *Fulton*'s facilities in Milne Bay would save her submarines time on patrol and bring support closer in an emergency. A new chapter was opening for *Fulton*, Task Force 72, and Brisbane's submarine war.

18

MILNE BAY

Hugh Story, arriving at Milne Bay aboard *Bluegill* in March 1944, observed, "Milne Bay was obviously the U.S. Army's staging port for the campaign up the north coast of New Guinea. They must have expected heavy casualties, for there was a whole string of general hospitals. . . . In the jungle we passed an oil storage dump of . . . drums, stacked twenty feet high and running a quarter of a mile."[1]

Fulton's arrival was welcomed by the fleet at large. Her facilities and skilled technicians were unique and would assist all vessels operating in the forward area. On the day after her arrival *Fulton's* first customer, *LST201*, arrived alongside. A fortnight later she left *Fulton* transformed into USS *Pontus*, a motor torpedo boat tender. In the following months *Fulton* repaired and refitted a wide variety of vessels, including the cruiser *Nashville*. One of her humbler jobs was salvaging a Japanese landing barge. Put into service as the garbage scow *Tojo Maru*, it dumped *Fulton's* refuse at sea.

Les Cottman recalled how hard *Fulton* worked in Milne Bay: "Our two big cranes worked overtime . . . as they were the only cranes in the area. During this time *Fulton* was often referred to as the 'Can-Do' ship, as no task was ever set aside."[2]

Fulton maintained a twenty-four-hour day. The workload remained heavy and constant. Clarence Hebb, who worked in *Fulton's* metal shop throughout the war, described life aboard as "routine and repetitive. The only changing aspect was moving from one location of operation on to the next. Always the same old 'office,' and the same old 'house.' Only the views from different dots on the map changed from time to time."[3]

For *Fulton's* men, Milne Bay was a stark contrast from the comforts of Brisbane. The climate was hot and humid, and tropical infections were rife. There were few attractions ashore, although visiting artists such as John Wayne and the Artie Shaw Band performed aboard. Wayne Jemmett considered Milne Bay "the worst place on earth . . . rain, heat, sweat, heat rash on my back that got infected, athlete's foot on my toes until the nails came off, dandruff in my hair, scabies. . . . Every fourth day they'd let us off the ship. They'd give us four cans of beer, warm beer. It was hot as the weather, and then we'd march through the mud over to a certain play area they had. . . . Anyway, we'd sit in the shade and drink our warm beer and walk back to the ship. That was our recreation."[4] Others like Clarence Hebb did not even bother to go ashore.

But Les Cottman found more to interest him in this new and rough environment: "While ashore at Milne Bay many remains of the fighting were seen. . . . An Aussie canteen provided cordial and tinned fruit (one can per person). Two-up games if you had the money to chance. The giant spider with a strong web strung between two trees that trapped many small birds. The Aussie soldier who hired native women to make sarongs to sell to the Yanks. The beautiful moths and butterflies which I helped a friend net for his collection."[5]

At Milne Bay the men were conscious they were much closer to the enemy. Antitorpedo nets surrounded the ship, and three times her crew was called to "action stations" for air raids. Relief crews moved submarines to an emergency dispersal area while crews stood to their antiaircraft guns. None of these alarms developed into attacks, and *Fulton's* men returned quickly to their tasks.

By far the more dangerous enemy was the unhealthy environment of heat, humidity, swamp, jungle, crocodiles, snakes, mosquitoes, scorpions, and lice. Men soon learned about unfamiliar ailments like dengue, malaria, heat rash, and fungus growth in the ear ("tropical ear").

Despite *Fulton's* departure, the Submarine Repair Unit, Navy 134, remained in Brisbane. The comprehensive repair and support facilities continued to refit submarines and rest their crews. Under the new arrangement Task Force 72 became a forward echelon at Milne Bay and the established facilities in Brisbane a rear echelon. Fife, appointed commodore in November 1943, left Brisbane with his operational staff on 2 December 1943 to command the task force from *Fulton* at Milne Bay. The rear echelon was under Fife's second in command, the commander of Squadron 8, Capt. W. M. Downes. On 12 February 1944 Capt. E. H. Bryant succeeded Downes in Brisbane.[6]

At Milne Bay, *Fulton* built in a coconut plantation a crew's rest and recuperation camp, which was opened on 11 December 1943. It was called Camp Beeman after Chief Pharmacist's Mate A. C. Beeman, killed in a gun action aboard *Amberjack* on 4 February 1943. Camp Beeman and later ones were poor substitutes for the facilities in Brisbane, Toowoomba, Surfers Paradise, or Coolangatta. Charles Schechter described life at these forward camps: "We were given all the beer we could drink at the rest camps only. Maybe they thought we needed a drink after the patrol? What else could we do on an island with no girls but play softball and drink beer."[7]

Despite its limitations and the regular tropical downpours, Camp Beeman enabled crews to "let their hair down" and generally unwind after a stressful patrol. *Dace* crewmen recalled: "A various assortment of casual attire was worn. . . . An occasional whitehat could be seen turned inside out. . . . Smiles were on their faces for the most part, as pale-skinned warriors swapped tales about their patrols. It was nice to be away from the boat for a couple of weeks."[8]

There were also occasions of civilized respectability for officers. Hugh Story recalled times in Milne Bay when "we invited a group of army nurses to be our guests for dinner in the tender's wardroom, a treat for them, white linen, polished silver, etc., and a treat for us to be with young ladies. We joined an Australian tank outfit for lunch at their base in the mountains. . . . The tablecloths were various pastel colors, and there was a native servant behind each of us."[9]

With *Fulton* at Milne Bay, submarines could refit and replenish alongside between patrols while the crew drank beer at Camp Beeman. However, this arrangement provided only limited relief, and a pattern developed whereby the submarines continued to Brisbane after every second patrol. There the crews enjoyed all the recreation facilities available while the submarines were inspected and cleaned in dry dock. Outbound, the boats exercised with their escorts while traveling north, then called briefly at Milne Bay for orders and to top up fuel before continuing on patrol.

Another development was the "double-barrel" patrol, whereby the submarine briefly returned to *Fulton* or *Coucal* in the middle of a sixty-day patrol to replenish fuel, torpedoes, or supplies. *Balao* (Lt. Comdr. R. Crane) conducted an early double-barrel patrol in October 1943. Firing ten torpedoes at a large convoy on 23 October, she was recalled to Tulagi to top up her fuel, returning to sea on the twenty-eighth. After another three weeks *Balao* terminated her patrol, coming alongside *Fulton* at Milne

Bay on 16 November 1943. Double-barrel patrols became common for Brisbane submarines as their tenders moved forward with the Allied advance.

In late 1943 Task Force 72 achieved greater success against shipping. In fourteen out of sixteen patrols from Brisbane and Milne Bay between November 1943 and February 1944, twenty-three enemy vessels were sunk. These included the task force's two major convoy victories. With the torpedo problems finally cleared during January 1944, the task force's prospects looked bright.

Less than three days after *Fulton* reached Milne Bay, Allied forces went ashore at Torokina to establish an airfield. Six weeks later there were landings on New Britain. These advances, on opposite sides of Rabaul, tightened the noose around the enemy strong point and strengthened the Allied position for further advances.

Meanwhile, Nimitz's powerful fleet of fast aircraft carriers made the first assault in its drive through the central Pacific. The first objective was Makin and Tarawa in the Gilbert Islands, with landings on 20 November 1943 in Operation Galvanic. These islands were captured within a few days, although Tarawa's casualties were horrific.

Submarines were deployed for Operation Galvanic in activities typical of later assaults. These included providing weather reports, photographic reconnaissance of landing beaches, and landing commando parties. However, their main employment was blockading enemy ports and sinking warships coming to the battle.

Operation Galvanic also saw another activity added to the submarines' repertoire: "lifeguarding." This involved submarines standing off enemy positions during an air strike to rescue any ditched airmen. The task was not new to Brisbane's submarines, *Triton* having done it off Wake Island in December 1942.

Captain Fife had previously introduced lifeguard submarine placements to support Fifth Air Force raids on Rabaul. An example was positioning *Guardfish* (Lieutenant Commander Ward) off Rabaul for two days in mid-October 1943. The downside was that, to avoid revealing the submarine's presence, two targets were allowed to pass. After this, submarine lifeguarding became an integral component of air offensives.

As the central Pacific assault proceeded, most submarines deployed for Operation Galvanic came from Pearl Harbor. However, two Brisbane boats, *Blackfish* and *Drum,* took part in the ambush around Truk to prevent enemy warships from interfering with the landings. *Drum* scored a major success when she sank *Hie Maru* (11,621 tons) on 17 November

1943. Five days later she attacked another convoy, but was caught and so damaged that she was forced to return to the United States for repairs.

Mike Rindskopf, her executive officer, described what happened: "We evaded deep, but Bill [Williamson, *Drum*'s captain] wanted to see what was going on. When we broke through the thermocline at maybe 120 feet, the escorts detected us and dropped half a dozen *big* charges just above the engine room. One of these split the after bulkhead of the conning tower.... That sent us to Pearl.... During the ensuing deep dive, I noticed that the whole conning tower was showing signs of collapse at two hundred feet. We surfaced, and then were sent to Mare Island for a new four-hundred-foot test conning tower."[10]

Another submarine near Truk for Operation Galvanic was not so fortunate. *Corvina* (Comdr. R. S. Rooney) on her first patrol to join Task Force 72 passed to Fife's control on 2 December 1943 and was ordered to retire south and report. No answer was received, but considering the amount of radio interference in the area, this did not cause alarm, and a surface escort was sent to meet her off Tulagi on 9 December. *Corvina* did not arrive and was never seen again. On 23 December 1943 she was posted missing, presumed lost. After the war it was discovered that *Corvina* had been torpedoed by the Japanese submarine *I-176* on 16 November 1943 and sunk with all eighty-two crew. *Corvina* was the only American submarine known to have been sunk by a Japanese submarine.

There was a note of irony in *Corvina*'s loss. The American submarines off Truk had received an "ultra" telling them that a Japanese submarine was coming through the area. U.S. code-breakers read a signal from *I-176* saying, "Received direct torpedo hit en route to Truk, no damage," which suggested that the Japanese boat could have been hit by a dud torpedo.[11] The tables were apparently then turned and *Corvina*, the probable hunter, was sunk.

The top priority for radio intelligence was major enemy warships, and Fife attempted wherever possible to use that intelligence to direct submarines to a position for attack. But until late in 1943, radio intelligence made little contribution to success against major warships. In two years of war, American submarines sank only two major Japanese warships, the cruisers *Kako* and *Tenryu*. Brisbane submarines sank both, but neither sinking resulted from radio decryption.

A golden opportunity came during November 1943 after Allied air raids damaged several warships at Rabaul. Intelligence learned that the modern cruiser *Agano*, badly damaged in the raids, was being towed to Truk. Fife sent *Scamp* (Commander Ebert) to sink her. Ebert located *Agano* on 12 November being towed by her sister *Noshiro,* surrounded by destroyers. *Scamp* fired six torpedoes. One hit amidships, stopping the cruiser. However, that was *Scamp's* only opportunity as the destroyers drove her away while the tow resumed.

Fife directed a second submarine to intercept, *Albacore* (Lt. Comdr. O. E. Hagberg). However, *Albacore* was discovered before she could fire and was depth-charged for four hours, allowing *Agano* to escape.

This disappointment was the climax of a nightmare patrol. *Albacore* had been bombed by Allied aircraft twice within the space of just a few days. The first incident occurred when she was chasing a convoy. Two days later a second attack almost sank her. The day after the second attack, *Albacore* was sent against *Agano.* The full impact of the attack is described by one of *Albacore's* crew members, Willard Devling:

We were to be part of a joint attack of navy ships and marine planes from Guadalcanal. The *Albacore* was assigned the northeast area of the entry to [St. George's Channel], and as planes attacked the fleet and it dispersed to open water, we were in position to torpedo them. . . . At about the time of the raid, we were straddled with two near misses of bombs. We were damaged quite severely but managed to operate. Commander Hagberg was on the bridge and sustained severe burns. He was able to identify the plane as a Marine Corps plane. As we were in no condition to participate in the raid, . . . we moved out of the area so as to try and repair the damage. We then broke radio silence and asked permission to return to Brisbane.

We were granted permission but were given the location of a Japanese cruiser that had been torpedoed by one of our subs and was dead in the water. We were told to finish it off. We located it and were ready to fire torpedoes when . . . our sonarman reported two Japanese destroyers making a run on us. Not having time to fire we went deep to avoid depth charges. They crisscrossed us for what seemed like an hour dropping I don't know how many depth charges, causing so much damage we could not maintain a safe depth. Our skipper told us our only chance was to blow to the surface, with only one gun our chances were almost zero. . . . At that time the sonarman reported an explosion on the horizon and that the destroyers were leaving us. We surfaced and headed for Brisbane.[12]

To prevent any recurrence of *Albacore*'s experience, MacArthur imposed bombing restrictions on aircraft in areas beyond the Bismarck Archipelago north of 2°S.

Task Force 72 was reduced to eight submarines on 11 December 1943 when *Raton* and *Ray* left Milne Bay to join Christie's command. Attrition was further reducing Fife's numbers following the loss of *Corvina* and the damage to both *Drum* and *Guardfish*. On 9 December, Fife noted that he had only one submarine, *Peto*, on patrol north of the Bismarcks. The situation improved a week later when *Balao* and *Gato* took up positions, enabling Fife to cover the three convoy routes from Saipan, Palau, and Truk.[13]

Gato (Comdr. R. F. Foley) was lucky to survive the patrol. Foley was fearlessly aggressive, his motto being, "If I hit him first, he's not going to hit me."[14] Five days before Christmas 1943, *Gato* attacked a convoy, sinking one ship and damaging another. The escorts dropped nineteen depth charges—apparently right on top of *Gato*. When *Gato* surfaced later, the bridge crew were horrified to find an unexploded depth charge on deck aft. An escort burst through a rain squall, but Foley was able to dodge back into the squall. The depth charge was loaded onto a rubber raft, which was punctured and pushed overboard to sink slowly in *Gato*'s wake.

Foley was later chasing another convoy when *Gato* was sighted by a Japanese floatplane and the convoy changed course. Foley surfaced to "end around," but again the floatplane dived at *Gato*. Foley decided to stay on the surface and fight it out, meeting the aircraft's approach with *Gato*'s antiaircraft guns. The floatplane pulled up out of range "with surprise written all over both floats" and eventually flew away, while the convoy escaped. Admiral King, commander in chief of the U.S. Navy, heard of this incident and forcefully expressed his disapproval.[15]

January 1944 saw Fife's second convoy victory as three submarines combined to sink two out of three tankers bound for Truk. The principle of submarines working together for greater success, pioneered by the successful German "wolf packs," was gaining support and encouraging initiative by submarine captains.

The central Pacific offensive moved into top gear in early 1944. American forces in late January captured Kwajalein, Maloelap, and Mili. Other Japanese positions were bypassed to wither in the "island-hopping" strategy. Yet threatening any further advance was the Japanese fleet base at Truk. Heavy aircraft carrier strikes pounded Truk on 17 and 18 February 1944, effectively destroying this base.

During these operations submarines were placed around Truk, initially to blockade the base and sink any warships sailing to oppose the Allied assaults. During the raids on Truk the submarines' dual roles were picking off any Japanese vessels trying to escape and picking up any American airmen shot down. Units of Task Force 72 supported all these operations.

For the initial assaults, only one Brisbane submarine was deployed. This was *Guardfish* (Lieutenant Commander Ward), stationed south of Truk to intercept enemy shipping. On 1 February 1944 Ward made a textbook torpedo attack on the destroyer *Umikaze* to blow off her stern and sink her.

Three of Fife's submarines were off Truk during the strikes in mid-February. *Darter* was close offshore as a lifeguard. Farther out, *Dace* and *Gato* waited to intercept Japanese ships fleeing the raids. No downed airmen were rescued, and no shipping attack was successful. Only two weeks previously, in an exposed bay on New Britain, *Gato* had saved twelve Allied airmen shot down while raiding Rabaul.

Farther west, *Balao* (Lt. Comdr. C. C. Cole) was off Palau to intercept shipping leaving to give aid during the Allied attacks on Truk. She was still there when American aircraft struck enemy positions in the Marianas on 22 February. In the following week *Balao* sank three Japanese ships totaling more than 15,000 tons.

With benefit of hindsight, some recent writers have criticized the use of submarines to support major fleet operations. One analyst wrote:

> With such advanced weapon systems, technologically superior to the defence, and with intelligence from decrypts of what U.S. code-breakers termed the *"Maru* code" detailing convoy routes and schedules, it is abundantly clear that a concentrated campaign against merchant shipping could have cut off Japan from her southern sources of supply and crippled her war effort in a relatively short time. . . . Clear as it is in retrospect, Nimitz's and MacArthur's staff were intent on their own plans for direct assaults, and Lockwood and Christie complied. . . . At Nimitz's daily conferences Lockwood provided the submarine force input, tying his command tactically into the C-in-C's plans; thus submarines continued to be used as they had been from the start, in reconnaissance for the fleet, in patrols off Japanese fleet bases and island targets, and in the new tasks of weather reporting, photo-reconnaissance of potential invasion beaches, and "lifeguarding." . . . In the south-west Pacific area MacArthur continued to demand submarines for special tasks.[16]

Although these criticisms appear valid in retrospect, U.S. admirals had made great strides in adjusting submarine use in only two years. Prior to 1941, submarines were an adjunct of the fleet for use against enemy warships. War against commerce, limited by the London Treaty, had not been seriously considered.

The accelerating advances across the Pacific in 1944 needed all resources available, and the submarines' part was significant. By February 1944 antishipping strategies based on experience were employed, and only now was a reliable torpedo available. This year would see results.

Less than a fortnight after the Truk operation, on 29 February 1944, MacArthur's forces landed on the Admiralty Islands to take Manus Island and magnificent Seeadler Harbor. After a month, this island group was under Allied control, placing the Allies northwest of Rabaul and Kavieng, isolating them from any further part in the war.

Neutralizing Truk and Rabaul early in 1944 changed Task Force 72's operational environment. Fife's submarine patrol areas in the Bismarcks and north of New Guinea became empty of enemy shipping and subject to Allied air power.

By February 1944 all Squadron 8 submarines were due for relief. All Task Force 72 submarines deployed for the Marshalls, Truk, and Palau operations were on patrols that would transfer them to or from the Brisbane command. *Balao, Gato,* and *Guardfish* returned for refit in the United States. New submarines *Dace* and *Darter* were on their way to join the Brisbane command. Both made the most of this double-barreled patrol under Fife's control.

Fulton had also spent almost eighteen months in the Southwest Pacific without docking, and she too was overdue for overhaul at home. Her replacement, USS *Euryale,* reached Milne Bay on 14 March 1944. The next day all work was transferred to *Euryale,* and *Fulton* prepared for home. On 17 March 1944 *Fulton* stood out to sea bound for Pearl Harbor and Mare Island shipyard in California.

As she sailed she received messages. From Vice Admiral Kinkaid, successor to Carpender as Seventh Fleet commander, came "a 'Well Done' to all hands for a grand job from beginning to end." The commander of Task Force 72 sent the message, "You will be greatly missed, and long remembered. Well done."[17]

In contrast with her journey to Brisbane, *Fulton*'s voyage home was peaceful. She crossed the Equator where it intersects with the International Date Line (0° latitude and 180° longitude) at noon on 22 March 1944, making her crew "golden shellbacks" in the lore of the sea. *Fulton*

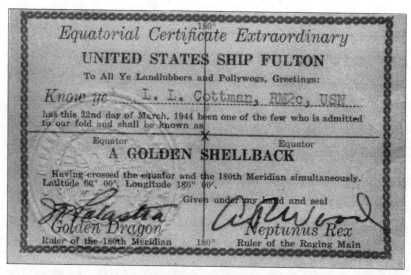

Golden Shellback Ticket.
Courtesy of L. L. Cottman

reached Mare Island Navy Yard on 24 April, after two years away from the continental United States. Her crew went on long leave while *Fulton* underwent modernization.

On the day *Fulton* handed over to *Euryale,* Commodore Fife also surrendered command of Task Force 72. Recently reduced to only eight submarines, Task Force 72 no longer merited an officer of Fife's seniority and experience. He transferred command to Capt. J. M. Haines, then flew home to take up a position on Admiral King's staff in Washington.

Commencing the war in the Philippines, Fife worked with submarines through many setbacks to see them on the road to success when he left Milne Bay. Reflecting on these events many years later, Admiral Fife considered the Allies' holding Guadalcanal in 1942 and 1943 to have been crucial. Reaching this turning point was the greatest satisfaction of his career, and he believed that it was during this period of the war that he made his greatest contribution to victory.[18]

19

A NEW SQUADRON

Replacing *Fulton* was the new tender *Euryale* (Capt. H. A. Guthrie). The navy took her over before completion as a freighter and converted her to a submarine tender, commissioning her in December 1943. *Euryale* reached Brisbane on 5 March 1944, delivering torpedoes, stores, and personnel to the submarine repair base. Five days later she sailed, arriving in Milne Bay on 14 March.

Euryale was flagship for the new submarines of Squadron 18 (Capt. E. H. Bryant). These submarines, all either straight from their builders or having completed only one or two patrols, were manned by crews blending experienced men with those fresh from training. Their commanders were experienced in combat.

The first of the squadron's submarines to join, *Cero*, reached Milne Bay on 12 January 1944. She was followed over the next two months by *Dace*, *Darter*, *Bashaw*, *Flounder*, and *Bluegill*. The last Squadron 8 time-expired boats, *Blackfish* and *Scamp*, left Task Force 72 in April, replaced by *Bream* and *Guavina*.

The new submarines carried improved radar and sonar capable of navigating through a minefield. Surface-search radars had the now familiar "plan position indicator" (PPI), a circular screen showing all contacts within range, with the submarine at the center. The PPI was a radical innovation that allowed range and bearing of the target to be measured and other contacts to be seen as on a map.

Also introduced around this time was the Mark 18 torpedo, powered by electricity rather than steam. Steam torpedoes left a wake of bubbles, while the electric ones left no wake. Although the Mark 18 was slow in reaching the fleet and some flaws remained, it was welcomed by the submarine force despite its slower thirty-knot speed.

The Southwest Pacific situation had improved with the neutralization of Truk and Rabaul, and ensuing strategic moves needed to be determined. U.S. leaders differed on the strategy for final victory. MacArthur wanted an advance on Japan via the Philippines, while Nimitz wanted to advance more directly across the central Pacific.

After considering each approach, the Joint Chiefs of Staff on 12 March 1944 approved a policy of "two roads to Japan," whereby mutually supporting advances would converge on the Philippines. Later that month Nimitz traveled to Brisbane to meet MacArthur and discuss implementation and coordination of their offensives. The two conferred at MacArthur's headquarters on 26 and 27 March. Agreement was reached on a program that saw MacArthur's forces advancing through the Southwest Pacific while Nimitz's fleet struck westward through the central Pacific.

This coordinated strategy commenced with American landings protected by Nimitz's fleet at Hollandia and Aitape on 22 April 1944, and Australian troops capturing Madang two days later. These moves isolated Wewak and Hansa Bay. A month later MacArthur took Biak. During this period Nimitz's aircraft carriers were targeting Japanese airfields in island groups to reduce opposition to Allied advances.

From March 1944, Task Force 72's patrol areas moved farther west through waters between western New Guinea and the Dutch East Indies to Mindanao in the Philippines where, in Davao Gulf, the Japanese had a forward fleet base. Brisbane submarines were now operating close to areas patrolled by Christie's Fremantle submarines. As a result, Task Force 72's operations were integrated more closely with those of Task Force 71, with Rear Admiral Christie exercising a more unified command.

Brisbane's submarines were also closely supporting the Allies' advances. Their role involved blockading enemy ports to intercept escaping merchant shipping or warships sailing to attack landing forces. When aircraft carriers struck deep within enemy waters at Palau, five Task Force 72 submarines were in positions to support the operation. An unusual role that the submarines played in the invasion of Hollandia was deception: leaving empty life rafts to drift ashore, implying that a reconnaissance party had landed.[1]

Dace (Commander Claggett) came to this operation directly from the "Blue" Harris special mission near Hollandia. On 31 March 1944, *Dace* was off Davao Gulf awaiting enemy shipping. Aircraft patrols kept her submerged much of the day. Once a twin-engine bomber attacked, but *Dace* was undamaged. On 5 April a Japanese aircraft carrier passed too far away for an attack. The next day *Dace* attacked three speeding cruisers, but her torpedoes missed. *Bashaw* also sighted the aircraft carrier, and *Darter* and *Scamp* saw the cruisers, but none was able to close to attack.

After being driven off by the cruisers' escorts, *Scamp* (Comdr. J. Hollingsworth) surfaced in daylight to send a contact report. A Japanese seaplane surprised her and dropped a bomb close to her port side, sending the submarine out of control to 320 feet. Eventually the crew brought the boat under control, and they surfaced that night. After repairing the radio they called for help. *Dace*, sent by Captain Haines, escorted the listing *Scamp* for six days on the surface to Milne Bay. After docking, *Scamp* left for the United States and more repairs on 22 April 1944. *Dace* reached New Farm on 13 May for leave.

Task Force 72 now found the enemy using new tactics. Convoys, frequently supported by aircraft, hugged island coasts with escorts to seaward. The land made detection by radar or sight difficult. Also, the shallower coastal water hindered attacks and evasion. The many small transport craft merited only risky gun attacks. Still, surprise attacks with more and heavier deck guns became more common. In two actions in March 1944, *Gato* destroyed an 870-ton freighter and two trawlers by gunfire off northwestern New Guinea. Three weeks later *Scamp*'s deck gun failed after she set a 200-ton trawler afire off Davao. During her first war patrol, *Bashaw* (Comdr. R. E. Nichols) sank one 60-ton trawler and damaged three others in a "battle surface" attack.

One of Task Force 72's new submarines was *Bluegill* (Lt. Comdr. E. L. Barr). Barr was fearlessly aggressive, inspiring the same zeal in his crew: "I went out there to sink ships. . . . I'd lost too many shipmates, too many classmates, too many friends. . . . After the commissioning ceremony I said, 'We're going to get this ship's nose bloody,' and we did."[2]

Hugh Story, a junior officer, later outlined *Bluegill*'s delivery voyage and first patrol: "We departed San Salvador, Galapagos Island, February 25, 1944, and arrived Milne Bay March 27th. . . . We departed Milne Bay 1 April and proceeded to Langemak, New Guinea, to top up our fuel supply. Departed on first war patrol 3 April. First war patrol lasted sixty-eight days, sunk Japanese cruiser *Yubari* and two freighters, *Asosan Maru* and *Miyaura Maru*, sixty-eight depth charges. As we started down the east coast of Australia the seas really got rough, and after two months of tranquil seas there was a fair amount of queasiness aboard as we approached Brisbane. Tied up at New Farm Wharf 7 June."[3]

Lt. Comdr. E. L. Barr displays *Bluegill*'s battle flag
in Brisbane at the end of her first war patrol.
Official U.S. Navy photo, courtesy of H. Story

The sinking of *Yubari* resulted from an "ultra" message received on 26 April 1944. Barr was informed that a Japanese cruiser was carrying troops to Sonsorol in the Caroline Islands. Located by radar before dawn next day, *Yubari* passed too far from *Bluegill* and disembarked the troops. Barr stalked *Yubari* and later made an attack, firing six torpedoes. Three hit, and *Yubari* sank. *Bluegill* was depth-charged but eventually escaped.

After two years of disappointment, *Yubari*'s destruction showed that American torpedoes and directions based on "ultra" intelligence worked. A further "ultra" success came to another Brisbane submarine two months later.

Darter (Comdr. D. H. McClintock) was patrolling west of Morotai on 29 June 1944. An "ultra" advised that an important ship was nearby "with VIPs aboard." That afternoon *Darter* sighted a large minelayer escorted by two submarine chasers and a patrol aircraft. McClintock fired six torpedoes for two hits, sinking the new 4,000-ton *Tsugaru*. Her escorts counterattacked, and although McClintock found maneuvering difficult in the strong current, *Darter* escaped at extreme depth.[4]

American submarines now had reliable torpedoes and radar. Experienced officers and senior sailors led them, and they were well served with decryption intelligence. However, the waters between northern New Guinea and Mindanao did not present easy targets. This area was now the front line, and heavily escorted Japanese ships moved with extreme caution.

Between March and August 1944, Brisbane's submarines sank sixteen enemy ships by torpedo and additional small craft by gunfire. The most successful boat was *Bluegill,* sinking six ships in two patrols, but others found enemy shipping elusive and enemy air patrols strong.

One submarine suffering disappointing patrols was *Flounder.* Her experience became more common as Japanese shipping was driven from the seas or imprisoned in guarded ports. *Flounder*'s crew had painted their namesake fish on the bow, and when they returned from patrol, the fish would show either a smile if *Flounder* had been successful or tears if no ships had been sunk.[5] On her first three patrols between March and October 1944, *Flounder* sank only one ship. Her first patrol of fifty-four days into the Halmaheras brought numerous aircraft sightings, restricting her freedom of movement, but few shipping contacts. Assigned to Davao Gulf in her second patrol, *Flounder* sank *Nipponkai Maru* (2,681 tons) on 17 June but was depth-charged in return. Later she was surprised on the surface and damaged by enemy aircraft. After repairs in Brisbane, *Flounder* embarked on a third patrol that included lifeguarding, but few enemy ships were seen, and only one attack (unsuccessful) was made in sixty-one days at sea.

The Admiralty Islands assault gave the Allies Manus Island's spacious Seeadler Harbor. Northwest of the Bismarcks and just 2 degrees south of the Equator, Seeadler Harbor provided an ideal anchorage for assembling invasion convoys to continue the offensive westward.

Japanese forces in the Admiralties strongly resisted the landings, and it was almost two weeks before Seeadler Harbor was safe for shipping. Organized resistance did not end until late March 1944, and isolated fighting continued afterward. Once Seeadler Harbor was secured, forward base units and facilities moved there from Milne Bay.

With forces about to land in Biak, *Euryale* arrived in Seeadler Harbor on 28 May 1944. This brought *Euryale* six hundred nautical miles closer to the front line and gave submarines clear ocean to traverse to their patrol areas, saving them the hazards of narrow waters in the hostile Bismarck Archipelago.

Euryale with two submarines in Seeadler Harbor,
Manus Island, May 1944.
U.S. National Archives, Record Group 80-G, 380204

Preceding *Euryale* into Seeadler Harbor was *Coucal,* which arrived in mid-March 1944. *Coucal* proved useful in the combat zone, towing barges to Seeadler Harbor and carrying American casualties and Japanese prisoners on her return trips. For two days she supported American troops on two islands by shelling enemy positions. During April and May her divers assisted in repairing Allied ships and inspected a Japanese wreck. She also carried on her routine duties supporting submarines and built a rest camp in Seeadler Harbor.

Darter also preceded *Euryale* into Seeadler Harbor, arriving there on 23 May 1944 and mooring alongside *Coucal.* An unusual rest period followed, as Ira King, *Darter*'s communications officer, later explained:

The powers that be neglected to tell us that the island had not been secured. . . . We awaited the arrival of the tender with shooting going on all around us. The Seabees "gave" us an island in the harbor . . . probably one hundred yards by two hundred yards. In a day they put a generator and a reefer [refrigerated container] on the island along with two jeeps and more beer than could be consumed in a year. . . .

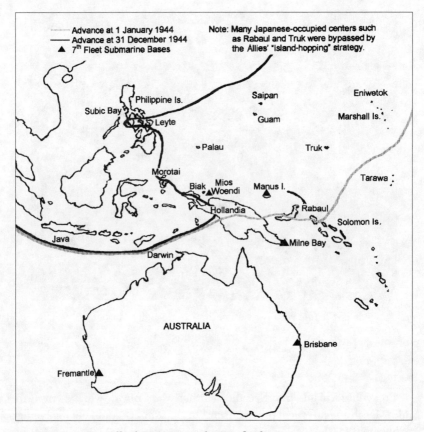

Allied Progress in the Pacific during 1944.

A lot of the ratings wanted souvenirs, so they went over to the army to shoot a few Japs and liberate some Japanese trinkets. Another officer and I frequented the airstrip and took a couple of rides in B24 Liberators and bombed Palau and the Philippines. That was our R&R.[6]

After capturing Aitape and Hollandia, MacArthur's forces landed at Biak on 27 May, then at Noemfoor a month later. These advances were coordinated with those in the central Pacific at Saipan on 15 June and Guam on 21 July. The Saipan assault brought a response from the Japanese fleet. The ensuing Battle of the Philippine Sea saw more than three hundred Japanese aircraft destroyed in what the Americans called the "Great Marianas Turkey Shoot," and three enemy aircraft carriers sunk.

These moves involved Task Force 72 in blockading enemy ports, lying along enemy intervention or escape routes, and lifeguarding. The most successful lifeguarding operation of a Task Force 72 submarine occurred between 2 and 21 July 1944 during Fifth Air Force raids on Yap in the Caroline Islands when *Guavina* rescued twelve aircrew.

While Task Force 72's forward echelon was advancing in New Guinea, the rear echelon continued in an active role. On 27 March 1944, after taking charge of Task Force 72, Captain Haines moved headquarters from *Euryale* back to Brisbane, closer to the Seventh Fleet's headquarters and the Submarine Repair Unit's well-established facilities.

Despite Task Force 72's reduced strength, American submarine numbers in the western Pacific were increasing. Now with spare capacity, Brisbane's repair facilities would also be used by submarines from other commands. So submarine entries to South Brisbane Dry Dock in 1944 matched those for 1943.

Stores, torpedoes, and personnel came to New Farm Wharf on tenders from the United States. The first to arrive after *Fulton* moved to Milne Bay was *Orion*, calling on Christmas Eve 1943 en route to Fremantle. *Euryale* called in March 1944 before taking over at Milne Bay, and a familiar profile arrived on 22 April when *Griffin* berthed at New Farm Wharf en route to Fremantle.

Other personnel and stores came to Brisbane aboard transport vessels, but not necessarily directly. Warren Shaw, gunner's mate, traveled to Australia during 1944 aboard a Liberty ship. The freighter left San Francisco for Milne Bay, then to Hollandia and finally to Sydney. From there Shaw traveled to Brisbane, spending a few months attached to the armory before moving to Fremantle.[7]

Squadron 18 submarines visited Brisbane regularly for refit, dry docking, and two weeks' liberty for their crews. They called after every second patrol, or when significant repairs were required.

Brisbane was also convenient for resting and refitting some submarines from Pearl Harbor supporting aircraft carrier offensives in the western Pacific. For these boats a Brisbane refit was regarded as a real favor. *Pollack*'s patrol report rises above formal expression when it records on 27 August 1944, "Received glad tidings that we were to be routed to Brisbane."[8]

The first visiting submarine refitted in Brisbane was a Brisbane alumnus, *Silversides* (Lt. Comdr. J. S. Coye), which arrived on 8 April 1944. She was followed three days later by *Tunny*, badly damaged by a near-miss bomb off Palau.

Silversides spent two and a half weeks in Brisbane, then sailed on a patrol that added luster to her already brilliant record. *Silversides* sank three vessels of a convoy on 10 May 1944 and dispatched another three ships before the end of the month. Days later, with two torpedoes remaining, Coye guided a "wolf pack" to two more convoys before turning for home.

Two more Pearl Harbor submarines arrived about a month later. *Mingo* (Lt. Comdr. J. Staley), transferring from Pearl Harbor to Fremantle, was delayed in Brisbane with engine trouble. *Seahorse* (Lieutenant Commander Cutter), another successful boat, sank four ships on her next patrol departing Brisbane on 3 June 1944. Paul Snyder said of Cutter, "He was a rare individual . . . a football hero and a gifted musician . . . gentle, humorous, highly intelligent, and able to fight physically and mentally when called upon—and, as my wife says, 'a handsome cuss also.'"[9]

After a relaxed rest period, *Seahorse* sailed to take up a blockade and reporting position for the American invasion of Saipan in mid-June 1944. On the fifteenth, *Seahorse* shadowed the Japanese battle fleet all day, reporting their movements. Another submarine, *Flying Fish* (Lt. Comdr. R. D. Risser), shadowed the Japanese aircraft carrier force on the same day farther north. Reports from these two submarines enabled American aircraft carriers to defeat them four days later in the "Great Marianas Turkey Shoot." Following this battle, *Flying Fish* also came to Brisbane for four weeks to rest her crew and refit the boat.

As new submarines joined the fight, older S-boats became available for antisubmarine training. Between April and July 1944, *S42*, *S45*, and *S47* joined the Seventh Fleet to help train air and surface antisubmarine units. All were assigned to Task Force 72, based with *Euryale* at Milne Bay and, later, Seeadler Harbor. Their duties were unspectacular but necessary. Nevertheless, there were occasional operations, and *S42* and *S47* each conducted a low-risk special mission from Manus Island.[10]

While the war was swinging in the Allies' favor and Japanese forces were being driven farther away from Australia, the danger of "friendly" attack continued. On 16 August 1944 *Seawolf* was attacked (though not damaged) by an Allied bomber. A further danger developed in 1944 as the Allies relaxed the convoy system in quieter waters and Allied merchant vessels sailed independently. Submarines on the surface came under fire from merchant ships whose crews acted on the principle of "shoot first, ask questions later." *S38* was shelled by a merchant ship off New Caledonia on 21 April 1944. Three weeks later an American Liberty ship fired at *Bream* on passage from Brisbane to Milne Bay. Neither submarine was hit.[11]

In July 1944 Brisbane hosted top-level talks. The two Pacific submarine force commanders, Vice Admiral Lockwood at Pearl Harbor and Rear Admiral Christie at Fremantle, had not met face to face since February 1943. With the war moving westward, their patrol areas were coming closer together, and there was an urgent need for a coordinated strategy and common understanding on a wide range of issues.

The admirals arrived in Brisbane with their staffs on 5 July 1944. Christie and all Lockwood's staff preferred Perth, while Lockwood did not want to leave Pearl Harbor. Brisbane was the compromise location. Daytime discussions and evening social functions saw the agenda completed. By 8 July, agreement had been reached on a wide spectrum of subjects including patrol areas, communications frequencies, location of forward bases, rotation of boats, and deployment of crews and spare parts.[12]

The issue that more than any other affected Task Force 72 was the location of forward bases. The submarine advanced bases needed to move with the Allies' front. At the time of the conference, the latest conquests were Biak in the Southwest Pacific area and Saipan in the central Pacific. Both were suitable for advanced bases, and Lockwood planned to move a tender to Saipan as soon as possible, while Christie would move one to Biak. *Holland* arrived at Saipan late in July, while *Orion* anchored at Mios Woendi, near Biak, on 26 August.

These developments had a direct effect on Task Force 72. Mios Woendi was sufficiently west to be used by Fremantle submarines as well. In addition, *Orion* was part of Task Force 71. Once she arrived at Mios Woendi, there would be no need for *Euryale* at Seeadler Harbor. The move would further integrate the operations of Task Force 72 submarines with those from Fremantle, as Brisbane submarines would now proceed on patrol through Mios Woendi or Darwin, both Fremantle forward bases.

Euryale remained at Seeadler Harbor until 11 August 1944, when she weighed anchor for Brisbane, arriving five days later. Awaiting her at New Farm Wharf was *Orion,* on passage to Mios Woendi. For the next three days the two tenders transferred equipment and stores, then *Orion* steamed north. *Euryale* left Brisbane the next day for Fremantle.

By late August 1944, Task Force 72 no longer had a tender, and its fleet-submarines had been reduced to only six of Squadron 18. *Coucal* transferred to Darwin on 12 August, where she continued to support Brisbane submarines passing through.

Although Task Force 72's front-line strength had declined, it still included three S-boats on training duties. In addition, submarines used for special missions to the Philippines were now transferred to the Brisbane command. These missions were pioneered from Brisbane, but later the submarines were based at Fremantle, operating through Darwin.

With the arrival of British submarines in Fremantle and increasing numbers of American boats, that port's accommodation was stretched to the limit. Brisbane had spare capacity, and they could still operate through Darwin. In addition, Cairncross Dock's completion in June 1944 enabled *Narwhal* and *Nautilus,* fully employed on Philippine special missions, to be fully refitted in Brisbane. The first Philippines submarine to refit in Brisbane was *Seawolf,* arriving on 23 August 1944.

20
PHILIPPINE "SPY SQUADRON"

"I shall return"—Gen. Douglas MacArthur's simple words reverberated around the world and down the years. He had escaped from Corregidor to carry on the battle from Australia. Returning to the Philippines became his unswerving goal and "I shall return" an inspiration to Americans and Filipinos alike.

Gudgeon (Lt. Comdr. W. Stovall) sailed from Brisbane on 27 December 1942, marking the first active step in fulfilling MacArthur's promise. On board were Maj. Jesus Villamor, six other Filipinos, and a ton of supplies including weapons, a radio, money, medicines, candy, and cigarettes.

After Corregidor's surrender on 6 May 1942, escaping personnel as well as radio messages told of guerrilla groups throughout the islands. In October that year, as the Japanese hunted these "bandits," the Allied Intelligence Bureau (AIB) set up a Philippines subsection to aid and organize guerrillas.

In early December, MacArthur directed his senior intelligence officer to dispatch a group to the islands to ascertain the situation and set up an intelligence organization. The group would organize a radio network for internal communication and link with Darwin, using an Australian-developed powerful battery radio small enough to fit through the submarine hatch when broken into four components. They would also contact prominent local citizens and organize military action and sabotage. It was a daunting assignment for Jesus Villamor and his six former messboys.

Villamor already had a distinguished record as a fighter and a leader. He had led a squadron of obsolete fighters into action over Luzon and had sailed a small boat from Manila to escape to Australia. He eagerly accepted leadership of Operation Planet and reported to the Tabragalba training camp. Over the next three intensive weeks of training, Villamor and his party practiced the skills of guerrilla fighters and intelligence operatives. They also worked hard to assume their cover identities as farmers down from the hills.

Early on 27 December the party arrived at New Farm Wharf to toil with *Gudgeon's* crew loading supplies. But at day's end, the working party stayed on board. Their supplies were already there. The operation was on.[1]

At night on 13 January 1943, Stovall closed the coast of Negros, but lights ashore forced the landing's postponement. The next night all seemed well, and Villamor crammed his men and their equipment into two rafts. As the party paddled toward land, *Gudgeon* resumed her patrol.

A month after leaving Brisbane, Villamor made radio contact with Australia, establishing his mission's success. *Gudgeon* sank no enemy vessels on this patrol, but on 9 February Stovall rescued twenty-one Australians, one Englishman, one Portuguese, and five Timorese from enemy-occupied Timor.

When MacArthur returned to the Philippines in 1944, he acknowledged "the enormous volume of valuable military information sent by the various guerrilla units . . . [and] . . . those great patriots both Filipino and American who had led and supported the resistance movement." The general continued:

> Through the understanding assistance of our navy I was able to send in by submarine, in driblets at first, arms, ammunition, and medical supplies. News of the first shipment spread rapidly throughout the Philippines to electrify the people . . . that America had neither abandoned them nor forgotten them.
>
> Since then, as resources increased, I was enabled . . . to send vitally needed supplies in ever increasing quantities . . . by four submarines finally committed exclusively to that purpose.[2]

This last reference was to SpyRon, the so-called Spy Squadron. *Gudgeon* was the first of nineteen submarines to make the hazardous trip in support of the Philippines guerrillas. Initially the navy was reluctant to divert any of its few submarines from their primary mission, but senior naval staff officers appreciated the importance of intelligence received from the partisans, so they provided boats (in the words of "Chick" Parsons,

The two mainstays of SpyRon's Philippines service, *Nautilus*
(left, with fleet submarine *Gabilan* outboard) and *Narwhal*
at New Farm Wharf in December 1944.
Courtesy of L. L. Cottman

the U.S. officer who liaised with the guerrillas) "with more frequency than
I had ever dreamed possible."[3]

As new fleet-boats swelled submarine numbers, older submarines could
be released from war patrols. The first assigned exclusively to Philippines
special missions were the old giants *Narwhal* and *Nautilus*. Their size, combined with sluggish maneuverability, detracted from their performance in a
combat role but suited them to supply missions. Later in the war the veteran *Seawolf* and *Stingray* joined SpyRon.

Just days after Villamor sailed on *Gudgeon*, Lt. Comdr. "Chick" Parsons,
USNR, made the first of many wartime appearances in Brisbane. Before
the war, Parsons had traveled all over the Philippines mastering several
dialects as he rose to the presidency of the Luzon Stevedoring Company.
Steeped in Philippines culture and languages and with a stocky build and
brown complexion, Parsons could mingle and travel easily in the islands.
After months in occupied Manila, Parsons and his family had been repatri-
ated to the United States.

MacArthur wanted an American's assessment of the situation in the
occupied Philippines and assigned Parsons to contact self-styled "General"

Wendell Fertig on Mindanao. Fertig, with years of experience in the islands, was the first guerrilla leader to radio compliance with MacArthur's conditions for recognition. Parsons was to deliver supplies and confer with him.

On 5 March, Parsons's party landed from *Tambor* (Lt. Comdr. S. Ambruster) on Mindanao's south coast. To Fertig's group they delivered U.S. $10,000 in pesos, ammunition, and other stores. During his conference with "General" Fertig, Chick delivered the rank badges of a full colonel and reiterated MacArthur's message: "There are no generals in the Philippines guerrilla army." Parsons then left to visit other groups. At the end of July he reappeared in Brisbane.[4]

Narwhal (Comdr. F. Latta) berthed at New Farm on 2 October 1943 to begin regular deliveries to Philippine guerrillas. During refit, all reload torpedoes and their handling gear were removed and their place taken by ninety-two tons of ammunition and stores. On 13 November, Chick Parsons and his nine men took half of this ashore seventy-five miles south of Manila. Colonel Fertig received the remaining forty-six tons two days later. The return trip brought to Darwin thirty-two evacuees including eight women, one baby, and two other small children.

This summary understates the hazards faced during this pioneering patrol. Eighteen days out, Parsons first experienced submarine combat. One of *Narwhal*'s officers, Robert Griffiths, later explained:

> On receiving a message that a large tanker with escorts was proceeding eastwards through Mindanao Sea, we delayed slightly so as to contact it at night. . . . We fired four torpedoes for no hits. In return we took about a dozen depth charges, none close. We surfaced to get away and were chased into what looked like a blind alley. When we asked Chick Parsons if he recognized the surrounding mountain peaks, he said, "Yes, keep going, straight ahead." With the Jap patrol boat chasing us, the captain ordered "emergency speed." . . . We circled around Siquijor Island and came out between Siquijor and Negros. As a result of this escape the captain (who was a religious man) named the engines Matthew, Mark, Luke, and John. Their names were painted on the engines.[5]

At the height of the chase the engineering officer called the bridge: "Captain, if we don't slow down pretty soon, we're not going to have any engines left." With enemy shells splashing him, Latta replied, "If we slow down we won't need those damn engines."[6]

The first drop-off was made without incident, and *Narwhal* continued to Mindanao to deliver supplies to Fertig's guerrillas. As Robert Griffiths explained:

> We observed the security signals on the beach, which were two white sheets. . . . We met a motor launch with friendly guerrillas and . . . started up the Agusan River. We had a Filipino pilot aboard who didn't speak English, and we didn't know Spanish. So in spite of Chick acting as interpreter, we ran aground at one point, and had visions of becoming guerrillas ourselves. . . . We got afloat in ten to fifteen minutes. Continuing up the river, we soon circled 'round to tie up at a small wooden dock built especially to receive us. As we approached, the Filipino band began playing "Star-Spangled Banner" and other favorite American military music. It was a tremendous thrill to hear such music right in the middle of enemy territory. . . . The unloading took about four hours.[7]

Despite the welcome, *Narwhal* never attempted to enter the river again, and future cargoes were unloaded onto a barge.

Mary Maynard, then a nine-year-old girl, was among those who boarded *Narwhal* that night. After subsisting on local foods, the taste of fresh sandwiches brought back memories of home, and on board, the children were treated royally. There were tears from both sides as they disembarked in Darwin.[8]

Narwhal's return journey was typical of all her SpyRon missions. Upon emerging from Surigao Strait into the Pacific all her passengers became seasick, but the voyage was otherwise uneventful.

With Fremantle being closer to the Philippines, many SpyRon missions sailed from there. Then, as Darwin became safer, the northern town embarked and landed passengers and supplies.

Highlights of SpyRon's operations included smuggling millions of pesos' worth of counterfeit Japanese occupation currency into the Philippines, supporting the guerrillas' operations and devaluing Japanese money. Along with fighting materiel, the submarines delivered medicines and luxuries like chocolate and cigarettes.

Further positive results came from Parsons's "Padre Kits." The overwhelmingly Catholic Philippines produced neither wheat nor grapes, so very soon after the occupation cut off altar bread and wine supplies, priests began celebrating Mass using wine measured out with a dropper and slivers of Hosts. Parsons then "contacted the head man of the Catholic

Propaganda Matchbox Cover.
Courtesy of L. L. Cottman

Church in Australia." Soon submarines were delivering four-gallon sealed kerosene tins containing bottles of Mass wine and wheat flour. Religious medals filled any spaces.

Bowfin (Comdr. J. Willingham), commissioned 1 May 1943, reached Brisbane in August for voyage repairs and final indoctrination. Before sailing on her first patrol, she took on weapons and ammunition, radios, medicines, and counterfeit pesos. On 2 September the submarine began unloading her cargo for Fertig's Moros off Mindanao. Willingham proudly offered refreshments: thickly sliced ham on fresh bread, pie, and coffee. He was shocked when Fertig's men tossed the ham overboard. A quiet word from Fertig ensured that *Bowfin* never again served pork to Muslims.

In all, forty-one SpyRon missions to the Philippines delivered more than 330 agents and 1,325 tons of supplies. More than 470 passengers made the return trip to Australia. Nineteen submarines took part, with *Narwhal, Nautilus,* and *Stingray* undertaking the lion's share of the missions.[9]

On 21 September 1944, a month before MacArthur fulfilled his promise of returning to the Philippines, *Seawolf* (Lt. Comdr. A. Bontier) sailed from Brisbane. In fourteen patrols since the beginning of the Pacific War, *Seawolf* had covered herself in glory. Now the veteran boat was on her second SpyRon mission. At Manus Island *Seawolf* topped up on fuel, took aboard a seventeen-man army reconnaissance party and ten tons of supplies, then sailed to land them on Samar, north of MacArthur's planned invasion island of Leyte.

At 7:56 AM on 3 October, *Seawolf* exchanged recognition signals with *Narwhal*. Both vessels were in a safety lane where U.S. forces were forbidden to attack any submarine unless it was positively identified as enemy. Ten minutes later, just over the horizon, the Japanese submarine *RO-41* torpedoed the destroyer escort USS *Shelton*. Her sister ship, *Richard M. Rowell* (Comdr. H. A. Barnard, Jr.), stood by.

Three hours later, an aircraft from the carrier *Midway* sighted a submarine in the safety lane and dropped two bombs as the boat submerged. *Rowell* raced in, and at 1:10 PM her sonar registered a contact. As the escort prepared to attack, the sonar operator reported that his instrument was receiving dots and dashes from the submarine. Dismissing these signals as an attempt to jam his sonar, Barnard pressed on with his forward-firing Hedgehog mortar, whose charges exploded only on hitting the target. At 1:16 PM, after the second pattern of twenty-four projectiles had been fired, *Rowell*'s log recorded, "Three explosions heard. Two large boils [bubbles] observed off port beam. Debris observed in the boils."[10]

Four submarines were in the safety lane at the time. Urgent calls to report their positions brought responses from three, but *Seawolf* was never heard from again. *RO-41* escaped.

Two days later an inquiry into the incident was held at Manus Island. The finding was that *Rowell* had sunk *Seawolf*. Barnard was censured for not having made positive efforts to identify his target in the safety lane before dismissing the sound signals and attacking.

So famous *Seawolf*, which had survived many enemy attacks, became a victim of the "friendly" fire that so concerned American submariners throughout the war. One of the United States' own ships sent *Seawolf*, with her eighty-two crew and seventeen passengers, ninety-six hundred feet down to the ocean floor.

21
FINAL SUCCESS

The two Pacific offensives converged on 15 September 1944 with assaults on Morotai and Palau, only five hundred miles apart. The Allied drive now pointed at the Philippines. American aircraft raids prior to the landings attracted less opposition than expected. As a result, Admiral Halsey proposed, and General MacArthur immediately agreed, that the Allies' next step be directly to the Philippines. It was a bold move, striking at Leyte in the central Philippines, bypassing Mindanao, and cutting two months off the war.

A strong Japanese reaction was expected, as the Philippines stood directly between Japan and its source of oil, rubber, and other raw materials in the East Indies and Southeast Asia. Although Japan's aircraft carrier force had been reduced at the Battle of the Philippine Sea, its intact surface fleet of battleships and heavy cruisers posed a serious threat to invasion convoys.

As the Allies rapidly progressed through their island possessions, Japan anticipated that a strike in their inner defensive perimeter was only a matter of time, and they prepared a plan, "Sho Go," for implementation when this occurred. Invading the Philippines was one possibility envisaged.

To meet this threat, all American Pacific naval forces concentrated to support the assault, with Kinkaid's Seventh Fleet supporting the landings and Halsey's Third Fleet covering out to sea. The operation, planned in the greatest secrecy, was set for 20 October 1944.

Forty submarines would be deployed around the Philippines and Japan and in the southern approaches to Leyte. Of Task Force 72's six fleet-submarines, *Bashaw, Flounder,* and *Guavina* were in Brisbane during the invasion and *Cero* was on a SpyRon mission. Only two Brisbane submarines, *Dace* and *Darter,* participated in this great endeavor.

Darter and *Dace* ended their third patrols with Task Force 72 on 8 and 12 August 1944 respectively. Both refitted and were docked while their crews enjoyed two weeks' leave. They left Brisbane on 1 September for a scheduled two-month war patrol. For the next five days they exercised with the corvettes HMAS *Warrnambool* and *Whyalla.* They topped up their fuel from *Coucal* at Darwin on 10 September, then entered enemy waters.

Dace's captain was Comdr. B. D. Claggett. His considerable combat experience since 1941 included patrols against German U-boats and Pacific operations on *Guardfish* and *Pargo.* He had concentrated on training his crew as an effective fighting team. He was also a gracious and considerate captain, showing concern for his men, and they had great respect for him.[1]

Comdr. D. H. McClintock was captain of *Darter.* He was a veteran of nine war patrols conducted since his submarine was strafed off Hawaii on Pearl Harbor day. A crewman described him as "a good disciplinarian. A man of few words, yet you just knew that when he said something he knew what he was talking about, and meant it."[2]

McClintock and Claggett graduated from the Naval Academy in 1935, but McClintock was marginally senior to Claggett. In this patrol, *Darter* and *Dace* would operate most of the time together as a two-boat "wolf pack" with McClintock in charge.

Their initial mission was to join a submarine patrol line across the Celebes Sea in support of the Morotai and Palau assaults. Both *Darter* and *Dace* registered numerous aircraft contacts and were frequently forced to submerge, but no enemy ships were seen.

In late September both submarines called at Mios Woendi to replenish fuel and stores alongside *Orion.* After leaving together on 1 October 1944, *Dace* had to return for minor repairs, but *Darter* continued, passing near newly recaptured Morotai on the third. This coincided with the sinking of USS *Shelton.* Although *Darter* was in the safety lane, she was menaced by carrier aircraft and two destroyers. Eventually McClintock, who stayed on the surface, satisfied them of *Darter*'s identity and continued. *Seawolf* was not so lucky.

On 10 October, *Darter* and *Dace* met to patrol their area, Balabec Strait between Borneo and Palawan, and Palawan Passage—a narrow channel along the west of 250-mile-long Palawan Island. Bounding the passage's west was a broad, unsurveyed area of reefs called Dangerous Ground. At its narrowest, Palawan Passage is only twenty-five miles wide.

Two days later, *Darter* detected seven southbound vessels with two escorts. McClintock maneuvered for three hours, then fired four torpedoes. Hits were heard. That night the submarines met to plan their next move.

Dace relocated the convoy just before midnight the following night. One of her officers, Harry Caldwell, recalled what happened: "*Dace*, in a night surface attack, fired ten torpedoes for four hits resulting in two ships sunk and one heavily damaged. The action was enlivened by number 3 torpedo, which circled. While the ship control team struggled to sidestep the erratic torpedo, the fire control party tried to concentrate on shooting the seven remaining torpedoes at selected targets. Both submarines departed the scene at high speed in order to reach deep water by dawn."[3]

It had not been straightforward, but *Dace* had sunk *Eikyo Maru* and *Nittetsu Maru* and heavily damaged *Taizen Maru*, totaling 18,337 tons. Task Force 72 had come a long way in its convoy battles since the lean months of 1943.

Unknown to *Darter* and *Dace*, great events were unfolding to the east and south. While they were attacking their convoy, Allied assault convoys were bound for the Philippines. At 8 AM on 17 October 1944, Allied cruisers commenced bombarding enemy positions at Leyte Gulf, and the Japanese high command activated "Sho 1," their response to landings in the Philippines.

The Japanese navy made ready for sea at Singapore and in Japan. From Japan would come their aircraft carrier force—only a shadow since being decimated in the Marianas four months earlier. Their role would be to lure Allied forces away from guarding the Leyte beachhead.

Japan's strongest force was the battleships, heavy cruisers, and destroyers near Singapore. This fleet had proved itself a formidable fighting force in all surface battles and was little diminished from when Japan entered the war. It now comprised seven battleships, including *Yamato* and *Musashi*, the largest battleships ever built, eleven heavy cruisers, two light cruisers, and nineteen destroyers.

Commanded by Vice Adm. T. Kurita in the heavy cruiser *Atago*, this mighty fleet sailed on 18 October 1944 for Leyte Gulf. It fueled at Brunei Bay and split into two groups, a Southern Attack Force of the two oldest battleships, one heavy cruiser, and four destroyers, and a formidable Center Force comprising the remaining thirty-two warships. Both forces left Brunei on 22 October to approach Leyte by different routes.

On 19 October, *Darter* and *Dace* sighted two destroyers in Palawan Passage, apparently carrying out an antisubmarine sweep. When they met that night, the two captains considered whether the destroyer sweep heralded some movement of larger warships.

The next morning American troops stormed ashore at Leyte Gulf. That afternoon General MacArthur waded ashore to announce, "People of the Philippines, I have returned." His unswerving goal maintained through two and a half years of exile had been achieved. For security reasons, no warning of the Philippine assault had been given to submarine captains. The first inkling Darter and Dace received of these events came by radio that night—ironically, from Tokyo Rose. Ira King, Darter's communications officer, recalled hearing the news: "We were practically out of food and out of fuel . . . and were about to depart the area and return to Perth. We heard a broadcast from Tokyo Rose stating that the Americans had landed in Leyte and they would all die. . . . We had received no such information from our own forces, but Dave [McClintock] said we'd better stick around for a day or two and see if anything came up the slot [Palawan Passage] from the south."[4]

That night Vice Admiral Lockwood and Rear Admiral Christie advised their submarines of the Leyte landings and issued orders. First priority would be to report any enemy fleet movements, and only after this were they permitted to attack.

Just before midnight on 21/22 October 1944, Darter's new, sophisticated SG surface-search radar detected three targets at a range of twenty-six thousand yards. Darter chased at top speed through the dark, sending two contact reports to Christie and eleven to Dace, farther north. However, the enemy warships were faster, leaving Darter farther behind as morning approached. Dace made a high-speed dash to intercept at dawn but saw nothing, as the Japanese had turned away.

This squadron of six ships was not moving to attack American landing forces but was transporting troops to the front line. Other submarines farther north kept watch, and the next evening Bream torpedoed the cruiser Aoba, crippling her for the remainder of the war.

The next night Darter and Dace met while their captains consulted by megaphone. At sixteen minutes past midnight on 23 October, as they cruised together, Darter's radar operator reported numerous contacts about thirty thousand yards to the south, adding that it was probably a rain squall. Looking at the screen himself, McClintock disagreed: "Rain squall hell, those are enemy ships!"[5]

For the second night the submarines began a high-speed dash to close and identify the enemy vessels and then attack. At first they could barely keep pace, but during the night the Japanese squadron reduced speed, allowing *Darter* and *Dace* to reach a favorable position ahead.

As they rushed through the night *Darter*, as senior ship, sent contact reports to Christie, with the final one identifying a "large task force of eleven heavy ships." This was the major Japanese force, and *Darter*'s reports were all relayed to Admirals Halsey and Kinkaid by 6:20 AM. It was their first news in a week of the main Japanese force, and it allowed Halsey to position his aircraft carriers to attack the Japanese the next day.

The Japanese also heard *Darter*'s signals, and at 3 AM Kurita warned his ships to be on their guard against American submarines signaling nearby.[6] Ira King, as communications officer, was responsible for these messages: "I encrypted a message, and it was receipted for by the navy in Washington, D.C. It was addressed to 'Any ship or station' for retransmission. In any event, when the Japanese heard us transmit they always came on the air and receipted for our message in an attempt to deceive us into believing it was delivered. That was standard practice. All radiomen could tell a Japanese 'fist' from an Allied one."[7]

Lt. Comdr. R. C. Benitez described the tension aboard *Dace* in the five hours between first sighting and the attack: "The odds were not exactly even but we were more than willing to take the chance. . . . As the night approached its end, however, tension heightened throughout the boat. The jokes became fewer and fewer as the conversation gradually died out. . . . At 0500 the word was passed to man battle stations. It was a useless command. The men during the night had slowly gravitated towards their stations, and in a matter of seconds each man was reported at his appointed place."[8]

Ten minutes later *Darter* dived to an attack position on the west side of the passage. A few minutes later *Dace* also dived five miles to the northeast, where she could attack from the opposite side.

The vast naval strength confronting the submarines was in two columns of heavy warships two nautical miles apart with a column of destroyers a mile farther out on either side. The fleet was in two groups extending more than eight miles in length. Both submarine captains could see only the first group, and each concentrated on the closest column of heavy warships. In the narrow waters this great fleet was limited in its zigzag course. In addition, Admiral Kurita had not positioned destroyers in an antisubmarine screen ahead.

First to attack was McClintock's *Darter*, ahead of the western column comprising three heavy cruisers and the battleship *Nagato*. Conditions were clear and calm as the column approached in the early dawn. McClintock selected the leading cruiser and at 5:32 AM commenced firing *Darter's* six bow torpedoes at 980 yards' range.

As soon as the sixth torpedo had gone, he swung *Darter* to fire four stern torpedoes at the second cruiser. As the first stern torpedo left its tube, the first hit was heard. McClintock described the scene: "Whipped periscope back to first target to see the sight of a lifetime. . . . She was a mass of billowing black smoke from the number one turret to the stern. Bright orange flames shot out from the side along the main deck from the bow to the after turret. Cruiser was already down by the bow, which was dipping under. Number one turret was at water level. She was definitely finished."[9]

With destroyers rushing in, it was time for *Darter* to take evasive action. As the submarine dived deep, further hits were heard on the second cruiser. Four destroyers passed overhead, and five minutes later depth-charging began.

Darter's torpedo explosions were heard aboard *Dace*, and Claggett noted, "*Darter* is really having a field day. Can see great pall of smoke completely enveloping spot where ship was at last look. . . . Ship to left is also smoking badly. . . . It is a great show."[10]

Claggett had little time to enjoy the scene, as the starboard column was rapidly approaching. The first two ships he identified as heavy cruisers, but the third appeared to be larger. Thinking this was a battleship, Claggett selected this vessel, saying, "Let the first two go by, they are only heavy cruisers."[11]

Twenty-two minutes after *Darter* fired her first torpedoes, Claggett commenced firing *Dace's* six bow tubes. At the end of a long patrol, no stern torpedoes remained. Two minutes after firing, the first of four hits was heard, followed at 6:01 AM by two tremendous explosions.

Lieutenant Commander Benitez described the dreadful sound heard inside *Dace*: "On our way down, a crackling noise . . . soon enveloped us. . . . Those of us experienced in submarine warfare knew that a ship was breaking up. . . . Could the Jap be breaking up on top of us? We were making full speed in an attempt to clear the vicinity of the attack, but that crackling noise was still all around us. . . . Then relief came with a rush. We were leaving the noise astern. We not only had hit but had sunk a major Japanese warship."[12]

The heavy cruiser *Atago*, flagship of Admiral Kurita,
sunk by *Darter* on 23 October 1944.
Naval Historical Center photo NH 86889

In minutes the first depth charges exploded nearby. The destroyer counterattack came progressively closer for half an hour. Altogether forty-one depth charges were dropped. Then the Japanese task force hurried away, leaving the submarine to creep away at deep submergence.

They left behind a disaster. *Darter* had scored four hits along the length of Kurita's flagship *Atago*. Ablaze from stem to stern, *Atago* foundered in eighteen minutes, taking 360 crewmen with her. Vice Admiral Kurita was forced to jump into the oily water and swim for his life.

One minute after *Atago* was hit, two torpedoes struck the second heavy cruiser, *Takao*. The first hit flooded three of *Takao*'s boiler rooms while the second blew off her rudder and two of her screws. Thirty-three crewmen were killed and another thirty wounded. Crippled and dead in the water, *Takao* was out of the fight. Also removed from battle were two destroyers ordered to stand by and escort her to safety.

Dace's target was not a battleship, as Claggett had thought, but the heavy cruiser *Maya*. Hit by four torpedoes, *Maya* was shaken by powerful explosions, listed, and sank in only eight minutes. Three hundred and thirty-six crewmen were killed.[13]

There was confusion as the two columns steered clear of the wrecks and increased speed to hurry away. Second in command was Rear Admiral Ugaki, who, seeing his admiral's flagship devastated, immediately took command. Within minutes *Maya*, directly ahead of him, also erupted in a huge explosion, and Ugaki recalled, "When the spray and smoke cleared, nothing of the mighty cruiser remained to be seen."[14] Vice Admiral Kurita, after some minutes in the oily water, was rescued by the destroyer *Kishinami*. He transferred to *Yamato* later and resumed command as his force, depleted but still formidable, continued to Leyte.

Darter's torpedoes were the first shots of the Battle of Leyte Gulf, the biggest and most decisive naval battle of World War II. By destroying Vice Admiral Kurita's flagship, those torpedoes had a profound effect on the following four-day battle. Kurita's command team was scattered when *Atago* sank. Many were killed and the remainder divided among rescuing destroyers. One, *Asashimo,* separated to escort the *Takao* to Brunei.[15] The dislocation of Kurita's communication staff resulted in vital messages between different Japanese forces not being received the next day, hindering coordination. Captain Ohmae, senior staff officer with the Japanese aircraft carrier force, stated, "Four messages were sent on 24th from the Japanese [aircraft carrier] Fleet to Tokyo and [Kurita's] Fleet. They were not received, and I think the lack of success of the entire operation depended on that failure of communication."[16]

In addition, later in the battle Kurita's cruisers engaged a weak American group that stood alone between his fleet and the invasion convoy. Confused and lacking clear information from his forward units and other Japanese forces, and possibly still shaken from having to swim for his life when his flagship was sunk, Kurita broke off the action prematurely and withdrew.

By contrast, *Darter's* sighting reports led to Halsey moving his aircraft carriers to attack Kurita's force on 24 October. Throughout that day waves of aircraft assailed the Japanese warships, sinking the mighty *Musashi*. Vice Admiral Kinkaid, commander of the Seventh Fleet, commended *Darter's* part in this success: "The information, which was promptly transmitted, was the first tangible evidence of the size and magnitude of the forces which the enemy was assembling to dislodge our positions in Leyte. The early receipt of this information enabled our forces to formulate and put into execution the countermeasures which resulted in a major disaster for the Japanese in [the Battle of Leyte Gulf]."[17]

General MacArthur also recognized the importance of *Darter* and *Dace's* action: "Before sunrise on 23 October the first blows of the fateful Battle for Leyte Gulf had been struck, with U.S. submarines performing yeoman service in their running fight with the enemy's large surface units. Not only did the submarines strike the first damaging blows against Admiral Kurita's ships but they alerted all United States forces to the approach of the main Japanese striking force two full days in advance of the final battle."[18]

After the depth-charge attacks, McClintock brought *Darter* to periscope depth to find *Takao* dead in the water with two destroyers and patrolling aircraft protecting her. During the day he approached *Takao* twice but both times was driven off by the escorts.

For *Dace* the depth-charge attacks were more severe, and tension remained high throughout the morning as destroyers continued charging overhead. At 11 AM Claggett looked through his periscope and found nothing in sight. Four hours later *Dace* located *Takao* and her escort. Claggett decided to attack that evening with his four remaining torpedoes.

That night the two captains discussed tactics while recharging batteries. The night was dark and visibility poor, but *Takao*'s crew had started her moving slowly ahead. McClintock and Claggett decided they would make a night attack from positions on either side ahead of the enemy. Both submarines set off at full speed.

Darter sped down the west of Palawan Passage until, at five minutes past midnight on 24 October 1944, she came to an abrupt stop. The bridge watch saw the bow suddenly rear out of the sea as, with a deafening roar and scraping metal, *Darter* came to a halt.[19] Ira King, inside the control room, recalled, "I thought we had been torpedoed. . . . I hit the collision alarm behind my head and for a couple of hours we tried to sally ship [rock the boat free by means of a group of men repeatedly running back and forth between bow and stern], pump fuel, dump stores to lighten ship, but it was hopeless."[20] A couple of minutes later McClintock radioed *Dace*, "We are aground."

Darter had grounded on the edge of Bombay Shoal, a half-mile-wide reef, just an hour before high tide. Overcast skies and constant enemy contact had prevented navigational sights for the past twenty-four hours. In addition, the waters were treacherous, with reefs and swift-flowing currents. *Darter* was not greatly off track when she hit Bombay Shoal. Just one hundred yards east was safe water. *Darter*'s stranding was one of the hazards of wartime operations. It was a calculated risk, but this time the submarine lost.

When he heard *Darter*'s message, Claggett had to decide whether to attack *Takao* or break off pursuit to rescue his teammate. There was little doubt where his priorities lay: he turned away. To his control room Claggett explained, "I went to Annapolis with McClintock, and you all have friends on *Darter*, so we're going over and get them."[21] Claggett's decision was unequivocally supported by Rear Admiral Christie: "There was no chance of getting *Darter* off, but the feat of saving all of her crew from certain capture by the enemy was of far-reaching importance."[22]

The sound of *Darter* hitting the reef had been heard aboard the nearest Japanese destroyer, *Naganami*, which turned toward the noise as *Darter's* crew anxiously watched on their radar. *Darter's* guns were manned to defend the heavily outgunned boat. However, when *Naganami* came to sixty-one hundred yards and saw nothing, she turned away.[23]

Darter's crew fruitlessly tried every means to save their ship. At 1:40 AM *Dace* arrived to find *Darter* "so high that even her screws were out of the water—she seemed like a ship in drydock."[24] It was the top of the tide, and it was obvious that *Darter* would never be refloated.

Despite concerns expressed by McClintock that *Dace* too might strike the reef, Claggett maneuvered *Dace* to one hundred feet off *Darter's* stern and passed a line. After three hours, *Darter's* crew had been safely transferred. Aboard *Darter* all classified material was destroyed, machinery wrecked, and state-of-the-art equipment smashed.

Throughout this period Ira King was busy:

> As communicator I had a multitude of classified material to destroy even though we were on a "reduced" allowance. I started a fire on the control deck and one in the after battery and started burning. . . . The boat was full of smoke, there was a Japanese destroyer less than five miles away, and Dave McClintock and I were the last ones to leave. As we were leaving, dawn was starting to break. He told me to wait a second and ran back and left a picture of the *Atago* on his desk so the Japs knew who sank it. He then picked up a souvenir ashtray, which he promptly dropped on his toe. It was heavy and he limped for days.[25]

At 4:42 AM, with everyone safely aboard, *Dace* cast off to observe the explosion of *Darter's* demolition charges. However, only a dull "pop" was heard. Claggett fired two torpedoes that exploded harmlessly against the reef. Two more failed to damage the stranded vessel. *Dace's* 4-inch deck gun was fired into the wreck, inflicting little apparent damage.

With dawn breaking, a Japanese bomber appeared. *Dace* hurriedly dived, but the aircraft headed toward the stranded *Darter* and dropped its bombs on the reef near her. Later *Naganami* reappeared and sent a boat to inspect the abandoned submarine. With all torpedoes gone, *Dace* could only watch. That night *Dace* returned to *Darter* to put her own demolition charges aboard. However, this plan was aborted when a sonar ping was heard, indicating that an enemy submarine was targeting *Dace*.

Christie ordered *Dace* to Fremantle while another submarine, *Rock*,

Officers of *Darter* and *Dace* in Fremantle after returning from
their success in the Battle of Leyte Gulf.
Courtesy of H. H. Caldwell

was sent to complete the demolition of *Darter.* On 26 October, *Rock* fired
nine torpedoes, which detonated against the reef, leaving *Darter* untouched. Finally *Nautilus,* on a SpyRon mission, destroyed the boat with
her two 6-inch guns on 29 October.

Dace was crowded with two complete submarine crews, 155 men.
Darter survivors occupied every corner, every bunk, and every seat. Meals
were prepared around the clock for the doubled numbers.

As they moved south submerged, the air inside *Dace* deteriorated rapidly. However, once through Lombok Strait, *Dace* traveled on the surface.
The voyage took eleven days, and by the end the galley was reduced to
serving peanut butter sandwiches, mushroom soup, coffee, and dough-
nuts. Lieutenant Commander Benitez, *Dace's* executive officer, described
the conditions: "During that time we were always crowded, dirty, and
tired. The good food soon disappeared. We had eleven days of it, but we
were happy. Few submarines had accomplished what we had done."[26]

Finally, at 8 AM on 6 November 1944, *Dace* took her place alongside
Euryale at Fremantle. From her periscope flew a large flag, "Task Group
M," with eight flags depicting the naval and merchant ships sunk or damaged. The *M* signified McClintock, leader of the two-boat "wolf pack" that
had left Brisbane more than two months earlier. A band and cheering

crowds greeted their arrival. Benitez commented, "It was a great thrill for the *Dace* to return from that patrol."[27]

The Battle of Leyte Gulf was the greatest fleet battle of World War II, destroying the Japanese fleet as a significant force. Japanese losses totaled three battleships, four aircraft carriers, and ten cruisers as well as smaller ships, and others, like *Takao*, so damaged that they took no further part in the war.

Darter and *Dace*'s part in this battle was the crowning success of Brisbane's submarine task force. Coming at the twilight of the base's life, their success reflected back over the lean pickings and hard knocks of two and a half years' struggle. The lessons learned from bitter experience in those long years bore fruit in *Darter* and *Dace*'s achievements.

Their advanced radar enabled the captains to follow the enemy with confidence, their radio messages influenced the course of the battle, no torpedoes failed, and operating together doubled their success and brought both crews home safely. Above all, it was their captains and crews who had built on combat experience to face the Japanese fleet with calm efficiency and strike their blow with greatest effect.

Both captains recognized the importance of their crew's teamwork in achieving this great success. When Lieutenant Commander Benitez wrote the story of *Dace*, Claggett requested that *Dace*'s captain not be named.[28] Benitez later explained his reasons: "To mention any names, to single out any individual for what was accomplished, would be an injustice to others not so mentioned. We have always felt that our deeds were not the deeds of one man or of a group of men, but rather the work of all of us. . . . We prefer it that way."[29]

Commander McClintock requested that *Darter*'s crew be transferred intact to another submarine. Agreeing, Admiral King assigned them complete to a new submarine, *Menhaden*.

There was a signal honor in store for *Darter*'s crew. Ira King explained: "Admiral Nimitz said that he considered *Darter*'s fourth war patrol the outstanding patrol of any submarine because of the intelligence. To show he really meant that, when he gave up command of CinCPac/CinCPacFlt, he hauled down his flag on the USS *Menhaden*, the submarine manned by the old *Darter* crew. I believe the *Menhaden* was the only submarine to ever fly a five-star flag."[30]

Darter was the final loss suffered by Brisbane's submarine command. It bears a striking similarity to Brisbane's first loss, that of *S39* more than two years earlier. Both boats were lost by stranding, and, happily, both crews survived. Apart from these two, every other submarine out of Brisbane that failed to return was lost with all hands.

22
CLOSING DOWN

The Philippines invasion spelled the beginning of the end for the Brisbane base. Enemy shipping moved still farther west, and all Seventh Fleet submarine operations were controlled by Rear Admiral Christie in Fremantle. In addition, the Seventh Fleet commander's headquarters moved to Hollandia, New Guinea, at the end of October 1944. Commander Service Force, Seventh Fleet, Subordinate Command, in charge of all naval activities in Australia, remained in Brisbane for the rest of the war.

Squadron 18's final operation from Brisbane commenced on 27 October 1944 when *Bashaw, Flounder,* and *Guavina* left together for patrols in the South China Sea. The three submarines topped up on fuel and water in Darwin on 5 November. Urgent orders awaited them. Signals intercepted and decoded the previous day detailed the itinerary of one of the handful of German U-boats then in the Far East. *U537* was scheduled to leave Surabaya four days later for operations off Australia.[1]

After only a few hours, the three submarines rushed to intercept the U-boat. *Flounder* (Comdr. J. E. Stevens) was submerged at a checkpoint north of Lombok Strait at dawn on 10 November. Stevens watched a Japanese escort pass, followed two hours later by *U537*. Firing four torpedoes, *Flounder* sank *U537* with all hands. She was the last warship, and the only German vessel, sunk by Brisbane's submarines.

The three submarines patrolled as a "wolf pack" into the South China Sea. On 15 November, *Guavina* (Comdr. C. Tiedeman) came upon the freighter *Toyo Maru* stopped and on fire after an aircraft attack. Three torpedoes sank her. Six days later the pack attacked a convoy in the Dangerous Ground. At dusk, *Bashaw* torpedoed and damaged *Gyosan Maru.* Soon afterward *Flounder* blew off her stern, and two days later *Guavina* sank her remains. *Guavina* also destroyed a small freighter from this same convoy. Apart from this battle, the "wolf pack" found the sea empty of worthwhile targets before it ended the patrol in Fremantle.

By the time of this convoy battle, Task Force 72 had ceased to exist. On 15 November 1944, Task Force 72 was absorbed into Fremantle's Task Force 71. This brought all Seventh Fleet submarines under the direct command of Rear Admiral Christie, who had begun the Brisbane base in 1942. Christie formed the Brisbane command into Task Group 71.9, with Captain Haines continuing in charge and its duties unchanged. Further changes followed quickly as Capt. S. G. Barchet replaced Haines on 12 December 1944. Five days later the task group's decline was underlined when Captain Barchet was replaced by a commander: J. C. Broach.[2]

Rear Admiral Christie's command of Seventh Fleet submarines and Task Force 71 was also ending. After almost two years in this role, Christie was transferred to a nonoperational command, Bremerton Naval Shipyard. In Fremantle, Christie had earned his men's admiration, as Howard Smay recalled: "His practice of personally meeting every boat back from patrol with great fanfare and even awarding medals before thoroughly reviewing patrol reports had a very positive effect on submarine crews." Christie's reputation continued to shine in retirement, when he welcomed submariners of all ranks to his palatial estate on Diamond Head, Hawaii, which became "a tourist's paradise for old submariners."[3]

In a repetition of the events two years earlier in Brisbane, Christie's replacement was James Fife, now rear admiral. Once again Christie was unhappy to be leaving a front-line command, and once again he delayed his departure. However, the handover occurred on 30 December 1944, and Fife remained in control of Seventh Fleet submarines until the war ended.

By October 1944, Task Force 72's foremost activity was operating SpyRon special missions to the Philippines supporting guerrilla operations. After the loss of *Seawolf*, *Gar* temporarily joined *Narwhal*, *Nautilus*, and *Stingray* in SpyRon.

For the remainder of 1944, America strengthened its grasp on the central Philippines, advancing to Mindoro on 15 December and Luzon on 9 January. The need for submarine special missions there declined, and they stopped altogether that month. *Narwhal*, after nine successful missions, left Brisbane on 6 January 1945 to pay off. Her sister *Nautilus* had left three days earlier on her last run to the Philippines, and then followed her sister home.

As long as Submarine Repair Unit, Navy 134, remained and U.S. warships held first priority at Brisbane dockyards, submarines came for refit and rest. Fleet-submarines continued to pass through Brisbane's operational control en route to and from patrol areas. The last fleet-submarine refitted in Brisbane was *Pintado* (Comdr. B. A. Clarey), which arrived on New Year's Day 1945. Underlining just how remote Brisbane had become from the fighting, *Pintado*'s departure was delayed because no surface ships were available for prepatrol exercises. Her departure on 27 January 1945 was further delayed because "the upper echelons were puzzling over just what *Pintado*'s mission would be." On patrol in the South China Sea *Pintado* saw no targets worthy of a torpedo, and she reached Fremantle on 20 March 1945.[4]

Also under Brisbane's command were old S-boats used for antisubmarine training. Late in 1944, *S45* and *S47* trained air and surface escorts at Manus Island while *S42* operated from Brisbane. *S43* also trained Third Fleet escorts in the Solomons.

Earlier in the war, each of these old submarines had been part of Australia's first line of defense when the Brisbane base was first established. These S-boats now came to Brisbane for overhauls as they became due, and they would be the last submarines to use the Brisbane base.

Concurrently with Task Force 72's reduction to Task Group 71.9, the Brisbane repair unit prepared to transfer to the Philippines, close to the action. Plans for this originated while Christie was in command, and they were being developed when Fife took over. With characteristic energy, Fife flew to Brisbane during January 1945 to start closing down New Farm Wharf. He then flew to select a site at Subic Bay in southern Luzon for the new base. To Fife it was a question of effective use of his resources: "We had no use for the personnel that were tied up down there [in Brisbane], and I wanted to get them out so as to use them up in Subic Bay."[5]

Fife moved to place *Griffin*, which had inaugurated the Brisbane submarine base three years earlier, in Subic Bay. *Griffin* arrived on 10 February 1945 and began supervising construction and providing ship and submarine repairs.

The details of the "rolling up" of the Brisbane submarine base appear in the monthly war diary.[6] In January 1945, rooms in two hotels and five houses were canceled. More were canceled in succeeding months.

The closing down of Submarine Repair Unit, Navy 134, commenced on 16 February 1945 with stores, fittings, equipment, and heavy installations dismantled and packed for shipment. Days later the tender *Anthedon* arrived to load for the forward base. She was quickly followed by *Howard W. Gilmore*, named after the heroic captain of *Growler*. She too loaded stores, spare parts, and equipment from New Farm Wharf. The tenders sailed separately late in February for Subic Bay, arriving on 13 March 1945. A month later, Fife hoisted his flag aboard *Anthedon*. The hot, sodden, isolated, incomplete jungle camp was no comparison with Brisbane.

Dismantling New Farm Wharf continued through February while refits of the last submarines were completed. The S-boats departed singly for California, with *S47* the last to leave, casting off on 8 March 1945. She had been the first to sail on war patrol from the base almost three years earlier.

Three days later, Task Group 71.9's war diary ended: "At 0001 GCT on 11 March 1945, this Task Group was dissolved in accordance with dispatch orders from Commander Submarines, SEVENTH FLEET, and the functions of this command were absorbed into Commander Task Force SEVENTY-ONE."[7]

The Brisbane submarine base was no more.

Dismantling, packing, and loading equipment on USS *Crux* and *Ganymede* continued during March. Les Cottman was one of the last men of Navy 134 to leave, sailing on 30 March 1945 aboard HMAS *Westralia*. *Ganymede* sailed on 10 April 1945, leaving only bare sheds and an empty wharf. Admiral Fife recalled later, "What we couldn't move and what we didn't need we did turn over to [the Australians]."[8]

Vacating Brisbane properties took most of 1945. The Reciprocal Aid Review Board Report lists the dates.[9] The rest camps were vacated progressively, with Seabrae on 9 January and the Toowoomba camps on 28 February. The Coolangatta Rest Camp was transferred to the Royal Navy on 26 April. Also transferred to the Royal Navy were the Torpedo Repair Shop at the Benedict Stone Factory on 6 April and the Submarine Repair Unit at New Farm Wharf on 20 April. With the end of the war, the Mount Coot-tha Naval Magazine was closed on 31 August, and the Windsor Submarine Supply Center went to the Australian Military Forces on 24 October. Finally, the New Farm headquarters was vacated on 25 January 1946, and the last installation, the McLachlan Street Motor Pool, was handed over on 1 February.

Personal issues took longer to settle. *Mariposa* sailed from Brisbane packed with brides on 11 April 1946. Yvonne Cottman was aboard, along with other wives of submarine and tender crewmen. Years later the Cottmans returned to Brisbane.

The state funeral of an unknown American soldier on 22 December

1947 was a solemn event for which thirty thousand mourners lined the streets. His was the last of 1,409 servicemen's bodies carried to the *Goucher Victory* for burial in the United States. Led by mounted police, the procession wound through the crowds to the wharf gates where, as RAAF aircraft saluted overhead, official wreaths were laid. Before the coffin was carried aboard, seventy-year-old Mrs. L. Spillsbury laid her own tribute to "the Americans [who] came here to fight for us": a single hibiscus flower.[10]

23
THE BRITISH ARRIVE

By March 1945 the American submarines had left Brisbane, but this was not the end of Brisbane's submarine war.

Victory in Europe was now only a matter of time with Allied forces entering Germany, allowing the Royal Navy to release ships to join the war against Japan. The powerful British Pacific Fleet (Adm. Sir Bruce Fraser) joined the Americans tightening the noose around the Japanese home islands. The Royal Navy's support base in Brisbane, HMS *Furneaux*, was rapidly expanded. On 20 April 1945, New Farm Wharf and its facilities were transferred to the Royal Navy as a fleet repair base.

Among the Royal Navy's vessels was HMS *Bonaventure*, a converted cargo liner that, despite her inconspicuous appearance, was unique in the Allied navies: she was the only depot ship for midget submarines. Aboard she carried the 14th Submarine Flotilla, six small submarines numbered *XE1* to *XE6*. Each weighed 35 tons, was 53 feet long, and carried a crew of four.

Bonaventure's diminutive X craft were a wartime innovation that had already performed distinguished service. In September 1943 they had crippled the German battleship *Tirpitz*. During 1944, X craft surveyed the Normandy beaches for the D-Day landings and then guided the first assault wave in. They also made two successful raids on Bergen to sink an important floating dock.

Australian officers were well represented in these events. Three X craft captains for the *Tirpitz* attack were Australians—one, Lt. H. K. Hudspeth, subsequently commanding *X20* in the Normandy operations. Another Australian, Lt. M. Shean, commanded *X24* in the first attack on Bergen.

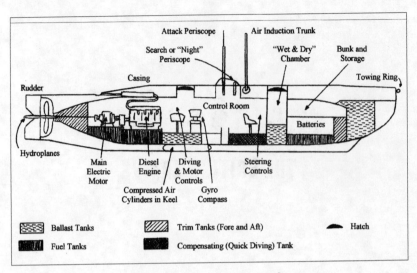

Exploded View of an XE Craft.

Australia already knew midget submarines through the Japanese attack on Sydney Harbour in 1942 and a tour of a salvaged midget through country towns. Italy and Germany also used midget submarines, but their achievements were few.

The British X craft differed from other navies' vessels. To describe them as midget submarines devalues their technology and capacity. Like their full-sized sisters, X craft had the full range of navigational equipment, both diesel and electric motors, and tanks for diving and trim. Their crews were highly skilled and well trained. Unlike all other contemporary submarines, X craft used divers who could enter and leave underwater through an air lock called a "wet and dry" chamber. These divers cut through net defenses so that heavy explosive charges could be laid under enemy ships.

X craft were built for stealth, with the silhouette of a floating log and a pencil-thin periscope. With a speed of only six knots, the X craft were intended to avoid detection. Their divers used closed-circuit oxygen, which did not emit air bubbles. However, these breathing sets were hazardous because of the danger of oxygen poisoning, and their use was strictly controlled.

A full-sized British submarine towed each X craft to within striking distance of its objective, but underwater towing was dangerous. Because high concentration was needed while under tow, a passage crew managed the submarine, handing it over to another crew for the operation.

Agreement to operate X craft in the Pacific was reached at the Quebec conference of September 1944 in private meetings between the chiefs of the British and American navies.[1] *Bonaventure* left the Clyde on 21 February 1945 for the Pacific with six X craft concealed in her holds and inside large crates on deck marked "aircraft." Reaching Pearl Harbor, the flotilla commander, Capt. W. R. "Tiny" Fell, consulted with Admiral Nimitz and other Pacific Fleet leaders on his submarines' future employment.

The news was devastating. These small submarines were completely new to the Americans, who saw them as similar to Japanese suicide craft, too dangerous for their crews and inappropriate for a civilized nation. Unspoken but suspected by the British was an American desire to avenge Pearl Harbor all by themselves.

Fell was advised that no use could be found for his X craft, and *Bonaventure* was sent to Brisbane to await orders. Morale plummeted, and *Bonaventure* sailed into Brisbane early on 27 April 1945, as Captain Fell put it, "with our tails right down, in black despair."[2]

However, Fell and his X craft had overcome seemingly impossible obstacles before, and he refused to accept defeat. Accordingly, he flew to Sydney to promote his flotilla personally with Admiral Fraser. But there too Fell met a negative response.

One small glimmer of hope remained. Fell flew to the Philippines to plead his case with Rear Admiral Fife, who received him warmly. From his stay in Great Britain in 1940–41, Fife had developed a high regard for the British fighting spirit. Furthermore, his patrols in three British submarines before America entered the war had been a valuable learning experience. Fife listened patiently to Fell but could say only that the X craft had arrived too late. He could have used them two months earlier, but targets had disappeared. Fell had found a friend, but he returned empty-handed.[3]

Meanwhile, *Bonaventure*'s crew enjoyed leave in Brisbane. Although the local hotels offered little comfort in the mere two hours a day they were open, the men found the food was good and plentiful after Britain's shortages, and they were welcomed in Brisbane homes. *Bonaventure* remained in Brisbane for two weeks, but inactivity on the long voyage had taken the edge off the submarine crews' skills. On 14 May, *Bonaventure* sailed for exercises, and finally the X craft were uncrated.

After stopping at Townsville, *Bonaventure* reached Cid Harbour in the Whitsunday Islands on 19 May. Here they were told that, as no work had yet been found for them, *Bonaventure* would pay off in Sydney. It was gloomy news, but a change was just around the corner.

The change came on 31 May when Captain Fell attended a conference in Sydney: "I chanced to overhear a remark about the difficulty the staff was having in breaking the Japanese submarine telegraph communication between Malaya, China, and Japan. I almost yelled that XE craft could do it, and within an hour had Sir Bruce's approval to fly to Manila once again and discuss it with the Americans. This time they were enthusiastic, and feverish plans and intensive training went forward."[4]

At this stage of the war, Allied forces were advancing through Burma, the Philippines, and East Indies, and assaults on Malaya and Singapore were planned for later in the year. Although the Allies could read Japanese radio traffic, the East Indies, Malaya, and Singapore communicated freely and securely with Japan and other Asian centers by long-distance telegraph cables laid in their own waters. Breaking these links would force Japanese communications onto the airwaves, where they could be intercepted and deciphered by the Allies.

However, cutting telegraph cables had never been a role for X craft, and there was much to be done. The task was urgent, and X craft crews needed to master a means of locating and cutting these cables. However, resourcefulness and adaptability were Fell's men's strong suit. Various types of grapnel were tested for their ability to pick up a cable on the seabed when towed behind a submerged X craft. Once located, the cable would be cut by the diver using enlarged net cutters. The most successful grapnel was a "flatfish" diamond plate with a horn plowing six inches into the sand. Given the right conditions, it worked the first time, every time.[5]

Initial trials were held at Cid Harbour, followed by more realistic exercises with a disused undersea cable in Hervey Bay. In these trials between 17 and 26 June two British officers, Lts. D. Carey and B. E. Enzer, were lost. Both were experienced X craft sailors, fit and strong, and they disappeared on successive days—a distressing tragedy for the close-knit crews, and one that caused much soul-searching.

The evidence pointed to oxygen poisoning. Breathing pure oxygen was dangerous at the best of times, gradually dulling the senses and causing a form of intoxication that often proved fatal. Daily training in the oxygen breathing apparatus built up the diver's tolerance, and the amount of time spent breathing pure oxygen needed to be limited. Neither of the missing officers had been under daily training, and it was believed that both had

*XE*3 on grappling trials in Hervey Bay in June 1945. On deck are Lt. David Carey (about to stream a reef anchor grapnel), Lt. Ian Fraser (center), and ERA Nairn. Lieutenant Carey was lost in a diving accident soon after this.

Courtesy of M. Shean

overexerted themselves, exceeded safety limits, and succumbed to oxygen poisoning. Strict controls were imposed over diving activities, and there were no further casualties.

Despite the deaths, the X craft and their crews were now ready for action. *Bonaventure* returned to Brisbane, where crew members renewed friendships from their previous visit. On 8 July 1945, *Bonaventure* left Brisbane after more than ten weeks in Queensland waters bound for the Philippines, where she arrived on 20 July.

Plans were well advanced for the invasion of Malaya, scheduled for the second half of August. Severing Japanese undersea telegraph cables to Singapore was one way X craft could contribute to this advance. Another, suggested by Rear Admiral Fife, was the X craft's more traditional employment.

Two Japanese heavy cruisers lay in Singapore, and although both were damaged, their heavy guns posed a threat to any Allied invasion. These cruisers became targets for the X craft. One was *Takao*, crippled by *Darter* at the Battle of Leyte Gulf. She had been brought to Singapore in January 1945 and had not moved since. The other cruiser, *Myoko,* had a similar story to tell after a Fremantle submarine blew her stern off in December 1944.

Bonaventure joined the Seventh Fleet at Subic Bay. She attracted great interest from the Americans, who had never seen such tiny submarines, and *XE4* gave a demonstration to Vice Admiral Lockwood. In a rare honor, Rear Admiral Fife raised his flag on *Bonaventure* on 24 July, remaining aboard until after the operations ended. Fife brought his ninety staff with him for the duration of his stay.[6]

The X craft cable-cutting operations—Operation Sabre off Saigon and Operation Foil at Hong Kong—would occur concurrently on 31 July 1945. The attack on the Japanese cruisers was called Operation Struggle. If these operations were successful, further cable cutting was envisaged off Singapore and Tanjong Priok, the main port of Java.[7]

Leaving *XE5* with HMS *Maidstone* at Subic Bay, *Bonaventure* sailed on 24 July for Labuan in northern Borneo, captured only six weeks earlier by the Australian 9th Division. Three days later the X craft were on their way. The closing words of the speech Fife made before their departure left the Labuan boats in no doubt of his admiration: "You're the little guys with a lotta guts. Good Luck!"[8]

The undersea cables to Singapore formed a triangular pattern. One went direct from Hong Kong to Singapore, while a second ran from Hong Kong to Saigon, then on to Singapore. Operation Foil's *XE5* (Lt. H. P. West-macott) targeted the direct cable. The task of Operation Sabre's *XE4* was to cut both Saigon's links where they came together off the mouth of the Mekong River.

There was a strong Australian presence in *XE4,* with Lt. Max Shean serving as commander and Sub-Lt. Ken Briggs as one of the divers. They had joined the Royal Australian Navy Volunteer Reserve before Japan entered the war. Sent to Great Britain, both served in antisubmarine escorts, and Shean spent three years with X craft from September 1942. With a fine technical mind, Shean drew on his engineering studies and small-boat experience to develop the successful "flatfish" grapnel they now took to war.

XE4 cast off from her towing submarine, HMS *Spearhead,* at 9:20 PM on 30 July in rising wind and sea. As *XE4* closed the coast, Shean was washed overboard but fortunately regained his hold. At dawn *XE4* submerged off the mouth of the Mekong River. Cable and Wireless Company had supplied charts of their cables' exact locations, but tides and silt might have moved and buried them, particularly off the entrance of a large, flood-prone river system.

Around 8 AM XE4 began dragging for the Saigon–Singapore cable. Shean navigated while Sub-Lt. Ben Kelly controlled trim. Engine Room Artificer V. "Ginger" Coles manned diving and surfacing controls and steered. The two divers, Sub-Lts. Ken Briggs and Adam Bergius, waited in the battery compartment, ready for when a cable was snagged.

Shean directed XE4's first sweep over a sandbank thirty feet deep across the line of the cable toward a submerged wreck, which XE4 bumped into at dead slow speed. The crash surprised the divers in the bow compartment, but no damage was done.[9] XE4 turned for a second pass ten feet deeper. Once again the grapnel failed to snag.

The third run was planned at a depth of fifty feet, where it was hoped the cable would not be silted over. At this depth the divers were in the danger zone for oxygen poisoning, and their time and efforts would need to be strictly controlled. Before the X craft had gone far, the grapnel caught. XE4 settled onto the seabed while Ken Briggs quickly moved into the wet and dry chamber. After filling it and equalizing the pressure, Briggs left the submarine. This sortie proved to be a false alarm when, feeling his way through murky water, Briggs found the grapnel caught on a rock. Releasing it, he was soon back inside.

Resuming her search, XE4 again stopped as the grapnel gripped another obstruction. Once again Briggs left, this time to find the cable. Cutting it in two places, he returned to XE4 within fifteen minutes, proudly grasping a short length of the Saigon–Singapore cable as evidence of his success. Shean continued along the fifty-foot depth contour to search for the Saigon–Hong Kong cable. He located it on the first run in its charted position, and the second diver, Adam Bergius, cut it. He too brought some cable on board for proof.

By 3 PM both cables were cut. The divers' task had not been easy, as the cables had been found at a deeper level than expected and a strong current made their work hazardous. The water was cloudy, and rocky outcrops made the seabed uneven—very different from their trials in Hervey Bay with clear visibility and a flat seabed. In the Mekong outflow, so close to an enemy port, it was vital that the X craft not break surface and reveal her presence. This was expertly achieved by Ben Kelly, who kept XE4 at a constant depth and correct trim, despite the added burden of the grapnel's drag.[10]

By midnight XE4 had rejoined *Spearhead*, and they reached *Bonaventure* on 3 August, the first X craft to return. XE4 had demonstrated the

Ken Briggs displays the section he cut from the telegraph cable
off Saigon on 31 July 1945.

Photo copyright *The Sunday Mail,* Brisbane, courtesy of Ken Briggs

professionalism of all X craft crews by making a difficult job, not even
imagined only two months earlier, look easy.

By contrast, the Hong Kong operation by *XE5* (Lt. H. P. Westmacott) was
beset with difficulties. Towed by HM submarine *Selene,* Westmacott had
a fright three days out when the crew found their vessel unaccountably
sinking. After a while they realized that the towrope had broken, and *XE5*
surfaced to find herself alone. More than two and a half hours later *XE5*
was again in contact with *Selene,* but this setback forced a twenty-four-
hour postponement of the operation.[11]

On 31 July *XE5* arrived in Hong Kong's West Lamma Channel, where
the cable was reportedly located. Westmacott and his crew found a fleet of
fishing junks in the area, twenty or thirty being in sight throughout their
operation. *XE5* commenced dragging the next day, but the cable proved
difficult to locate. The seabed was so soft that the crew thought the cable
was buried too deep in the mud for the grapnel.

After four and a half hours the grapnel snagged, and the diver, Lt. B. G. "Nobby" Clarke, left to investigate. The sea was so muddy that Clarke could see nothing, but by feel he applied the pneumatic cutter to the wire. In the poor visibility he almost severed a finger and was forced to return inside the X craft. In addition, Clarke had been stung all over by Portuguese men-of-war. XE5's second diver, Sub-Lt. Dennis Jarvis, cut the grapnel away from the snag, enabling XE5 to rush back to Selene, where Clarke received proper medical attention.

On the following morning Westmacott and his remaining crew returned to resume the search. Conditions did not improve, and Jarvis was working alone with no visibility, up to his waist in mud. For a day and a half XE5 trawled fruitlessly for the cable, then at midday on 3 August, Westmacott called off the search: "By now there was about two hours' oxygen left. . . . Three days dragging during which the estimated position of the cable was crossed seventeen times had been completely unrewarded. XE5 gave up."[12]

It was a subdued XE5 that arrived alongside Maidstone three days later. However, the X craft's efforts had not been wasted. When Allied forces reentered Hong Kong four weeks later, it was found that the Hong Kong–Singapore cable had gone out of service on the first day of Operation Foil. How this happened was unclear, but it was thought that the cable had been disabled by the movements of XE5 lying on the cable in the mud, snagging it, or by her divers' probing.[13]

Operation Struggle, the attack on the two Japanese cruisers at Singapore, was extremely hazardous. Both vessels were far up shallow, winding, and well-guarded Johore Strait. XE1 (Lt. J. E. Smart) and XE3 (Lt. Ian Fraser) were assigned to the operation. Their tow from Labuan covered four days before both were released late on 30 July 1945. They proceeded independently over a glassy sea and minefields, into the enemy harbor.

Just over twenty-four hours later XE3 returned to her parent submarine Stygian with her mission accomplished. But the day had been crowded with difficulties, proving the aptness of the operation's name.

Approaching the strait's entrance, XE3 had close encounters first with a fishing boat, then with an escorted tanker. Twice the tiny submarine dived to avoid the tanker and remained undetected. However, in diving, XE3 struck the shallow seabed, putting her distance-measuring log out of action. From here on her crew had to navigate without this aid.[14]

By 10:30 AM, more than three hours behind schedule, XE3 reached the boom net across the harbor entrance. This expected obstacle had been left

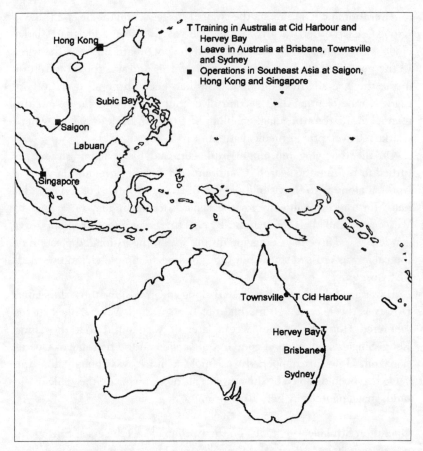

British X Craft Training and Operations in the Southwest Pacific.

open, and the submarine edged through at a depth of ten feet. In the clear, shallow waters the guard ship's crew could well have seen the X craft, but she passed undetected.

For the next two hours *XE3* threaded up the narrow strait. Because of the oily calm and the sea's clarity, only brief periscope glimpses could be made. Just before 1 PM *Takao* came into view, and Fraser could observe every detail.

Using the periscope sparingly, Fraser began his approach. Changing water density made depth-keeping difficult, and by now the crew had spent nine hours inside the hot, submerged submarine. Once, when Fraser raised the periscope, he was startled to find himself looking straight

into a boatload of Japanese sailors. He hastily lowered it, and *XE3* continued blind.

Creeping along at only thirteen feet, *XE3* suddenly collided with
Takao's hull. The craft was jammed for ten minutes as her crew revved the
motor backward and forward. Finally *XE3* burst free, and Fraser slithered
along *Takao*'s side until a seabed hole was found, allowing the craft under
the huge cruiser's keel.

So tight was the squeeze that the hatch could be only partially opened,
and *XE3*'s diver, Leading Seaman J. J. "Mick" Magennis, had to detach his
breathing set to exit. In the process he tore a hole in his breathing apparatus, and from then on a steady stream of oxygen bubbles rose to the surface, threatening to reveal his presence.

Magennis reported, "My first impression was how murky the water
was. The bottom of the target resembled something like an underwater
jungle and I had to clear a patch of undergrowth and barnacles off six
places in order to make sure the magnetic limpets (mines) would stick on.
. . . It took me about three quarters of an hour altogether before I got back
to *XE3*."[15]

The razor-sharp barnacles tore Magennis's hands and further damaged
his diving suit. He was exhausted when he returned inside. It had been
hard too for the other crew members. With fans stopped for quietness, the
inside of the submarine was like a boiler, and every minute Magennis was
working seemed like a day.

Once Magennis was inside, a 2-ton charge on *XE3*'s side was released,
timed to explode six hours later. When this task had been completed, a
further surprise was in store. The crew found that the balancing "limpet"
carrier on the other side of the X craft could not be removed. This left the
tiny submarine unbalanced. Added to this, *XE3* was again firmly stuck
under the cruiser.

The attack was planned for high tide at midday. It was now 4 PM, and
Takao was settling as the tide fell, threatening to crush *XE3*. Fraser struggled with every means he knew to dislodge the X craft. With motor racing,
XE3 finally moved out, but the dragging side weight remained. A diver had
to leave to release the burden.

Although Magennis was drained and breathless from his exertions,
there was no question in his mind that this was his job. He once more left
XE3 and within five minutes had freed the side carrier. Sitting on the side
carrier as it fell, he had to swim for his life after *XE3*. By the time he
returned inside he was barely conscious. At last *XE3* and her crew were
able to turn east to escape.

Their troubles continued as fresh water in the ebbing tide made depth-keeping difficult, and *XE3* briefly broke surface. They also had a close brush with a motor boat passing directly over the barely submerged *XE3*, but again she escaped detection.

They made faster time on the outward journey and passed the boom unseen in the growing darkness, three hours after leaving *Takao*. By midnight they had come once more under *Stygian*'s protection, having seen, on their way out, a big explosion at the time their charges were due to detonate.

For their courage in overcoming a succession of adversities inside the enemy's lair, Lieutenant Fraser and Leading Seaman Magennis were both awarded the Victoria Cross.

Sharing the attack on Singapore Harbor was *XE1* (Lt. Jack Smart). Casting off from HMS *Spark,* she entered Johore Strait at the same time as *XE3*. However, *XE1*'s part in Operation Struggle was plagued by delays.

The need to avoid numerous small craft slowed *XE1*'s progress, and she was an hour and a half behind *XE3* passing the entrance boom. Continuing up the shallow strait, Smart eventually saw the heavy cruiser *Myoko* a good distance farther on. Smart judged the distance to be too great to allow him to attack and exit the harbor before nightfall.

Faced with spending the night in the harbor with air and batteries expended, Smart decided to leave *Myoko* and attack *Takao*, two miles closer. This in itself was courageous, as Smart could not know whether an alarm had already been raised or whether *XE1*'s movements would set off her companion's charges. Nevertheless, *XE1* added her explosives to *XE3*'s beside *Takao*. Smart then headed his craft to sea.

Unable to contact *Spark* that night, *XE1* spent the next day on the seabed and rendezvoused with *Spark* the following night to make the four-day tow to *Bonaventure* at Labuan.

XE3 and *XE1* returned to *Bonaventure* on 5 and 6 August respectively. The return of all four X craft was a huge relief to both British and Americans. Admirals Lockwood and Fife, who had questioned the risk, were amazed and relieved. On the lower deck, the Americans were delighted that the X craft had sunk their enemy.

However, by the time *XE1* and *XE3* returned, air reconnaissance had shown that, although there was much oil around *Takao*, the two cruisers were still in their places. This was enormously disappointing to crews convinced that *Takao*, at least, had been destroyed. In fact *Takao* had a massive hole sixty by thirty feet in her hull, and her gun turrets and control systems were out of action. Compartments were flooded, and *Takao* sat on the harbor bottom, upright but no longer a fighting ship.[16]

Nevertheless, *Myoko* had been untouched, and because *Takao* still appeared to be a threat to the Allied assault planned for later that month, a second raid was planned. Fraser and his crew in *XE3* and Shean in *XE4* were assigned the task. After the initial raid, a return visit seemed suicidal, but they began preparations.[17]

On 12 August 1945 the X craft were shackled to their towing submarines with crews embarked, ready for the new operation. But less than an hour before sailing, the operation was canceled. It was a great relief to crews who had not yet recovered from the stress of their previous operations.

Other forces were at work as news broke of a new weapon, the atomic bomb. One of these had flattened the entire city of Hiroshima on 6 August. Another bomb had destroyed Nagasaki three days later.

Over fifty years later *XE4*'s crew discovered that their cable-cutting operation had a very secret link with these events, unknown to them for all those years.[18] In July 1945, with Germany defeated, the leaders of Great Britain, the United States, and the USSR met at Potsdam. Although the USSR was not then at war with Japan, ending the Pacific war was one matter discussed. During the conference President Truman was told of the atomic bomb's successful testing. Knowing this, Truman and Prime Minister Churchill issued the Potsdam Proclamation defining terms for unconditional surrender by Japan. Issued on 26 July, the declaration stated that "prompt and utter destruction" would follow if the terms were not accepted. The Japanese response two days later was interpreted as rejection.

In the complex situation arising from the Potsdam Proclamation, the Allied leaders needed the best information obtainable about Japanese intentions. Throughout the war this had come from radio interception. Cutting their telegraph cables returned Japanese communications in Southeast Asia to the airwaves, where they were open to interception. This most likely explained the presence of Fife's full staff aboard *Bonaventure*.[19]

However, events moved quickly, and on 2 August presidential clearance was given for use of the atomic bomb. The Japanese seriously considered surrender only after a second atomic bomb had fallen. After several days the Japanese emperor accepted the Allied terms, and on 15 August 1945, World War II was finally over. *Bonaventure* and her flotilla were released from the Seventh Fleet four days later. With peace, much work had to be done removing Japanese forces, rescuing prisoners of war, and restoring civil authority and services. There was little need for X craft, and *Bonaventure* retired to Sydney, arriving on 3 September.

Bonaventure's submarine equipment was removed, and she became a cargo transport carrying supplies to the occupation forces. It was a far cry from her recent operations, in which her flotilla had won twenty-seven bravery decorations, including two VCs. However, one moment of glory still remained for *Bonaventure*. In Sydney, word of her secret cargo leaked to the press. Reporters visited her in Athol Bight to hear the stirring stories of her men. In addition, *XE4* gave a demonstration, making a circuit around Sydney Harbour. But the days of the flotilla were numbered. The X craft were unloaded at Woolloomooloo and quickly broken up. Only *XE4* was spared, briefly, for some antisubmarine trials, then she too was scrapped.[20]

For *Bonaventure*'s crew also, it was a time of change. Their leave in Sydney was welcome, but the splendid team of men—skilled, resourceful, and brave—who had mastered this new form of undersea warfare and struck telling strategic blows would soon be dispersed. The VC winners, Fraser and Magennis, were flown home as VIPs. In Singapore they visited the hulk of *Takao*, seeing the wide, jagged hole in her side as she rested on the harbor bottom.[21] Most X craft crews were assigned to other submarines before returning home to Britain. The Australians Max Shean and Ken Briggs, already close to home, were quickly released to civilian life.

Bonaventure made several trips to the Far East before returning to Britain in 1946 for conversion to mercantile service as *Clan Davidson*. *Bonaventure* and her flotilla had faded from the scene, but they had written a shining page in submarine history.

In Brisbane, HMS *Furneaux* at New Farm Wharf continued to support Royal Navy ships after the war ended. As Britain restored Singapore and Hong Kong, the need for Brisbane's support diminished. *Furneaux* was decommissioned in December 1945, and New Farm Wharf returned to commerce.

CONCLUSION

The Silent Service's contribution to victory in the Pacific is not well known. Yet the losses that submarines inflicted starved Japan of the resources necessary to continue the war and ground its fighting forces and industry to a halt.

A professional tribute came from Vice Adm. Sir John Collins, who commanded the Seventh Fleet's Task Force 74. Australia's most distinguished sailor wrote, "[A] big factor, at the time little known, was the U.S. submarine campaign in the Pacific which practically annihilated the once flourishing Japanese merchant marine. Great credit is due to the American submariners for their success in a difficult task."[1]

Much of the experience that led to this victory was learned the hard way by the men and their leaders operating submarines from Brisbane. The Brisbane submarine task force reached its peak when the going was hardest. By the time effective strategy and tactics were developed, torpedo faults corrected, and sufficient submarine numbers built up, the war had moved on and Task Force 72 had been reduced. When *Fulton* left Brisbane on 25 October 1943 for Milne Bay, it was just over eighteen months since *Griffin* had set up the base on 15 April 1942. Just under eighteen months later, on 20 April 1945, the American Submarine Repair Unit moved out from New Farm Wharf.

Of Brisbane's war patrols, two-thirds (122) sailed in the first eighteen-month period. Only fifty-nine sailed in the second half of the base's life, twenty-one leaving from forward bases. By contrast, Brisbane's role as a maintenance center did not diminish over the three years, the eighty-nine submarine entries to Brisbane's dry docks being spread evenly between the two eighteen-month periods.

Patrols under Brisbane's submarine command resulted in 117 ships totaling around 515,000 tons being sunk, and others damaged. This represents about one-tenth of the 5.32 million tons of Japanese shipping sunk by American submarines during the war. Among the Brisbane total were a respectable number of Japanese warships, including three heavy and two light cruisers.

Added to this are less quantifiable tasks of support for coastwatchers and guerrillas in special missions, people rescued from enemy territory, reconnaissance information gained, and training for Allied antisubmarine units.

But the success was gained at a cost. Seven U.S. submarines were lost while under Brisbane task force control, and three more were lost on patrols to or from Brisbane while under the orders of other command areas. In all but two of these losses, there were no survivors. Another eleven submarines, formerly under Brisbane control, were lost later in the war.

Brisbane's submarines battled through tough fighting, heavy losses, and modest successes to share in the American Submarine Service's eventual victory.

Most enduring of all the dividends of Brisbane's submarine war is the powerful bond of friendship forged between U.S. sailors and the Australian people. A few reflections by American submariners convey the depth of their appreciation:

> "[Australians] took us into their homes and hearts with open handed hospitality at a time when we were badly beaten down and a long way from home. The beer is excellent, the beaches are better than many of our own, and the girls are good to look upon."
>
> (Vice Adm. C. A. Lockwood)[2]

> "We were extremely well received. The Australians, with their menfolk away, felt that here were a few people come to help protect us. On that basis we were very welcome."   (Adm. James Fife)[3]

> "The people of Brisbane treated us like their own, and my heart will always go out to them."   (Capt. Ira King, USS *Darter*)[4]

> "I, as well as all of us stationed in Brisbane, found it to be the perfect place to be, and the people were just wonderful to us."
>
> (Larry Hall, USS *Guardfish*)[5]

Wartime American submariners continue to feel a strong attachment to Australia long after the war has ended: "The official headgear of the United States Submarine Veterans of World War Two is modeled after the 'Digger' hat, complete with plume, worn by Australian soldiers. This because of the fond memories we all have of Australia."[6]

With the return of peace, New Farm Wharf resumed commercial activity. Peacetime business overtook the other premises that had heard American submariners' accents, and the Australians who had known them went on with their lives.

American submarines visit Brisbane from time to time, and Australia remains a popular leave destination. Celebrations of trans-Pacific friendship continue in Coral Sea Week commemorations and activities of the Australia-America Association.

Ghosts of the past were revived on 10 November 1966 when another American submarine, USS *Tiru*, entered South Brisbane Dry Dock to inspect damage after grounding on Frederick Reef. In 1992 the U.S. Navy acknowledged Brisbane's former submarine base by sending the tender *Proteus*, sister of *Fulton* and *Sperry*, to Brisbane for the fiftieth anniversary of the Battle of the Coral Sea.

Fulton paid off in 1991 after fifty years of service, and a handful of wartime submarines remain as museum vessels in the United States, witnesses to their contribution to victory in the Pacific. Among them are two Brisbane veterans, *Silversides* at Muskegon, Michigan, and *Drum* at Mobile, Alabama.

Apart from the river, the face of Brisbane has changed almost beyond recognition from the one that American submariners knew during the war. The Port of Brisbane has moved to the mouth of the river, and New Farm Wharf was demolished in 2000 to make way for a luxury housing development. South Brisbane Dry Dock ceased operations in 1971 and is now home to the Queensland Maritime Museum. An exhibit was opened in 1999 commemorating the men and vessels of Submarine Base–Brisbane. A memorial at Burnett Heads near Bundaberg honors the two British officers lost while preparing for action in their X craft.

Just downstream from New Farm Wharf, in tranquil Newstead Park, a plaque sponsored by the Queensland Branch of the Submarines Association Australia was unveiled in August 1995. It lists the submarines, American and British, that passed through Brisbane on their way to war. It is a fitting site, and an old submariner who passed that way reminds us of its importance: "When we came up the river returning from a patrol the people in the park, especially the children, would wave and cheer. The captain would salute them with the ship's whistle. It was as if we had come home, and in a sense we had."[7]

At home in a land on the far side of the Pacific Ocean—in war, and then in peace, for both American and Australian, this is the proud legacy of U.S. Subs down under.

APPENDIX 1
AMERICAN SUBMARINES USING BRISBANE BASE

TF42/72 Submarines

NAME	SERVICE WITH TF42/72	NO. OF PATROLS*	NOTES
Albacore	Dec 42–Jan 44	7	Sank cruiser *Tenryu*
Amberjack	Oct 42–Mar 43	3	Lost in action ca. 16 Feb 43
Argonaut	Dec 42–Jan 43	1	Lost in action 10 Jan 43
Balao	Jul 43–Mar 44	4	
Bashaw	Mar–Nov 44	4	
Blackfish	Sep 43–Apr 44	3	
Bluegill	Mar–Jun 44	1	Sank cruiser *Yubari*
Bream	May–Jul 44	1	
Cero	Jan–Oct 44	5	
Dace	Jan–Oct 44	4	Sank heavy cruiser *Maya*
Darter	Jan–Oct 44	4	Sank heavy cruiser *Atago*, lost 24 Oct 44
Drum	Apr–Nov 43	4	Damaged 22 Nov 43
Flounder	Mar–Nov 44	4	Sank German *U537*
Flying Fish	Nov 42–Jan 43	2	
Gar	Oct–Dec 44	2	Both special missions
Gato	Dec 42–May 43	3	Badly damaged 4 Apr 43
	Oct 43–May 44	3	
Grampus	Oct 42–Mar 43	3	Lost in action Mar 43
Grayback	Oct 42–May 43	4	
Greenling	Dec 42–Sep 43	4	
Grouper	Dec 42–Sep 43	5	Damaged 30 July 43
Growler	Nov 42–Oct 43	5	Badly damaged 7 Feb 43, bow replaced

NAME	SERVICE WITH TF42/72	NO. OF PATROLS*	NOTES
Guardfish	Jan 43–Feb 44	5	
Guavina	Jul–Nov 44	3	
Gudgeon	Oct 42–Jan 43	2	First special mission to Philippines
Narwhal	Oct–Nov 43	1	Special mission to Philippines
	Nov 44–Jan 45	—	Refit and withdrawal from service
Nautilus	Dec 42–Mar 43	1	
	Nov 44–Jan 45	1	Special mission to Philippines
Peto	Mar 43–Mar 44	5	
Plunger	Nov–Dec 42	1	
Pompon	Jun–Sep 43	1	
Raton	Oct–Dec 43	1	
Ray	Oct–Dec 43	1	
S37	Apr–Nov 42	3	
S38	Apr–Oct 42	4	
S39	Apr–Aug 42	2	Stranded 14 Aug 42
S40	Apr–Nov 42	4	
S41	Apr–Oct 42	3	
S42	Apr–Nov 42	4	Sank first ship sunk by TF42
	Mar 44–Feb 45	1	Mainly used in A/S training
S43	Apr–Nov 42	3	
S44	Apr–Nov 42	4	Sank heavy cruiser *Kako*
S45	Apr–Nov 42	3	
	July 44–Feb 45	—	A/S training
S46	Apr–Nov 42	3	
S47	Apr–Nov 42	4	First to patrol from Brisbane
	Mar 44–Mar 45	1	A/S training and last to leave Brisbane
Sailfish	Sep 42–Jan 43	2	
Sargo	Nov 42–Jan 43	1	
Saury	Oct–Dec 42	1	
Scamp	May 43–Apr 44	6	Badly damaged 6 Apr 44
Sculpin	Aug 42–Jan 43	2	
Seadragon	Nov 42–Jan 43	1	
Seawolf	Aug–Oct 44	1	Sunk in error 3 Oct 44
Silversides	Nov 42–Jan 43	2	
	Jun–Oct 43	3	
Snapper	Nov 42–Mar 43	2	
Spearfish	Nov 42–Jan 43	1	
Stingray	Jun–Sep 43	2	
	Oct–Dec 44	1	Special mission
Sturgeon	Aug–Dec 42	2	

NAME	SERVICE WITH TF42/72	NO. OF PATROLS*	NOTES
Swordfish	Oct 42–Feb 43	2	
Triton	Jan–Mar 43	2	Lost in action ca. 15 Mar 43
Trout	Oct–Nov 42	1	
Tuna	Dec 42–Aug 43	5	Badly damaged 29 July 43
	Dec 44–Jan 45	1	Special mission
Wahoo	Dec 42–Jan 43	2	

* Patrols include those wholly or for a substantial portion controlled by TF42/72.

Visiting Submarines

NAME	PERIOD IN BRISBANE AND COMMENTS
Billfish	Brisbane 1–12 Aug 43 on passage to Fremantle
Bluefish	Brisbane 21 Aug–1 Sep 43 on passage to Fremantle
Bonefish	Brisbane 30 Aug–8 Sep 43 on passage to Fremantle
Bowfin	Brisbane 10–16 Aug 43 on passage to Fremantle
Capelin	Brisbane 13–22 Oct 43 on passage to Fremantle, lost in action Dec 43
Cisco	Brisbane 1–9 Sep 43 on passage to Fremantle, lost in action 28 Sep 43
Cod	Brisbane 2–14 Oct 43 on passage to Fremantle
Corvina	Assigned to TF72 in Dec 43 but never joined, lost in action 16 Nov 43
Crevalle	Brisbane 11–20 Oct 43 on passage to Fremantle
Flying Fish	Brisbane 5 Jul–1 Aug 44 for refit between patrols
Gabilan	Brisbane 24 Nov–19 Dec 44 for refit between patrols
Mingo	Brisbane 9 May–10 Jun 44 for emergency repairs
Nautilus	Brisbane 14–20 May 44 on passage to Fremantle
Perch	Brisbane 24 Nov–19 Dec 44 for refit between patrols
Permit	Brisbane 13 Aug–21 Sep 44 for refit between patrols
Pintado	Brisbane 1–27 Jan 45 for refit between patrols
Pollack	Brisbane 12 Sep–6 Oct 44 for refit between patrols
Puffer	Brisbane ?–30 Aug 43 on passage to Fremantle
Rasher	Brisbane 11–24 Sep 43 on passage to Fremantle
S31	Brisbane 18 Sep–5 Dec 43 for refit–A/S training with 3rd Fleet and 1 patrol
S38	Brisbane 5 Jan–12 Feb 44 for refit–A/S training with 3rd Fleet
S43	Brisbane ? Jan–2 Mar 45 for refit–A/S training with 3rd Fleet
Seahorse	Brisbane 11 May–3 Jun 44 for refit between patrols
Silversides	Brisbane 8–26 Apr 44 for refit between patrols
Tunny	Brisbane 11–29 Apr 44 for emergency repairs

Ships Supporting Brisbane's Submarine Task Force

NAME	YEAR COMPLETED	DISPLACEMENT TONNAGE	SERVICE WITH TF42/72
Griffin	1940	8,600	Tender to SubRon 5 in Brisbane, 15 Apr–11 Nov 42
Fulton	1941	9,734	Tender to SubRon 8 in Brisbane, 9 Nov 42–25 Oct 43, and Milne Bay, 29 Oct 43–17 Mar 44
Sperry	1942	9,734	Tender to SubRon 10 in Brisbane, 13 Nov 42–17 Jan 43
Euryale	1943	8,282	Tender to SubRon 18 in Brisbane, Milne Bay, and Manus Island, 5 Mar–20 Aug 44
Tulsa	1923	1,200	Escort and support ship for TF42, 15 Apr 42–mid-43
Coucal	1943	1,653	Submarine rescue vessel for TF72, 23 Jun 43–Aug 44

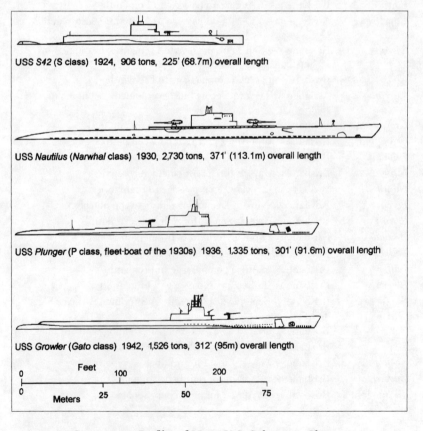

USS *S42* (S class) 1924, 906 tons, 225' (68.7m) overall length

USS *Nautilus* (*Narwhal* class) 1930, 2,730 tons, 371' (113.1m) overall length

USS *Plunger* (P class, fleet-boat of the 1930s) 1936, 1,335 tons, 301' (91.6m) overall length

USS *Growler* (*Gato* class) 1942, 1,526 tons, 312' (95m) overall length

Comparative Profiles of Major U.S. Submarine Classes.

APPENDIX 2
ENEMY SHIPPING SUNK BY SUBMARINES OF TF42 AND TF72

DATE		NAME	TONNAGE	TYPE	SUBMARINE
1942					
May	11	Okinoshima	4,400	Minelayer	S42
	12	Shoei Maru	5,644	Salvage ship	S44
June	21	Keijo Maru	2,626	Auxiliary gunboat	S44
July	8	Tenzan Maru	2,775	Passenger-cargo	S37
Aug	7	Meiyo Maru	5,627	Transport	S38
	10	Kako	8,700	Heavy cruiser	S44
Sep	19	Shirogane Maru	3,130	Passenger-cargo	Amberjack
Oct	1	Katsuragi Maru	8,033	Seaplane tender	Sturgeon
	7	Senkai Maru	2,101	Freighter	Amberjack
	7	Naminoue Maru	4,731	Transport	Sculpin
	14	Sumiyoshi Maru	1,921	Freighter	Sculpin
	21	Choko Maru	6,783	Passenger-cargo	Gudgeon
Dec	10	Kamoi Maru	5,355	Freighter	Wahoo
	17	Bandoeng Maru	4,003	Passenger-cargo	Grouper
	18	Tenryu	3,230	Light cruiser	Albacore
	21	I-4	1,970	Submarine	Seadragon
	22	Patrol Boat No. 35*	750	Frigate	Greenling
	30	Hiteru Maru	5,857	Freighter	Greenling
	30	Unnamed maru*	4,000	Freighter	Greenling
1943					
Jan	9	Yoshinogawa Maru	1,422	Freighter	Nautilus
	12	Patrol Boat No. 1	1,215	Frigate	Guardfish
	16	Chifuku Maru	5,857	Passenger-cargo	Growler
	16	Kinposan Maru	3,261	Freighter	Greenling
	18	Toei Maru	10,023	Tanker	Silversides

DATE		NAME	TONNAGE	TYPE	SUBMARINE
Jan	19	*Myoho Maru*	4,122	Freighter	*Swordfish*
	20	*Surabaya Maru*	4,391	Freighter	*Silversides*
	20	*Meiu Maru*	8,230	Freighter	*Silversides*
	20	*Somedono Maru**	5,154	Passenger-cargo	*Silversides*
	21	*Kenkon Maru*	4,575	Transport	*Gato*
	22	Unnamed maru*	4,000	Freighter	*Guardfish*
	23	*Hakaze*	1,215	Destroyer	*Guardfish*
	26	*Buyo Maru*	5,447	Transport	*Wahoo*
	26	*Fukuei Maru No. 2*	1,901	Freighter	*Wahoo*
	26	Unnamed maru*	4,000	Freighter	*Wahoo*
	29	*Nichiun Maru*	2,723	Freighter	*Gato*
Feb	15	*Suruga Maru*	991	Freighter	*Gato*
	19	*Hibari Maru**	6,550	Ammunition ship	*Gato* and USAAF aircraft
	20	Unnamed frigate*	750	Frigate	*Albacore*
	20	*Oshio*	1,960	Destroyer	*Albacore*
Mar	6	*Kiriha Maru*	3,057	Freighter	*Triton*
	30	*Kurohime Maru*	4,697	Freighter	*Tuna*
Apr	9	*Oyama Maru*	3,809	Freighter	*Drum*
	18	*Nisshun Maru*	6,380	Freighter	*Drum*
May	11	*Yodogawa Maru*	6,441	Collier	*Grayback*
	17	*England Maru*	5,829	Freighter	*Grayback*
	28	*Kamikawa Maru*	6,853	Seaplane tender	*Scamp*
Jun	11	*Hide Maru*	5,256	Freighter	*Silversides*
	13	*Suzuya Maru*	897	Freighter	*Guardfish*
	17	*Myoho Maru*	5,086	Passenger-cargo	*Drum*
	19	*Miyadono Maru*	5,196	Passenger-cargo	*Growler*
Jul	25	*Thames Maru*	5,871	Freighter	*Pompon*
	27	*I-168*	1,400	Submarine	*Scamp*
Sep	4	*Heijo Maru*	2,627	Auxiliary gunboat	*Albacore*
	8	*Hakutetsu Maru No. 13*	1,334	Freighter	*Drum*
	18	*Kansai Maru*	8,614	Freighter	*Scamp*
Oct	1	*Kinkasan Maru*	4,980	Freighter	*Peto*
	1	*Tonai Maru*	4,930	Passenger-cargo	*Peto*
	8	*Kashu Maru*	5,460	Freighter	*Guardfish*
	18	*Tairin Maru*	1,915	Freighter	*Silversides*
	24	*Tennan Maru*	5,407	Tanker	*Silversides*
	24	*Johore Maru*	6,187	Passenger-cargo	*Silversides*
	24	*Kazan Maru*	1,893	Freighter	*Silversides*
Nov	10	*Tokyo Maru*	6,481	Passenger-cargo	*Scamp*
	17	*Hie Maru*	11,621	Transport	*Drum*

DATE		NAME	TONNAGE	TYPE	SUBMARINE
Nov	23	Yamato Maru No. 2	439	Transport	Blackfish
	25	Kenzan Maru	4,704	Freighter	Albacore
	26	Nikkai Maru	2,562	Transport	Ray
	26	Onoe Maru	6,667	Ammunition ship	Raton
	26	Kamoi Maru	2,811	Passenger-cargo	Raton
	28	Yuri Maru	6,787	Freighter	Raton
	28	Hokko Maru	5,346	Freighter	Raton
	30	Columbia Maru	5,617	Passenger-cargo	Gato
Dec	1	Konei Maru	2,338	Freighter	Peto
	20	Tsuneshima Maru	2,926	Freighter	Gato

1944

Jan	12	Choko Maru No. 2	2,629	Auxiliary gunboat	Albacore
	12	H-4	25	Motor gunboat	Albacore
	14	Sazanami	2,090	Destroyer	Albacore
	14	Nippon Maru	9,974	Tanker	Scamp
	14	Kenyo Maru	10,024	Tanker	Guardfish
	16	Kaika Maru	2,087	Transport	Blackfish
	27	Keikai Maru*	2,827	Naval auxiliary	Dace
Feb	1	Umikaze	1,685	Destroyer	Guardfish
	17	Jozan Maru*	1,086	Transport	Cero
	22	Nikki Maru	5,857	Passenger-cargo	Balao
	22	Yamashimo Maru*	6,777	Repair ship	Gato
	26	Daigen Maru No. 3	5,255	Passenger-cargo	Gato
	28	Akiura Maru	6,803	Passenger-cargo	Balao
	28	Shoho Maru	2,723	Freighter	Balao
Mar	4	Kayo Maru	4,368	Freighter	Peto
	12	Okinoyama Maru No. 3	871	Freighter	Gato
	16	Kofuku Maru	1,919	Freighter	Silversides
	28	SS-3	948	Landing craft	Silversides
	30	Fujikawa Maru	2,829	Freighter	Darter
Apr	27	Yubari	2,890	Light cruiser	Bluegill
May	1	Asosan Maru	8,811	Freighter	Bluegill
	20	Miyaura Maru	1,856	Freighter	Bluegill
	23	Taijun Maru*	2,825	Freighter	Cero
Jun	16	Yuki Maru	5,704	Freighter	Bream
	17	Nihonkai Maru	5,591	Transport	Flounder
	25	Yamamiya Maru	6,440	Freighter	Bashaw
	29	Tsugaru	4,000	Minelayer	Darter
Jul	4	Tama Maru	3,052	Passenger-cargo	Guavina
	27	Kyoei Maru No. 2	1,192	Tanker	Dace
Aug	5	Tsurumi	14,050	Tanker	Cero

DATE		NAME	TONNAGE	TYPE	SUBMARINE
Aug	7	*Yamatama Maru*	4,642	Passenger-cargo	*Bluegill*
	13	*Kojun Maru*	1,931	Passenger-cargo	*Bluegill*
	13	*Misago Maru*	154	Submarine chaser	*Bluegill*
	13	*No. 12*	290	Submarine chaser	*Bluegill*
Sep	8	*Yanagigawa Maru*	2,813	Freighter	*Bashaw*
	15	*T-3*	1,500	Fast transport	*Guavina*
Oct	14	*Eikyo Maru*	6,948	Tanker	*Dace*
	14	*Nittetsu Maru*	5,993	Tanker	*Dace*
	23	*Atago*	13,160	Heavy cruiser	*Darter*
	23	*Maya*	13,160	Heavy cruiser	*Dace*
Nov	10	*U537* (German)	1,144	Submarine	*Flounder*
	15	*Toyo Maru*	2,704	Freighter	*Guavina* and USN aircraft
	21	*Gyosan Maru*	5,698	Freighter	*Bashaw* and *Flounder*
	22	*Dowa Maru*	1,916	Freighter	*Guavina*

* Records vary as to details and validity of this sinking.

Note: In addition to the above, a further forty-five ships totaling 155,527 tons were sunk by submarines on patrols either commencing or concluding in Brisbane while under the control of the Pearl Harbor or Fremantle task forces. Also excluded are ships damaged but not sunk by Brisbane submarines, and some small craft under 500 tons.

Sources: Results of Joint Army Navy Assessment Committee (JANAC) investigations published in Theodore Roscoe, *United States Submarine Operations in World War II* (Annapolis, Md.: U.S. Naval Institute, 1949), pp. 527–65, supplemented by later research by Comdr. J. D. Alden, USN (Ret.), published in *U.S. Submarine Attacks during World War II* (Annapolis, Md.: Naval Institute Press, 1989).

NOTES

Abbreviations

CUOHROC	Columbia University Oral History Research Office Collection, New York
DANFS	U.S. Navy, *Dictionary of American Naval Fighting Ships*
DJ	David Jones
JOL	John Oxley Library, Brisbane
NAA	National Archives of Australia
PN	Peter Nunan
QMM	Queensland Maritime Museum, Brisbane
RG	Record Group
SDMM	San Diego Maritime Museum, San Diego, Calif.
USNA	U.S. National Archives
USNHC	U.S. Naval Historical Center, Washington, D.C.
USNI	U.S. Naval Institute, Annapolis, Md.

Introduction

1. *Courier-Mail* (Brisbane), 15 April 1942.
2. Ibid., 14 February 1942, p. 6.
3. I. King (*Portland* and *Darter*), letter to DJ, 30 December 1998.

Chapter 1. First Arrivals

1. Blair, *Silent Victory*, pp. 80–83.
2. Operation order S7-42 by Commander Submarine Squadron 5, dated 28 February 1942, appendix B, USNA, RG38, Records of the Office of the Chief of Naval Operations (hereafter CNO records), boxes 303 and 304.

3. Operation order S7-42 by Commander Submarine Squadron 5.
4. Mailgram from ComSubRon 5, dated 20 March 1942, USNA, RG38, CNO records, boxes 303 and 304.
5. *DANFS*, 6:199–203.
6. Holmes, *Undersea Victory*, p. 102.
7. H. C. Smay (*Griffin* and *S47*), taped interview (2000), SDMM.
8. H. C. Smay (*Griffin* and *S47*), letter to DJ, 27 April 2000.
9. War diary of naval officer in charge, Brisbane, 1 February–30 June 1942, p. 3, Australian War Memorial, Canberra, AWM78, 398/1; Pilot Attendance Book for the port of Brisbane for April 1942, Queensland State Archives, Brisbane, PRV 8594-1-2.
10. Operation order S1-42 by Commander Task Group 42.1, dated 21 April 1942, USNA, RG38, CNO records, boxes 303 and 304.
11. Smay interview (2000).
12. Ibid.
13. Ibid.
14. T. Parks (*S39* and *Sailfish*), letter to DJ, 2 December 1999.
15. Account drawn from *DANFS*, 6:204; Lundstrom, *First South Pacific Campaign*, p. 143; and Morison, *Coral Sea, Midway, and Submarine Actions*, p. 225.
16. *DANFS*, 6:200–208.

Chapter 2. The Navy Comes Ashore

1. Letter from secretary of Australian Naval Board to district naval officer, Brisbane, 29 March 1942, NAA, Brisbane, BP132/2.
2. War diary of naval officer in charge, Brisbane, 1 February–30 June 1942, Australian War Memorial, Canberra, AWM78, 398/1.
3. "Defense-Aid Reciprocal Aid Review Board Report," item 40, USNA, RG71, Records of the Bureau of Yards and Docks.
4. South Brisbane Dry Dock register, QMM.
5. NAA, Melbourne, MP138/1, 603/223/1464.
6. Reminiscences of Rear Adm. A. H. McCollum (1971), USNI, pp. 489–95.
7. Lardner, *Southwest Passage*, pp. 144–50.
8. Potts, *Yanks Down Under*, p. 85.
9. D. C. Peto (*Greenling*), letter to DJ, 3 August 1999.
10. H. Story (*Bluegill*), letter to DJ, 2 October 2000.
11. S. Larsen (*Greenling*), letter to DJ, 9 October 2000.
12. Lardner, *Southwest Passage*, pp. 52, 150–55.
13. H. Smay (*S47*), letter to DJ, 27 April 2000.
14. Mendenhall, *Submarine Diary*, p. 93.
15. Gugliotta, *Pigboat 39*, pp. 178–81.
16. Quoted in Potts, *Yanks Down Under*, p. 131.
17. Finnane, *Policing in Australia*, p. 161.

18. F. J. White, constable 3479, arrest report of 12 January 1943, Queensland State Archives, Brisbane, A12030, 1268M.

Chapter 3. S-Boats

1. Ruhe, *War in the Boats*, pp. 26, 63.
2. T. Parks (*S39*), letter to DJ, 12 December 1999.
3. *DANFS*, 6:201.
4. Ruhe, *War in the Boats*, pp. 16, 38.
5. Blair, *Silent Victory*, p. 297.
6. T. Parks (*S39*), letter to DJ, 12 December 1999.
7. P. D. Snyder (*Guardfish*), letter to DJ, 26 March 2001.
8. S37 fifth war patrol report, p. 21, USNA, RG38, publication M-1752.
9. Padfield, *War beneath the Sea*, p. 249.
10. Ruhe, *War in the Boats*, p. 35.
11. T. Parks (*S39*), letters to DJ, 7 and 12 December 1999.
12. Gill, *Royal Australian Navy, 1942–1945*, pp. 75–76.
13. D. C. Peto (*Greenling*), letter to DJ, 13 May 2000.
14. Operation plan B-42 issued by Commander Task Group 42.1, dated 26 June 1942, USNA, RG38, CNO records, boxes 303 and 304.
15. Ibid.
16. T. Parks (*S39* and *Sailfish*), letter to DJ, 16 December 1999.
17. *DANFS*, 6:206.
18. H. C. Smay (*S47*), letter to DJ, 24 March 2001.

Chapter 4. S-Boats in the Solomons

1. Operation plan B-42 issued by Commander Task Group 42.1, dated 26 June 1942, p. 2, USNA, RG38, CNO records, boxes 303 and 304.
2. Morison, *Struggle for Guadalcanal*, p. 18.
3. Blair, *Silent Victory*, p. 299.
4. The following section on *S39*'s loss is drawn from Gugliotta, *Pigboat 39*, pp. 186–212; Roscoe, *United States Submarine Operations in World War II*, pp. 153–54; and Blair, *Silent Victory*, pp. 300–301.
5. A. P. Cousin (commanding officer, HMAS *Katoomba*), "Report of Proceedings Concerning U.S. Submarine S.39 Ashore on Rossel Island Reef," dated 17 August 1942, Australian War Memorial, Canberra, AWM78, 185/1.
6. Ibid.
7. Ibid.
8. Nesdale, *Spin Me a Dit*, p. 22.
9. S37 fifth war patrol report, p. 16, USNA, RG38, publication M-1752.
10. Ruhe, *War in the Boats*, p. 36.
11. Ibid., p. 41.

12. Morison, *Coral Sea, Midway, and Submarine Actions*, pp. 224–25.
13. Ruhe, *War in the Boats*, p. 38.
14. Ibid., pp. 41–42.

Chapter 5. New Tasks

1. Operation order S7-42 issued by Commander Task Group 42.1 to Commander USS *S39*, dated 9 May 1942, USNA, RG38, CNO records, boxes 303 and 304.
2. Holmes, *Undersea Victory*, p. 202.
3. Operation order S7-42 to *S39*.
4. Gill, *Royal Australian Navy, 1942–1945*, p. 72.
5. I. Pryce-Jones, "Report on Coastwatching, Solomon Islands, April 1943–January 1944," USNHC, p. 2.
6. This account is drawn largely from Pryce-Jones, "Report on Coastwatching," and *DANFS*, 6:205.
7. Wright, *If I Die*, foreword by E. Feldt.
8. Ibid., pp. 9–11.
9. The following account is drawn from Lord, *Lonely Vigil*, p. 85, and H. Josselyn, "Report, Part II, Events Leading to Final Establishment of Station NRY on Vella Lavella Island," USNHC.
10. Josselyn, "Report," para. 18.
11. Lord, *Lonely Vigil*, pp. 85–86.
12. Josselyn, "Report," para. 19.
13. This account is drawn from Josselyn, "Report," paras. 19–22, and J. Keenan, "Report," USNHC, sec. 3, paras. 2–5.
14. Reminiscences of Rear Adm. A. H. McCollum (1971), USNI, p. 556.
15. Firkins, *Of Nautilus and Eagles*, p. 214.
16. Ibid., pp. 207, 209.
17. Josselyn, "Report," para. 21.
18. Keenan, "Report," sec. 3, para. 4.
19. W. J. Read, "Report on Coastwatching Activity Bougainville Island, 1941–1943," typescript copy in QMM.
20. This account is drawn from Sister M. Celestine, "A Short History of the Sisters of St. Joseph of Orange in the Island of Buka," typescript, 13 May 1970, USNHC; Feuer, "Secret Mission to Teop"; and Read, "Report on Coastwatching Activity."
21. Read, "Report on Coastwatching Activity."
22. Eckert, "Left Overboard from a Diving Submarine," pp. 40–41.

Chapter 6. New Submarines Arrive

1. Mendenhall, *Submarine Diary*, pp. 32, 92, 93.
2. T. Parks (*Sailfish*), letters to DJ, 24 November 1999 and 23 January 2000.

3. T. Parks (*Sailfish*), letter to DJ of 24 November 1999.
4. *DANFS*, 6:660; Blair, *Silent Victory*, p. 305.
5. T. Parks (*Sailfish*), letter to DJ, 23 January 2000.
6. T. Parks (*Sailfish*), letter to DJ, 2 December 1999
7. Reminiscences of Rear Adm. N. G. Ward (1996), USNI, #4, pp. 163–64.
8. T. Parks (*Sailfish*), letter to DJ, 2 December 1999.
9. Blair, *Silent Victory*, p. 303.
10. Lockwood, *Sink 'Em All*, p. 47.
11. Ruhe, *War in the Boats*, pp. 83–104; Mendenhall, *Submarine Diary*, pp. 121–33.
12. Blair, *Silent Victory*, pp. 305–6.

Chapter 7. Boats from Pearl Harbor

1. Reminiscences of Adm. James Fife (1961–62), CUOHROC, pp. 302, 313.
2. Ibid.
3. P. Snyder (*Guardfish*), letter to DJ, 2 April 2000.
4. C. Hebb (*Fulton*), letter to DJ, 22 May 1999.
5. USS *Fulton*, war diary, 1–30 November 1942, entry for 3 November 1942, USNA, RG38.
6. R. C. Heath (*Fulton*), letter to C. J. Meyer, 8 December 2001, copy provided to DJ by C. J. Meyer; USS *Fulton* (*AS11*), *50th Anniversary*, p. 30.
7. R. C. Heath (*Fulton*), letter to C. J. Meyer, 8 December 2001; W. E. Jemmett (*Fulton*), interview with DJ, 27 October 2001.
8. L. L. Cottman, unpublished manuscript supplied by him to the authors, p. 5.
9. Reminiscences of Vice Adm. Lawson P. Ramage (1975), USNI, pp. 83–84.
10. U.S. Navy Base Brisbane, war diary, January 1943, USNA, RG38.
11. D. Peto (*Greenling*), letter to DJ, 3 August 1999.
12. *Guardfish* third war patrol report, entry for 28 January 1943, 1103L to 1513L, USNA, RG38, publication M-1752.
13. E. L. Schwab (*Guardfish*), article "Too Good to Be True," copy supplied to DJ by P. Snyder (no publication details available).
14. *Guardfish* third war patrol report.
15. U.S. Navy Base Brisbane, war diary, January 1943.
16. H. C. Smay (*Griffin and S47*), letter to DJ, 24 March 2001.

Chapter 8. The Compound and the City

1. M. K. Browne, "Memo to Miss Hannah Moore Frazier," 28 December 1943, p. 4, in MacArthur Papers, JOL.
2. *Fulton Bow Plane*, 1943, p. 9, in authors' collection.
3. C. J. Meyer, unpublished paper detailing his naval experiences, supplied by him to the authors.
4. USS *Fulton*, war diary, 1–30 November 1942, USNA, RG38.

5. Meyer paper.
6. *Fulton Bow Plane*, 1943, p. 16.
7. W. E. Jemmett *(Fulton)*, interview with DJ, 27 October 2001.
8. Meyer paper.
9. *USS Fulton (AS11)*, 50th Anniversary, p. 30; *Fulton Bow Plane*, 1943, p. 17.
10. *Truth* (Brisbane), 3 January 1943.
11. Program provided to DJ by P. Snyder *(Guardfish)*.
12. Brisbane City Council, *Brisbane Statistics, 1946*, 8:89–93.
13. Longhurst, *Friendship Is Life*, pp. 172–73.
14. *Courier-Mail* (Brisbane), 15 September 1943, p. 3.
15. L. L. Cottman, unpublished manuscript supplied by him to the authors.
16. D. Peto *(Greenling)*, letters to DJ, 3 August 1999 and 23 March 2001.
17. W. Turbeville *(Silversides)*, letter to DJ, undated.
18. D. Peto *(Greenling)*, letter to DJ, 23 March 2001.
19. W. E. Jemmett *(Fulton)*, interview with DJ, 27 October 2001.
20. Cottman manuscript.
21. Mendenhall, *Submarine Diary*, p. 254.
22. Letter from Lt. R. W. Sauer to Queensland police commissioner, dated 6 July 1943, Queensland State Archives, Brisbane, A12039, Police Department Correspondence File.
23. Queensland Police Brisbane Control Centre log, 14/3/42–21/5/43, Police Museum, Police Headquarters, Brisbane.
24. Report from Sergeant Bateson, 7 June 1943, Queensland State Archives, Brisbane, A12036.
25. Peter Winter, interview with PN, December 2000.
26. Marie Doyle, letter to DJ, 27 May 2001.
27. M. Sturma, "The Decorum of U.S. Servicemen in Queensland, 1942–45," unpublished thesis in JOL.

Chapter 9. A New Leader

1. Reminiscences of Adm. James Fife (1961–62), CUOHROC, pp. 130–33.
2. Ibid., p. 418.
3. Transcript of interview with Rear Adm. T. B. Klakring (1975) by C. and J. Blair, pp. 5–6, provided to DJ from P. Snyder's collection.
4. Blair, *Silent Victory*, p. 372.
5. Fife reminiscences, pp. 309–11.
6. Signal 260159 of 26 December 1942 from CSWPF to U.S. Navcom Port Moresby, USNA, RG313, item 23-C, Dispatches of Commander Submarines, Pacific Fleet Folders, Task Force 42.
7. Operation order S12-43 issued by Commander Task Force 42 for sixth war patrol of USS *Triton*, dated 15 February 1943, USNA, RG38, CNO records, boxes 303 and 304.

8. Blair, *Silent Victory*, p. 372.

9. Signal 180335 of 18 March 1943 from RDO Noumea (Vice Admiral Halsey) to RDO Honolulu (Admiral Nimitz), USNA, RG313, item 23-C, Dispatches of Commander Submarines, Pacific Fleet Folders, Task Force 72.

10. Reminiscences of Rear Adm. N. G. Ward (1996), USNI, #3, p. 150.

11. Blair, *Silent Victory*, p. 346.

12. O'Kane, *Wahoo*, p. 117.

13. *Wahoo* third war patrol report, USNA, RG38, publication M-1752.

14. Ibid.

15. O'Kane, *Wahoo*, pp. 136–39.

16. Ibid., p. 127

17. *Wahoo* third war patrol report.

18. Ibid.

19. John Clary, motor machinist's mate diary, entry for 26 January 1943.

20. DeRose, *Unrestricted Warfare*, pp. 77, 83, 94.

21. *Wahoo* third war patrol report.

22. O'Kane, *Wahoo*, p. 162.

23. *Wahoo* third war patrol report.

24. Clary diary, entry for 27 January 1943.

25. Blair, *Silent Victory*, p. 385.

26. Lockwood, *Sink 'Em All*, p. 66.

27. *Courier-Mail* (Brisbane), 16 March 1943.

28. Capt. J. H. Brown (acting commander, Submarine Force, Pacific Fleet), endorsement to *Wahoo* third war patrol report.

29. Alden, *U.S. Submarine Attacks during World War II*, pp. 30–31.

Chapter 10. Hard Times

1. O'Kane, *Wahoo*, p. 116.

2. Commander Submarine Force, *U.S. Submarine Losses, World War II*, p. 35.

3. D. D. Ames, "WWII Submariner's Dolphins Still on Active Duty," published online at http://www.csp.navy.mil/centennial/jenkins.htm, October 2000.

4. *Growler* fourth war patrol report, USNA, RG38, publication M-1752.

5. Quoted in Lanigan, *Kangaroo Express*, p. 82.

6. Quoted ibid., pp. 80–81.

7. Quoted ibid., p. 82.

8. Commander Submarine Force, *U.S. Submarine Losses, World War II*, pp. 37–38.

9. Signal 281221 of 28 March 1943 from U.S. Naval Communication Service, transmitted by *Fulton*, USNA, RG313, item 23-C, Dispatches of Commander Submarines, Pacific Fleet Folders, Task Force 72.

10. Commander Submarine Force, *U.S. Submarine Losses, World War II*, p. 43.

11. *Courier-Mail* (Brisbane), 14 June 1943.

12. D. Peto (*Greenling*), letter to DJ, 17 January 2000.
13. W. C. Turbeville (*Silversides*), letter to J. M. Allen, 26 June 1995; W. Devling (*Albacore*), letters to Mrs. J. M. Allen, 19 April and 15 October 1996, provided to DJ by J. M. Allen.
14. R. Brown (*Greenling*), letter to DJ, 6 January 2000.
15. Quoted in Blair, *Silent Victory*, p. 376.
16. Reminiscences of Adm. James Fife (1961–62), CUOHROC, p. 334.
17. Blair, *Silent Victory*, p. 377.
18. Memorandum from Rear Adm. Christie to Captain Fife, 25 March 1943, "Submarine Operations—Notes on Methods of Control," USNA, RG313, Messages, COMSUBPAC, CTF72, Most Secret In and Out, box 25.
19. Memorandum, 5 April 1943, "Method of Operational Control of Submarines of Task Force SEVENTY TWO," USNA, RG313, Messages, COMSUBPAC, CTF72, Most Secret In and Out, box 25.
20. Fife reminiscences, p. 333.
21. Commander Submarine Force, *U.S. Submarine Losses, World War II*, pp. 38–44.
22. Nevitt, *Who Sank the Triton?*
23. J. McKenzie Allen, letter to DJ, 11 July 2001, with results of research she had arranged by a Japanese historian of Japanese papers attached to JANAC report of sinking of *Triton*.
24. *Gato* fifth war patrol report, p. 7, USNA, RG38, publication M-1752.
25. Reminiscences of Rear Adm. N. G. Ward (1996), USNI, #3, p. 149.
26. *Gato* fifth war patrol report, pp. 7–8.

Chapter 11. Further Operations

1. U.S. Navy Base Brisbane, war diaries, January–June 1943, USNA, RG38.
2. Reminiscences of Adm. James Fife (1961–62), CUOHROC, p. 332.
3. Capt. J. Fife, endorsement to *Drum* fifth war patrol report, USNA, RG38, publication M-1752.
4. Quoted in Blair, *Silent Victory*, p. 379.
5. Capt. J. Fife, endorsement to *Gato* sixth war patrol report, USNA, RG38, publication M-1752.
6. Fife reminiscences, p. 340.
7. M. H. Rindskopf (*Drum*), letter to DJ, 25 December 2001.
8. Reminiscences of Vice Adm. Lawson P. Ramage (1975), #2, USNI, p. 82.
9. D. C. Peto (*Greenling*), letter to DJ, 23 March 2001.
10. C. Schechter (*Drum*), letter to DJ, 30 December 1998.
11. T. Parks (*S39* and *Sailfish*), letter to DJ, 7 December 1999.
12. P. Snyder (*Guardfish*), letter to DJ, 21 January 2001.
13. Kimball, "History Ignored Must Be Relived," p. 21.

14. T. Parks (*S39* and *Sailfish*), letter to DJ, 23 January 2000.

15. P. Snyder (*Guardfish*), letters to DJ, 20 and 23 April 2000.

16. F. Medina (*Guardfish* and *Tuna*), letter to DJ, 15 March 2000.

17. Capt. J. Fife, endorsement to *Drum* sixth war patrol report, USNA, RG38, publication M-1752.

18. Ruhe, *War in the Boats*, p. 92.

19. D. Peto (*Greenling*), letter to DJ, 17 January 2000.

20. Capt. J. Fife, endorsement to *Growler* fourth war patrol report, USNA, RG38, publication M-1752.

21. I. King (*Darter*), letter to DJ, 7 January 1999.

Chapter 12. Supporting the Coastwatchers

1. Wright, *If I Die*, pp. 31–32.

2. D. Peto (*Greenling*), letter to DJ, 17 January 2000.

3. *Gato* fifth war patrol report, USNA, RG38, publication M-1752.

4. J. Keenan, "Report," USNHC, sec. 5, paras. 1–2.

5. Ibid., sec. 6, paras. 2–4.

6. W. J. Read, "Report on Coastwatching Activity Bougainville Island, 1941–1943," typescript copy in QMM.

7. *Gato* fifth war patrol report.

8. Feldt, *Coast Watchers*, p. 271.

9. The following account is drawn from *Gato* report of second part of fifth war patrol, USNA, RG38, publication M-1752, and Read, "Report on Coastwatching Activity."

10. Curtis, "Memories on the 5th–6th Patrol."

11. Murray, *Hunted*, pp. 50–69.

12. Ibid., 132–79.

13. Ibid., p. 179.

14. Ibid., p. 226.

15. Feldt, *Coast Watchers*, p. 382.

Chapter 13. Buildup in Brisbane

1. Blair, *Silent Victory*, p. 371.

2. Reminiscences of Adm. James Fife (1961–62), CUOHROC, p. 346.

3. "Defense-Aid Reciprocal Aid Review Report," part B, item 51, USNA, RG71.

4. Commander Seventh Fleet, "Base Facilities Report," USNA, RG38, box 1408 P38A.

5. Fife reminiscences, p. 346.

6. E. George, letter to PN, 4 February 1997.

7. Ibid.

8. "Defense-Aid Reciprocal Aid Review Report," item 45.
9. F. H. G. Bolt, "Report of Torpedo Maintenance Facilities for USN and RN Submarines at Brisbane," NAA, Melbourne, MP1185/8, 2026/5/285.
10. "Defense-Aid Reciprocal Aid Review Report," item 44.
11. South Brisbane Dry Dock register, QMM.
12. Commander Seventh Fleet, "Base Facilities Report," p. 35.
13. NAA, Melbourne, MP1587/1, 340A.
14. Evans, *Report of the Department of Harbours and Marine for Year Ended 30 June 1945*, p. 2.
15. L. Curtis, letter to PN, 15 July 1998.
16. "A Brief History of the War Activities of the Ipswich Railway Workshops," pp. 20 and 29, Queensland State Archives, Brisbane, QSAA/9475, batch 710.
17. B. Ghormley, letter to PN, 8 October 1998.
18. Reminiscences of Capt. Slade D. Cutter (1985), USNI, pp. 219–21.
19. *Courier-Mail* (Brisbane), 1 July 1943, p. 3.
20. Fife reminiscences, p. 335.
21. Capt. J. Fife, endorsement to *Growler* fourth war patrol report, USNA, RG38, publication M-1752.
22. NAA, Melbourne, MP138/1, 603/223/1451.
23. Message from HMAS *Moreton* to Commander Task Force 42, dated 2 March 1943, re-repairs to *Growler*, NAA, Melbourne, MP138/1, 603/223/1451.
24. R. Ball, letter to PN, undated [1998].
25. A. Ullrich (*Growler*), letter to PN, 22 November 1997.
26. H. Caldwell (*Dace*), letter to DJ, 9 March 2002.
27. Mansfield, *Cruisers for Breakfast*, p. 42.
28. *Courier-Mail* (Brisbane), 1 December 1944, p. 3.
29. Ibid., 30 March 1943.
30. Foley, *Reef Pilots*, pp. 110–11.

Chapter 14. Leave in Queensland

1. Sterling, *Wake of the Wahoo*, p. 40.
2. Ibid., pp. 47–66.
3. O'Kane, *Wahoo*, pp. 111–15.
4. Ibid.
5. Grider and Sims, *War Fish*, p. 49.
6. Reminiscences of Capt. Slade D. Cutter (1985), USNI, pp. 221–23.
7. A. Ullrich (*Growler*), letter to PN, 22 November 1997.
8. L. Greenwood (*Growler*), letter to PN, 9 January 1998.
9. P. Toper (*Growler*), letter to PN, 22 November 1997.
10. M. Weymouth (*Growler*), letter to PN, undated [1997].
11. D. Peto (*Greenling*), letter to DJ, 3 August 1999.
12. L. Hall (*Guardfish*), letter to DJ, 17 February 2000.

13. I. King (*Darter*), letter to DJ, 1 January 1999.

14. T. Parks (*S39* and *Sailfish*), letter to DJ, 24 November 1999.

15. R. L. Griffiths (*Narwhal*), taped speech (1992).

16. Goodson and O'Rourke, "19 Upper Melbourne Street," pp. 28–29.

17. J. R. Bertrand (*Bowfin*), letter of 15 February 1995 to USS *Bowfin* Submarine Museum and Park, Honolulu, courtesy of that museum.

18. W. Devling (*Triton* and *Albacore*), letter to DJ, 4 April 2001.

19. W. Devling (*Triton* and *Albacore*), letter to DJ, 18 May 2001.

20. R. Brown (*Greenling*), letter to DJ, 6 January 2000.

21. W. Webb (*Darter*), letter to P. Ryan, Brisbane, 30 December 1998.

22. H. Story (*Bluegill*), letter to DJ, 2 October 2000.

23. Mansfield, *Cruisers for Breakfast*, p. 52.

24. Casey, *Battle Below*, pp. 15–17.

Chapter 15. The Rest Centers

1. Blair, *Silent Victory*, p. 371.

2. Reminiscences of Adm. James Fife (1961–62), CUOHROC, pp. 337, 348.

3. Commander Seventh Fleet, "Base Facilities Report," pp. 27–28, USNA, RG38, box 1408 P38A.

4. "Defense-Aid Reciprocal Aid Review Report," items 55 and 56, USNA, RG71.

5. H. Story (*Bluegill*), letter to DJ, 2 October 2000.

6. D. Peto (*Greenling*), letter to DJ, 23 March 2001.

7. Quoted in Mansfield, *Cruisers for Breakfast*, p. 56.

8. Fairhall, *Remember the War Years*, p. 41.

9. C. Meyer (*Fulton*), letter to DJ, 6 January 2003.

10. "Defense-Aid Reciprocal Aid Review Report," item 54.

11. Ibid., item 57.

12. Reminiscences of Rear Adm. N. G. Ward (1996), USNI, #4, p. 176.

13. Reminiscences of Capt. Slade D. Cutter (1985), USNI, pp. 223–25.

14. S. Larsen (*Greenling*), letter to DJ, 9 October 2000.

15. K. Moore, "History of the American Red Cross Officers' Rest Area, Surfers Paradise," n.d., three-page typescript in MacArthur Papers, JOL.

16. E. Williams, "Report of Recreation for February 1944, Naval Leave Area Coolangatta," in MacArthur Papers, JOL.

17. Kemper M. Moore, four-page typescript report on Red Cross activities at Surfers Paradise for November 1943 in MacArthur Papers, JOL.

18. Helen L. Swope, letter to H. M. Frazier on Representation at the Navy Club dated 20 November 1944 in MacArthur Papers, JOL.

19. Mendenhall, *Submarine Diary*, p. 252.

20. The following is drawn largely from Williams, "Report for February 1944."

21. Ibid.

22. R. Brown (*Greenling*), letter to DJ, 23 December 1999.

23. Moore, "History of the American Red Cross Officers' Rest Area."
24. J. Cran, "The American Red Cross Service Club, Brisbane," n.d., three-page typescript in MacArthur Papers, JOL.
25. M. K. Browne, "Report to Miss Helen Hall" (South and Southwest Pacific Director of American Red Cross), 27 November 1942, in MacArthur Papers, JOL.
26. M. K. Browne, seven-page typescript letter to Miss Hannah Moore Frazier dated 28 December 1943 in MacArthur Papers, JOL.

Chapter 16. Testing and Training

1. Capt. J. Ahern, "Ships Piloted," manuscript in collection of QMM.
2. Quoted in Lanigan, *Kangaroo Express*, p. 102.
3. Reminiscences of Rear Adm. N. G. Ward (1996), USNI, #4, pp. 160–61.
4. B. Claggett *(Dace)*, letter to DJ, 4 May 2000.
5. Reported in Lanigan, *Kangaroo Express*, p. 102.
6. O'Kane, *Wahoo*, p. 115.
7. *Growler* patrol report, quoted in Lanigan, *Kangaroo Express*, p. 94.
8. McDonell, *Australian Salvors of World War 2*, p. 148, quoting Chief Engineer Wheatley of the tug *St. Giles*.
9. Queensland Police Brisbane Control Centre log, p. 935.
10. "Report of Commanding Officer HMAS Lithgow to Commanding Officer HMAS Rushcutter," 22 May 1943, NAA, Melbourne, MP1049/5/0, 2002/2/177.
11. *DANFS*, 5:347.
12. Russell, *Hell Above, Deep Water Below*, p. 44.
13. Commanding officer, USS *Tunny*, to the naval officer in charge, New Guinea, "Escort Services Rendered by HMAS Katoomba," 6 May 1944, NAA, Brisbane, BP132/2, BNO431.
14. J. McGrievy *(Seahorse)*, letter to DJ, 28 May 2000.
15. L. Crabtree, "History of HMAS *Parkes*'s Voyages," 1994, quoted in V. Catchpoole, "Going to War on a Corvette," typescript in QMM, p. 3.
16. Commanding officer, HMAS *Stuart*, to the naval officer in charge, Brisbane, "Exercises with U.S. Submarine 'Scamp,'" 19 December 1943, NAA, Brisbane, BP132/2, BNO431.
17. Commanding officer, HMAS *Stuart*, to the naval officer in charge, Brisbane, "Exercises with U.S. Submarine 'Guardfish,'" 5 December 1943, NAA, Brisbane, BP132/2, BNO431.
18. Statement of commanding officer, USS *Guardfish*, dated 4 December 1943, re-collision at 2355 Love, 3 December 1943, with an unidentified vessel, USNA, RG313, Records of Naval Operating Forces.
19. L. Hall *(Guardfish)*, letter to DJ, 17 February 2000.
20. Commander Task Force 72, circular 0078, "USS S43 [sic] and USS S47—Employment for Anti-submarine Training of Units of SEVENTH FLEET—General Plan for," 22 March 1944, NAA, Brisbane, BP132/2, BNO431.

21. Commander Task Force 72, orders "Anti-submarine Training Exercises off Caloundra Head 10 to 12 August 1944," 4 August 1944, NAA, Brisbane, BP132/2, BNO431.

22. P. Snyder (*Guardfish* and *Seahorse*), letter to DJ, 28 February 2000.

23. Holmes, *Undersea Victory*, pp. 34–35.

24. P. Snyder (*Guardfish* and *Seahorse*), letter to DJ, 20 May 2000.

25. M. H. Rindskopf (*Drum*), letter to DJ, 28 December 2001.

26. G. Grider, quoted in Blair, *Silent Victory*, p. 315.

27. Sterling, *Wake of the Wahoo*, p. 72.

28. Holmes, *Undersea Victory*, pp. 201–2.

Chapter 17. Progress

1. G. H. Battershell (*Coucal*), interview with DJ, 23 May 2002.

2. D. Peto (*Greenling*), letter to DJ, 17 January 2000.

3. Interview with Vice Adm. A. S. Carpender, 11 July 1945, NAA, Melbourne, MP1587/1 3R, B6121.

4. Reminiscences of Rear Adm. N. G. Ward (1996), USNI, #4, p. 162.

5. Capt. J. Fife, endorsement to *Gato* sixth war patrol report, USNA, RG38, publication M-1752.

6. Reminiscences of Adm. James Fife (1961–62), CUOHROC, pp. 350–51.

7. *Growler* fifth war patrol report, USNA, RG38, publication M-1752.

8. Signal 210851 of 21 June 1943 from RDO Brisbane to Subs TF72, USNA, RG313, item 23-C, Dispatches of Commander Submarines, Pacific Fleet Folders, Task Force 72.

9. Blair, *Silent Victory*, pp. 477–78.

10. Ibid., pp. 480–81.

11. Capt. J. Fife, endorsement to *Drum* seventh war patrol report, USNA, RG38, publication M-1752.

12. Ward reminiscences, #4, pp. 179–80.

13. Signal 071037 of 7 April 1943 from RDO Brisbane to Subs TF72, USNA, RG313, item 23-C, Dispatches of Commander Submarines, Pacific Fleet Folders, Task Force 72.

14. F. Medina (*Tuna*), letter to DJ, 15 March 2000.

15. Maritime Trade Protection File, pp. 220–22, Australian War Memorial, Canberra, AWM54.

16. Signal 090535 of 9 August 1943 from Com 7th Fleet (Vice Admiral Carpender) to ComInCh (Admiral King), USNA, RG313, item 23-C, Dispatches of Commander Submarines, Pacific Fleet Folders, Task Force 72.

17. Montague, "Exploits of a WWII Submariner," p. 5.

18. Morison, *Breaking the Bismarck's Barrier*, p. 67.

19. U.S. Navy Base Brisbane, war diaries, August–October 1943, USNA, RG38.

20. Commander Submarine Force, *U.S. Submarine Losses, World War II*, pp. 61, 77–79.

21. Ruhe, *War in the Boats,* pp. 151–54.
22. Terzibaschitsch, *Submarines of the US Navy,* p. 69.
23. Report of trials of USS *Cisco,* dated 13 July 1943, USNA, RG19, General Correspondence—Bureau of Ships, 1940–45, file SS290, stack area 470, box 2127.
24. M. L. Coe (daughter of Comdr. J. W. Coe), letter to DJ, 10 August 1999.
25. Commander Submarine Force, *U.S. Submarine Losses, World War II,* pp. 59–60.
26. U.S. Navy Base Brisbane, war diary, December 1943, USNA, RG38.
27. W. Jemmett *(Fulton),* interview with DJ, 27 October 2001.
28. Joyce Barrett, phone interview with PN, 14 December 2000.
29. L. L. Cottman *(Fulton),* unpublished manuscript supplied by him to the authors, p. 7.

Chapter 18. Milne Bay

1. H. Story *(Bluegill),* letter to DJ, 2 October 2000.
2. L. L. Cottman *(Fulton),* unpublished manuscript supplied by him to the authors, p. 7.
3. C. T. Hebb *(Fulton),* letter to DJ, 22 May 1999.
4. W. E. Jemmett *(Fulton),* interview with DJ, 27 October 2001.
5. Cottman manuscript, p. 7.
6. U.S. Navy Base Brisbane, war diaries, November and December 1943, February 1944, USNA, RG38.
7. C. Schechter *(Fulton* and *Drum),* letter to DJ, 7 February 1999.
8. Mansfield, *Cruisers for Breakfast,* p. 49.
9. H. Story *(Bluegill),* letter to DJ, 2 October 2000.
10. M. H. Rindskopf *(Drum),* letter to DJ, 17 March 2001.
11. Alden, "Ultra Intercepts."
12. W. Devling *(Triton* and *Albacore),* letter to DJ, 29 March 2001.
13. U.S. Navy Base Brisbane, war diary, December 1943, USNA, RG38.
14. Reminiscences of Rear Adm. N. G. Ward (1996), USNI, #3, p. 149.
15. Blair, *Silent Victory,* pp. 483–84.
16. Padfield, *War beneath the Sea,* p. 386.
17. Messages published on *Fulton* plan of the day for Monday, 20 March 1944, copy provided to the authors by L. L. Cottman *(Fulton).*
18. Reminiscences of Adm. James Fife (1961–62), CUOHROC, pp. 562–65.

Chapter 19. A New Squadron

1. Morison, *New Guinea and the Marianas,* p. 66.
2. E. L. Barr *(Bluegill),* interview in "The Captains of World War II," part 2 of *The Silent Service,* television series screened on History Channel, January 2001.

3. H. G. Story (*Bluegill*), letter to DJ, 2 October 2000.

4. Mansfield, *Cruisers for Breakfast*, pp. 94–95.

5. S. Jordan (Women's National Emergency Service), interview with PN, 7 January 2003.

6. I. King (*Darter*), letter to DJ, 30 December 1998.

7. W. Shaw (*Bream*), letter to DJ, 28 December 1998.

8. *Pollack* eleventh war patrol report, USNA, RG38, publication M-1752.

9. P. Snyder (*Guardfish* and *Seahorse*), letters to DJ, 16 and 20 May 2000.

10. U.S. Navy Base Brisbane, war diaries, April 1944–March 1945, USNA, RG38.

11. Ibid., April and May 1944.

12. Blair, *Silent Victory*, pp. 672–74.

Chapter 20. Philippine "Spy Squadron"

1. Breuer, *MacArthur's Undercover War*, pp. 48–51.

2. Gen. Douglas MacArthur GHQ, SWPA, special release of 25 October 1944, quoted in Supreme Commander for the Allied Powers, *Campaigns of MacArthur in the Pacific*, p. 324.

3. "Chick" Parsons, quoted in Dissette and Adamson, *Guerrilla Submarines*, p. 75.

4. Breuer, *MacArthur's Undercover War*, p. 85.

5. R. L. Griffiths (*Narwhal*), taped speech (1992).

6. Wheeler, *War under the Pacific*, pp. 130–31.

7. Griffiths speech.

8. Maynard, "Anchor Aweigh in the Dark Night," pp. 11–12.

9. Dissette and Adamson, *Guerrilla Submarines*, pp. 72, 75–78, 235–36.

10. Kimmett and Regis, *U.S. Submarines in World War II*, p. 114.

Chapter 21. Final Success

1. Mansfield, *Cruisers for Breakfast*, pp. 43–46.

2. Ibid., pp. 83–85, 89.

3. H. H. Caldwell (*Dace*), letter to DJ, 27 March 2002.

4. I. King (*Darter*), letter to DJ, 4 January 1999.

5. Mansfield, *Cruisers for Breakfast*, p. 150.

6. Ibid., p. 153.

7. I. King (*Darter*), letter to DJ, 1 January 1999.

8. Benitez, "Battle Stations Submerged," p. 29.

9. *Darter* patrol report, quoted in Roscoe, *United States Submarine Operations in World War II*, p. 392.

10. *Dace* patrol report, quoted ibid., p. 393.

11. Mansfield, *Cruisers for Breakfast*, p. 165.

12. Benitez, "Battle Stations Submerged," p. 30.

13. Mansfield, *Cruisers for Breakfast,* pp. 162–63, 166–68.

14. Ibid., p. 168.

15. Ibid., p. 170.

16. Quoted in Roscoe, *United States Submarine Operations in World War II,* p. 396.

17. Vice Adm. T. C. Kinkaid, quoted ibid., p. 399.

18. General MacArthur, quoted in Supreme Commander for the Allied Powers, *Campaigns of MacArthur in the Pacific,* p. 208.

19. Mansfield, *Cruisers for Breakfast,* p. 179.

20. I. King (*Darter*), letter to DJ, 4 January 1999.

21. Mansfield, *Cruisers for Breakfast,* p. 180.

22. Ibid., p. 202.

23. Ibid., pp. 181–82.

24. Benitez, "Battle Stations Submerged," p. 31.

25. I. King (*Darter*), letter to DJ, 4 January 1999.

26. Benitez, "Battle Stations Submerged," p. 35.

27. Ibid.

28. B. D. Claggett (*Dace*), letter to DJ, 4 May 2000.

29. Benitez, "Battle Stations Submerged," p. 35.

30. I. King (*Darter* and *Menhaden*), letter to DJ, 1 January 1999.

Chapter 22. Closing Down

1. Stevens, *U-Boat Far from Home,* pp. 136–39.

2. U.S. Navy Base Brisbane, war diary, November and December 1944, USNA, RG38.

3. H. C. Smay (*S47* and *Searaven*), letter to DJ, 24 March 2001.

4. Mendenhall, *Submarine Diary,* pp. 253–68.

5. Reminiscences of Adm. James Fife (1961–62), CUOHROC, pp. 411, 414.

6. U.S. Navy Base Brisbane, war diaries, January–July 1945, USNA, RG38.

7. Ibid., March 1945.

8. Fife reminiscences, p. 411.

9. "Defense-Aid Reciprocal Aid Review Report," USNA, RG71.

10. *Courier-Mail* (Brisbane), 23 December 1947, p. 5.

Chapter 23. The British Arrive

1. Reminiscences of Adm. James Fife (1961–62), CUOHROC, p. 395.

2. Warren and Benson, *Above Us the Waves,* p. 216.

3. Fife reminiscences, pp. 115–33, 217–18.

4. Capt. W. R. Fell, article in *Blackwood's Magazine* 262, no. 1585 (November 1947), copy held by Royal Navy Submarine Museum Research Centre, Gosport, Hampshire, A1983/92.

5. M. Shean (*XE4*), letter to DJ, 25 January 2000.

6. Mitchell, *Tip of the Spear,* p. 160.

7. Fife reminiscences, p. 431.

8. Warren and Benson, *Above Us the Waves,* p. 220.

9. K. Briggs (*XE4*), interview with DJ, 31 January 2002.

10. K. Briggs (*XE4*), interview with DJ, 27 March 1999.

11. Lt. H. P. Westmacott, "Operation Foil," 8 August 1945, Royal Navy Submarine Museum Research Centre, Gosport, Hampshire, A1980/68/001.

12. Ibid.

13. Mitchell, *Tip of the Spear,* p. 177.

14. Fraser, *Frogman V.C.,* pp. 156–57.

15. Fleming, *Magennis VC,* p. 156.

16. Warren and Benson, *Above Us the Waves,* p. 227.

17. Shean, *Corvette and Submarine,* pp. 250–51.

18. M. Shean (*XE4*), letter to DJ, 25 January 2000.

19. Ibid.

20. K. Briggs (*XE4*), interview with DJ, 31 January 2002.

21. Fraser, *Frogman V.C.,* p. 197.

Conclusion

1. Collins, *As Luck Would Have It,* p. 135.

2. Lockwood, *Sink 'Em All,* p. 386.

3. Reminiscences of Adm. James Fife (1961–62), CUOHROC, p. 294.

4. I. King (*Darter*), letter to DJ, 28 December 1998.

5. L. Hall (*Guardfish*), letter to DJ, 10 February 2000.

6. T. Parks (*S39* and *Sailfish*), letter to DJ, 30 November 1999.

7. Ibid., 22 August 2000.

BIBLIOGRAPHY

Books

Alden, John D. *U.S. Submarine Attacks during World War II.* Annapolis, Md.: Naval Institute Press, 1989.

Alperovitz, Gar. *The Decision to Use the Atomic Bomb.* London: Harper Collins, 1995.

Bagnasco, Emilio. *Submarines of World War II.* London: Arms and Armour Press, 1977.

Blair, Clay, Jr. *Silent Victory.* New York: J. B. Lippincott, 1975.

Boyd, Carl, and Akihiko Yoshida. *The Japanese Submarine Force and World War II.* Shrewsbury: Airlife Publishing, 1996.

Breuer, William B. *MacArthur's Undercover War.* New York: John Wiley and Sons, 1995.

Brisbane City Council. *BCC Annual Report, 1939–40.* Brisbane: Brisbane City Council, 1941.

———. *Brisbane Statistics, 1946.* Vol. 8. Brisbane: Brisbane City Council, 1947.

Bureau of Yards and Docks. *Building the Navy's Bases in World War II.* Washington, D.C.: U.S. Government Printing Office, 1947.

Cairns, Lynne. *Fremantle's Secret Fleets.* Fremantle, Western Australia: Western Australian Maritime Museum, 1995.

"The Captains of World War II." Part 2 of *The Silent Service.* Television series, History Channel, January 2001.

Casey, Robert J. *Battle Below.* Indianapolis: Bobbs-Merrill, 1945.

Charlton, Peter. *South Queensland WWII, 1941–1945.* Brisbane: Boolarong Publications, 1991.

Cline, Rick. *Submarine Grayback.* Placentia, Calif.: R. A. Cline Publications, 1999.

Coletta, P. E., ed. *United States Navy and Marine Corps Bases, Overseas.* Westport, Conn.: Greenwood Press, 1985.

Collins, Sir John. *As Luck Would Have It.* Sydney: Angus and Robertson, 1965.

Commander Submarine Force, U.S. Pacific Fleet. *U.S. Submarine Losses, World War II.* Washington, D.C.: U.S. Government Printing Office, 1946.

Conner, C. C. *Nothing Friendly in the Vicinity.* Mason City: Savas Publishing Co., 1999.

Cracknell, W. H. *USS Barb (SS.220), Gato Class Submarine.* Windsor, Berks: Warship Profile, Profile Publications, 1973.

Creed, David. *Operations of the Fremantle Submarine Base, 1942–1945.* Garden Island, New South Wales: Naval Historical Society of Australia, n.d.

Davenport, W. *Harbours and Marine.* Brisbane: Department of Harbours and Marine, 1986.

DeRose, James F. *Unrestricted Warfare.* New York: John Wiley and Sons, 2000.

Dissette, E., and H. Adamson. *Guerrilla Submarines.* New York: Ballantine, 1972.

Evans, W. J. *Report of the Department of Harbours and Marine for Year Ended 30 June 1945.* Brisbane: Queensland Government Printer, 1945.

Fairhall, P. *Remember the War Years—Redcliffe.* Brisbane: Australia Remembers, 1995.

Feldt, Eric. *The Coast Watchers.* Garden City, New York: Nelson, 1979.

Finnane, M., ed. *Policing in Australia: Historical Perspectives.* Kensington: New South Wales University Press, 1987.

Firkins, P. *Of Nautilus and Eagles.* Stanmore, New South Wales: Cassell Australia, 1975.

Fleming, George. *Magennis VC.* Dublin: History Ireland, 1998.

Foley, John. *Reef Pilots.* Sydney: Banks, 1982.

Fraser, Ian. *Frogman V.C.* London: Angus and Robertson, 1957.

Gill, G. Hermon. *Royal Australian Navy, 1939–1942.* Canberra: Australian War Memorial, 1957.

———. *Royal Australian Navy, 1942–1945.* Canberra: Australian War Memorial, 1968.

Gray, Edwin. *Few Survived.* London: Futura Publications, 1986.

Greenwood, G., ed. *Brisbane, 1859–1959.* Brisbane: Brisbane City Council, 1959.

Greenwood, G., and J. Laverty. *Brisbane, 1859–1959: A History of Local Government.* Brisbane: Oswald L. Ziegler, n.d.

Grider, George, and Lytel Sims. *War Fish.* Boston: Little, Brown and Co., 1958.

Gugliotta, Bobette. *Pigboat 39.* Lexington: University Press of Kentucky, 1984.

Holmes, Harry. *The Last Patrol.* Annapolis, Md.: Naval Institute Press, 1994.

Holmes, W. J. *Double-Edged Secrets.* Annapolis, Md.: Naval Institute Press, 1979.

———. *Undersea Victory.* Garden City, N.Y.: Doubleday and Co., 1966.

Holthouse, H. *Looking Back: The First 150 Years of Queensland Schools.* Brisbane: Queensland Department of Education, 1975.

Hoyt, Edwin P. *MacArthur's Navy.* New York: Orion, 1989.

———. *Submarines at War.* New York: Stein and Day Publishers, 1984.

Humphris, Colin. *Trapped on Timor.* Victor Harbour, South Australia: Colin Humphris, 1991.

Ingham, T. *Rendezvous by Submarine*. New York: Doubleday, 1945.

Jenkins, David. *Battle Surface!* Milsons Point, New South Wales: Random House Australia, 1992.

Kimmett, Larry, and Margaret Regis. *U.S. Submarines in World War II: An Illustrated History*. Seattle: Navigator Publishing, 1996.

Lack, Clem. *Three Decades of Queensland Political History*. Brisbane: Queensland Government Printer, 1962.

Lanigan, Richard J. *Kangaroo Express*. Laurel, Fla.: RJL Express Publications, 1998.

Lardner, John. *Southwest Passage*. London: J. B. Lippincott, 1943.

LaVo, C. *Back from the Deep*. Annapolis, Md.: Naval Institute Press, 1994.

Lenton, H. T. *American Submarines*. London: Macdonald and Co., 1973.

Lenton, H. T., and J. J. Colledge. *Warships of World War II*. London: Ian Allen, 1962.

Lewin, Ronald. *The Other Ultra*. London: Hutchinson, 1982.

Lockwood, Vice Adm. Charles A. *Sink 'Em All*. New York: E. P. Dutton and Co., 1951.

———. *Down to the Sea in Subs*. New York: W. W. Norton and Co., 1967.

Long, Gavin. *The Six Years War*. Canberra: Australian War Memorial and Australian Government Publishing Service, 1973.

Longhurst, R. *Friendship Is Life: A History of Tattersalls Club, Brisbane*. Brisbane: Tattersalls Club, 1993.

Lord, Walter. *Lonely Vigil*. New York: Viking, 1977.

Love, Robert W., Jr. *History of the U.S. Navy, 1775–1941*. Harrisburg, Pa.: Stackpole Books, 1992.

Lowder, Hughston E. *The Silent Service*. Baltimore, Md.: Silent Service Books, 1987.

Lundstrom, John B. *The First South Pacific Campaign*. Annapolis, Md.: Naval Institute Press, 1976.

MacIntyre, Donald. *The Battle for the Pacific*. London: Angus and Robertson, 1966.

Manchester, W. *American Caesar*. New York: Dill, 1978.

Mansfield, John G., Jr. *Cruisers for Breakfast*. Tacoma, Wash.: Media Center Publishing, 1997.

Mars, Alastair. *Submarines at War, 1939–1945*. London: Corgi Books, 1974.

McDonell, Capt. R. F. J. *Australian Salvors of World War 2*. Melbourne: "Polly Woodside" Publishers, 1995.

Mendenhall, Rear Adm. Corwin. *Submarine Diary*. Annapolis, Md.: Naval Institute Press, 1995.

Mitchell, Pamela. *The Tip of the Spear*. Huddersfield, U.K.: Richard Netherwood, 1993.

Morison, Samuel Eliot. *Breaking the Bismarck's Barrier, 22 July 1942–1 May 1944*. Vol. 6 of *History of United States Naval Operations in World War II*. Boston: Little, Brown and Co., 1950.

————. *Coral Sea, Midway and Submarine Actions, May 1942–August 1942*. Vol. 4 of *History of United States Naval Operations in World War II*. Boston: Little, Brown and Co., 1949.

————. *Leyte, June 1944–January 1945*. Vol. 12 of *History of United States Naval Operations in World War II*. London: Oxford University Press, 1958.

————. *New Guinea and the Marianas, March 1944–August 1944*. Vol. 8 of *History of United States Naval Operations in World War II*. Boston: Little, Brown and Co., 1953.

————. *Struggle for Guadalcanal, August 1942–February 1943*. Vol. 5 of *History of United States Naval Operations in World War II*. Boston: Little, Brown and Co., 1955.

Murray, M. *Hunted—A Coastwatcher's Story*. Melbourne: Specialty Press, 1967.

Navy Department. *Dictionary of American Naval Fighting Ships*. 9 vols. Washington, D.C.: U.S. Government Printing Office, 1959–91.

Nesdale, Iris. *Spin Me a Dit*. Adelaide, South Australia: Iris Nesdale, 1984.

Nevitt, A. D. *Who Sank the Triton?* Published online at http://www.combined-fleet.com/triton.htm, 1998.

O'Kane, Rear Adm. Richard H. *Wahoo*. Novata, Calif.: Presidio Press, 1987.

Padfield, Peter. *War beneath the Sea*. New York: John Wiley and Sons, 1998.

Potter, E. B. *Nimitz*. Annapolis, Md.: Naval Institute Press, 1976.

Potts, Daniel E., and Annette Potts. *Yanks Down Under, 1941–45*. Melbourne: Oxford University Press, 1985.

Ralph, Barry. *They Passed This Way*. East Roseville, New South Wales: Kangaroo Press, 2000.

Roscoe, Theodore. *United States Submarine Operations in World War II*. Annapolis, Md.: U.S. Naval Institute, 1949.

Ruhe, Capt. William J. *War in the Boats*. Washington, D.C.: Brassey's, 1994.

Russell, D. *Hell Above, Deep Water Below*. Tillamook, Ore.: Bayocean, 1995.

Shean, Max. *Corvette and Submarine*. Claremont, Western Australia: Max Shean, 1994.

Silverstone, Paul H. *U.S. Warships of World War II*. London: Ian Allen, 1965.

Sterling, Forest J. *Wake of the Wahoo*. Philadelphia: Chilton, 1960.

Stern, Robert C. *U.S. Subs in Action*. Carrolltown, Tex.: Squadron/Signal Publications, 1983.

Stevens, David. *U-Boat Far from Home*. St. Leonards, New South Wales: Allen and Unwin, 1997.

Supreme Commander for the Allied Powers. *The Campaigns of MacArthur in the Pacific*. Vol. 1 of *Reports of General Douglas MacArthur, Prepared by His General Staff*. Washington, D.C.: U.S. Government Printing Office, 1966.

Terzibaschitsch, Stefan. *Submarines of the U.S. Navy*. London: Arms and Armour Press, 1991.

Trumbull, R. *Silversides*. New York: Henry Holt, 1945.

USS Fulton (AS11), 50th Anniversary. Paducah, Ky.: Turner, 1991.

Van Der Vat, Dan. *Stealth at Sea.* London: Weidenfeld and Nicolson, 1994.

Waldron, T., and J. Gleeson. *The Frogmen.* London: Evans Bros., 1950.

Warren, C. E. T., and James Benson. *Above Us the Waves.* London: George G. Harrap and Co., 1954.

Watts, Anthony J. *Japanese Warships of World War II.* London: Ian Allen, 1966.

Wheeler, Keith. *War under the Pacific.* Alexandria, Va.: Time-Life Books, 1982.

White, Michael W. D. *Australian Submarines—A History.* Canberra: Australian Government Publishing Service, 1992.

Winter, Barbara. *The Intrigue Master.* Brisbane: Boolarong Press, 1995.

Winton, John. *The Forgotten Fleet.* Wadhurst, East Sussex: Douglas-Boyd Books, 1989.

Worledge, G. R., ed. *Contact! HMAS Rushcutter and Australia's Submarine Hunters, 1939–1946.* Sydney: Anti-submarine Officers' Association, 1994.

Wright, Malcolm. *If I Die.* Melbourne: Landsdowne Press, 1965.

Articles

Alden, John D. "Ultra Intercepts Offer Clues to Unrecorded Japanese Ship Casualties in World War II." *Warships International,* no. 3 (1995): 242–52.

Benitez, Lt. Comdr. R. C. "Battle Stations Submerged." *U.S. Naval Institute Proceedings,* January 1948, pp. 25–35.

Blanch, Ken. "Those Mighty Midgets." *Sunday Mail* (Brisbane), 16 April 1995, pp. 52, 85.

Caldwell, H. H. "*Darter* and *Dace* at Leyte Gulf." *Submarine Review* (Naval Submarine League, Annandale, Va.), July 2001, pp. 63–68.

Curtis, K. "Memories on the 5th–6th Patrol." *G-Fish Herald* (USS *Guardfish* veterans newsletter), August 1997.

Eckert, P. "Left Overboard from a Diving Submarine." *Shipmate* magazine, June 1989.

Fell, Capt. W. R. Article in *Blackwood's Magazine* 262, no. 1585 (November 1947). Copy held by Royal Navy Submarine Museum Research Centre, Gosport, Hampshire, A1983/92.

Feuer, A. B. "Secret Mission to Teop." *Sea Classics* magazine, July 1991, pp. 10–15.

Goodson, A., and J. O'Rourke. "19 Upper Melbourne Street." *Polaris* magazine, June 1991, pp. 28–29.

Kimball, Frank. "History Ignored Must Be Relived." *Polaris* magazine, February 1999, p. 21.

Maryland Main Ballast (Delmarva Chapter of U.S. Submarine Veterans of World War II), no. 2, February 1985.

Maynard, Mary. "Anchor Aweigh in the Dark Night." *Polaris* magazine, June 2001, pp. 11–12.

Milford, F. J. "U.S. Torpedoes, Part Two: The Great Torpedo Scandal, 1941–43." *Submarine Review* (Naval Submarine League, Annandale, Va.), October 1996.

Montague, Albert A. "Exploits of a WWII Submariner—Albert A. Montague: His Story." *Patrol* magazine, 11 July 1986, p. 5.

Reisig, M. "Leslie Lloyd Cottman Remembers Arkansas." *Mena (Arkansas) Star,* 16 May 2000.

Ruddy, John. "Fulton's Final Voyage." *The Day* (New London, Conn.), 17 May 1991, pp. B1–B8.

Reports and War Diaries

Bolt, F. H. G. "Report of Torpedo Maintenance Facilities for USN and RN Submarines at Brisbane." National Archives of Australia, Melbourne, 2026/5/285.

Commander Seventh Fleet. "Base Facilities Report, 15 September 1944," revised 6 January 1945. U.S. National Archives, Record Group 38, Records of the Office of the Chief of Naval Operations.

Cousin, A. P. (commanding officer, HMAS *Katoomba*). "Report of Proceedings Concerning U.S. Submarine S.39 Ashore on Rossel Island Reef," dated 17 August 1942. Australian War Memorial, Canberra, AWM78, 185/1.

"Defense-Aid Reciprocal Aid Review Board Report." U.S. National Archives, Record Group 71, Records of Bureau of Yards and Docks.

Flemming, Lt. Col. P. V. Report on court of enquiry into "Entry to port of Brisbane by U.S. Submarine," dated 9 September 1942. Australian War Memorial, Canberra, AWM60, 9/615/42.

Josselyn, H. "Report, Part II, Events Leading to Final Establishment of Station NRY on Vella Lavella Island." U.S. Naval Historical Center, Washington, D.C.

Keenan, J. "Report." U.S. Naval Historical Center, Washington, D.C.

Official report on Operation Foil, dated 8 August 1945. Royal Navy Submarine Museum Research Centre, Gosport, Hampshire, A1980/68/001.

Pryce-Jones, I. "Report on Coastwatching, Solomon Islands, April 1943–January 1944." U.S. Naval Historical Center, Washington, D.C.

Read, W. J. "Report on Coastwatching Activity Bougainville Island, 1941–1943." Typescript copy in Queensland Maritime Museum, Brisbane.

Statement of commanding officer, USS *Guardfish,* dated 4 December 1943, re-collision at 2355 Love, 3 December 1943, with an unidentified vessel. U.S. National Archives, Record Group 313, Records of Naval Operating Forces.

U.S. Navy Base Brisbane. War diaries, 1 October 1942–31 July 1945. U.S. National Archives, Record Group 38, Records of the Office of the Chief of Naval Operations.

U.S. submarine war patrol reports, 1941–45. U.S. National Archives, Record Group 38, Records of the Office of the Chief of Naval Operations, publication M-1752.

USS *Fulton.* War diary, 1–30 November 1942. U.S. National Archives, Record Group 38, Records of the Office of the Chief of Naval Operations.

War diary of naval officer in charge, Brisbane, 1 February 1942–31 December 1944. Australian War Memorial, Canberra, AWM78, 398/1.

Westmacott, Lt. H. P. "Operation Foil," dated 8 August 1945. Royal Navy Submarine Museum Research Centre, Gosport, Hampshire, A1980/68/001.

Unpublished Papers

Ahern, Capt. J. "Ships Piloted." Manuscript in collection of Queensland Maritime Museum, Brisbane.

Celestine, Sister M. "A Short History of the Sisters of St. Joseph of Orange in the Island of Buka." Typescript, 13 May 1970. U.S. Naval Historical Center, Washington, D.C.

Clary, John (ex–USS *Wahoo,* lost aboard USS *Escolar* in October 1944). Motor machinist's mate diary made available by his son, Gilbert Clary.

Cottman, L. L. (ex–USS *Fulton*). Manuscript account of his six years in the U.S. Navy supplied to the authors by L. L. Cottman.

Crabtree, L. "History of HMAS *Parkes*'s Voyages," 1994. Quoted in V. Catchpoole, "Going to War on a Corvette." Typescript in collection of Queensland Maritime Museum, Brisbane.

Meyer, C. J. (ex–USS *Fulton*). Paper detailing his naval experiences supplied to the authors by C. J. Meyer.

Sturma, M. "The Decorum of U.S. Servicemen in Queensland, 1942–5." Thesis in John Oxley Library, Brisbane.

Oral Histories

Carpender, Vice Adm. A. S. Transcript of interview with Lt. J. S. Tarbell (1945). National Archives of Australia, Melbourne.

Cutter, Capt. Slade D. Transcript of reminiscences (1985). U.S. Naval Institute, Annapolis, Md.

Fife, Adm. James. Transcript of interview with J. T. Mason (1961–62). Columbia University Oral History Research Office Collection, New York.

Griffiths, Lt. Robert L. (ex–USS *Narwhal*). Tape of speech to the Honda Car Club, 19 September 1992. Copy provided to the authors by the Submarines Association, Australia—Queensland Branch.

Klakring, Rear Adm. T. B. Transcript of interview with C. and J. Blair (1975). Published in *G-Fish Herald* (USS *Guardfish* veterans newsletter), provided to the authors from P. Snyder collection.

McCollum, Rear Adm. A. H. Transcript of interview with J. T. Mason (1971). U.S. Naval Institute, Annapolis, Md.

Parks, Tom (ex–USS *S39* and USS *Sailfish*). Transcript of interview with John F. Wukovits for *Military History Magazine* (April 1992). Available online at http://www.geocities.com/Baja/Dunes/4791/interv2.html (Tom Parks's website).

Ramage, Vice Adm. Lawson P. Transcript of reminiscences (1975). U.S. Naval Institute, Annapolis, Md.

Smay, Howard C. (ex–USS *Griffin* and USS *S47*). Taped interview with Robert C. Wright (1 July 2000), San Diego Maritime Museum, San Diego, Calif. Copy provided to the authors by Douglas Smay.

Ward, Rear Adm. N. G. Transcript of interview with P. Stillwell (1996). U.S. Naval Institute, Annapolis, Md. Published in the *G-Fish Herald* (USS *Guardfish* veterans newsletter) and used by permission of USNI.

INDEX

ABOUT THE AUTHORS

David Jones is a native of Brisbane and has had a lifelong interest in maritime history, naval affairs, and ship photography. While shipping remained an interest, he made his career as a government auditor and retired in 2000 after thirty-seven years with the Queensland Audit Office. Jones is also the author of *The Whalers of Tangalooma*, first published in 1980. A member of the Queensland Maritime Museum Association and the Navy League of Australia, he lives with his wife, Heather. They have two adult children.

Peter Nunan taught high school English, history, and geography in Queensland, New South Wales, the United Kingdom, Alberta, and Ontario after completing his studies in education in 1959. Upon retirement in 1993, he joined the Queensland Maritime Museum, where he is currently the honorary librarian. He and his wife live in Brisbane with their two Australian-American sons.

The Naval Institute Press is the book-publishing arm of the U.S. Naval Institute, a private, nonprofit, membership society for sea service professionals and others who share an interest in naval and maritime affairs. Established in 1873 at the U.S. Naval Academy in Annapolis, Maryland, where its offices remain today, the Naval Institute has members worldwide.

Members of the Naval Institute support the education programs of the society and receive the influential monthly magazine *Proceedings* and discounts on fine nautical prints and on ship and aircraft photos. They also have access to the transcripts of the Institute's Oral History Program and get discounted admission to any of the Institute-sponsored seminars offered around the country.

The Naval Institute also publishes *Naval History* magazine. This colorful bimonthly is filled with entertaining and thought-provoking articles, first-person reminiscences, and dramatic art and photography. Members receive a discount on *Naval History* subscriptions.

The Naval Institute's book-publishing program, begun in 1898 with basic guides to naval practices, has broadened its scope to include books of more general interest. Now the Naval Institute Press publishes about one hundred titles each year, ranging from how-to books on boating and navigation to battle histories, biographies, ship and aircraft guides, and novels. Institute members receive significant discounts on the Press's more than eight hundred books in print.

Full-time students are eligible for special half-price membership rates. Life memberships are also available.

For a free catalog describing Naval Institute Press books currently available, and for further information about subscribing to *Naval History* magazine or about joining the U.S. Naval Institute, please write to:

Membership Department
U.S. Naval Institute
291 Wood Road
Annapolis, MD 21402-5034
Telephone: (800) 233-8764
Fax: (410) 269-7940
Web address: www.navalinstitute.org